Studies of the Americas

Series Editor
Maxine Molyneux
Institute of the Americas
University College London
London, UK

The Studies of the Americas Series includes country specific, cross-disciplinary and comparative research on the United States, Latin America, the Caribbean, and Canada, particularly in the areas of Politics, Economics, History, Anthropology, Sociology, Anthropology, Development, Gender, Social Policy and the Environment. The series publishes monographs, readers on specific themes and also welcomes proposals for edited collections, that allow exploration of a topic from several different disciplinary angles. This series is published in conjunction with University College London's Institute of the Americas under the editorship of Professor Maxine Molyneux.

More information about this series at
http://www.palgrave.com/gp/series/14462

Marieke Riethof

Labour Mobilization, Politics and Globalization in Brazil

Between Militancy and Moderation

palgrave
macmillan

Marieke Riethof
Modern Languages and Cultures/
Latin American Studies
University of Liverpool
Liverpool, Merseyside, UK

Studies of the Americas
ISBN 978-3-319-60308-7   ISBN 978-3-319-60309-4 (eBook)
https://doi.org/10.1007/978-3-319-60309-4

Library of Congress Control Number: 2018935678

© The Editor(s) (if applicable) and The Author(s) 2019
This work is subject to copyright. All rights are solely and exclusively licensed by the Publisher, whether the whole or part of the material is concerned, specifically the rights of translation, reprinting, reuse of illustrations, recitation, broadcasting, reproduction on microfilms or in any other physical way, and transmission or information storage and retrieval, electronic adaptation, computer software, or by similar or dissimilar methodology now known or hereafter developed.
The use of general descriptive names, registered names, trademarks, service marks, etc. in this publication does not imply, even in the absence of a specific statement, that such names are exempt from the relevant protective laws and regulations and therefore free for general use.
The publisher, the authors and the editors are safe to assume that the advice and information in this book are believed to be true and accurate at the date of publication. Neither the publisher nor the authors or the editors give a warranty, express or implied, with respect to the material contained herein or for any errors or omissions that may have been made. The publisher remains neutral with regard to jurisdictional claims in published maps and institutional affiliations.

Cover image: ANDRESSA ANHOLETE / Stringer
Cover design: Jenny Vong

Printed on acid-free paper

This Palgrave Macmillan imprint is published by the registered company Springer International Publishing AG part of Springer Nature.
The registered company address is: Gewerbestrasse 11, 6330 Cham, Switzerland

Voor Oskar

Preface

I began the project that would eventually result in this book, with a research trip to Chile. As a typically ambitious graduate student I hoped to develop a comparison between the political role of trade unions in Chile and Brazil. While in Santiago I had arranged interviews with several trade unionists to scope out the potential for this project. As I arrived at the union headquarters, however, I discovered that angry miners had occupied the building, while internal union elections revealed significant splits and disagreements. As the Chilean unions entered a major political crisis, I decided to switch my main focus to Brazil, a country still known internationally at the time for its strong and combative union movement. I discovered soon enough during my fieldwork that the crucial role of trade unionists in the Brazilian transition to democracy was only part of the story and that these unions faced their own political challenges. Nevertheless, my initial experience in Chile and my many conversations with labour activists in Brazil showed me that it is moments of crisis and conflict that reveal significant insights into how and why trade union political strategies evolve.

I was also fascinated when the trade unionists I interviewed connected their workplace struggles to a wider political agenda, which they considered a natural extension of their union work. They explained to me that they did not find these two levels of political activism always easy to reconcile but that political ideas and aspirations always informed what they did. Their political activism ranged from opposition to the dictatorship and protests, to participation in political parties, social movements, and even in government, yet I found that the literature on trade unions and labour studies paid relatively little attention to the political nature of collective labour action.

This discrepancy led me to a focus on trade union political strategies, telling the story of how Brazilian trade unions found space for political participation during the democratic transition, how they struggled with the impact of economic crisis, and, paradoxically, how they dealt with the ambiguities of a government led by their political ally, the Workers' Party.

The book presented here is the result of many years of study and research, a journey of discovery and learning. The opportunity to interview Brazilian trade unionists, to attend union meetings, and to interview members of organizations related to the trade union movement was one of the most rewarding aspects of the research project. I would particularly like to mention the following people who took the time to talk to me over the course of the project: Clara Ant, Valmir Barbosa, the executive board of the Central Única dos Trabalhadores of the Federal District, Maria Silvia Portella de Castro, Marcelo Sereno, Mônica Valente, Julio Turra, Kjeld Jakobsen, Francisco Alexandre, Cesário da Silva, Fernando Lopes, Tarcísio Secoli, Argemiro Pertence Neto, Luiz Vieira, Celso Vianna de Fonseca, Mozart Schmitt Queiroz, Baltazar, Wilson Almeida, and Uriel Villas Boas.

In addition to the interviews and observations, a significant part of my analysis focused on published and unpublished trade union documents, many of which had not been used for research before. The Centro de Pesquisa Vergueiro in São Paulo is an indispensable source for union publications and newspaper clippings, although its activities have suffered from financial restrictions in recent years. Other important sources for union material were the Centro de Documentação e Memoria Sindical, the Departamento de Estudos Socio-Econômicos e Políticos, the CUT's publication department, the Centro de Documentação of the Sindicato dos Bancários in São Paulo, the Arquivo Edgard Leuenroth, and the Fundação Perseu Abramo. The Sindicato dos Metalúrgicos do ABC, and the Federação Nacional dos Urbanitários in Rio de Janeiro provided me with ample access to their documentation. Closer to home, the International Institute of Social History in Amsterdam had a significant amount of archival material on the PT as well as on trade union action in the late 1970s and 1980s. I would also like to thank the Interunion Department for Statistics and Socio-Economic Research (DIEESE, São Paulo) for its invaluable assistance with statistical information and the analysis of union documents, particularly Ana Yara Paulino, Antonio Prado, and Ilmar Ferreira Silva. Through Carlos G.J. Pradez and Jan Tilma, of the Companhia Vale do Rio Doce (CVRD), I received a significant amount of information on the CVRD, while José Roberto Fagundes of the Human Resources Department organized interviews with the trade union and the investors' association. Furthermore, Kjeld Jakobsen and Odilon Faccio of the Observatório Social in Florianópolis invited me to an extremely useful seminar for academics and trade unionists on labour standards in multinational corporations.

The generosity and hospitality of many Brazilians, academics, trade unionists, and others, certainly turned my research trips into an excellent experience. Iram Rodrigues, Glauco Arbix, and Armando Boito Jr. all took considerable time to discuss my research and results at several stages. In addition, I would like to thank the Department of Sociology at the University of São Paulo for providing me with a position as visiting researcher during my first stay in Brazil. In addition, I have greatly benefited from conversations with the following people: Giovanni Alves, Nadya Araújo Guimarães, Francisco Galrão Carneiro, Lúcio Kowarick, Paulo Martins, Monica Paranhos, Salvador Sandoval, Adalberto Moreira Cardoso, José Ricardo Ramalho, Marco Aurelio Santana, and Tullo Vigevani. I would also like to thank Celso Peel for introducing me to the social impact of privatization in Cubatão, a town economically dominated by a now privatized industrial sector. A special mention goes to Susana Camargo Vieira, who introduced me to many people who proved to be very important for my project. In addition, she provided me with several opportunities to present my work and discuss my findings with experts.

I would like to thank the following people for their friendship and support over the years: Antonio Carmona Baez, Barbara Hogenboom, Christianne Jacobs, Claudia Sanchez Bajo, Courtney Lake, Christa Licher, Inês Trigo de Sousa, Jessica van der Wusten, Laura van Rossem, Martine Wolzak, Marianne Franklin, Maria Pia di Matteo, Mireille Codfried, Damian Raess, Nancy de Randamie, Paul Blokker, René Wiering, Lewis Taylor, Katinka Weber, Andy Stokes, Colin Irwin, Haekyung Um, Andrew Redden, Tom Whittaker, Mike Ogden, Charles Forsdick, John and Lynn Timm as well as many others. I would also like to thank my PhD supervisors Alex Fernández Jilberto, Marianne Marchand, and Gerd Junne for their support and advice. In particular, I have very fond memories of the many coffee breaks with Alex, and his experience has inspired me to focus my new research project on Chilean refugees and solidarity campaigns. Furthermore, I would like to thank my fellow PhD students at University of Amsterdam for their comments on my early work. I also benefitted greatly from conversations with Mahrukh Doctor, Fiona Macaulay, Alan Angell, and Leslie Bethell during my time at the Latin American Centre and the Centre for Brazilian Studies in Oxford. In recent years, working with fellow Latin Americanists in an interdisciplinary environment at the University of Liverpool has enriched my understanding of the region in a way that would have been difficult otherwise.

I am very grateful to my family for their support and generosity during all these years. A special mention to my nieces, Eline and Laura, and my nephew Jack, who always manage to take my mind far away from academic work. Sadly, my mother, Renée Riethof-Zanoni, saw the beginning but not the end of this project but I know she would have been very proud of me. I dedicate this book to our son, Oskar O'Sullivan-Riethof; he could not stay with us, but he will always be in our hearts. Finally, my husband, Tadgh O'Sullivan, lived through the many highs and lows of the research and writing process, across borders and sometimes even across continents. Not only this book, but also my life would not have been the same without his love and support.

Liverpool, UK   Marieke Riethof

Contents

1 **Introduction**   1
   1.1 Militancy, Moderation, and Political Strategies: Explaining the Political Dimensions of Labour Militancy   4
   1.2 Turbulent Political Trajectories: Understanding Cycles of Militancy and Moderation   7
   1.3 Approaching Brazilian Labour: Contexts and Outline   10
   Bibliography   16

2 **Labour Movements, Globalization, and the Dilemmas of Development**   19
   2.1 Globalization and Labour: Beyond Structural Explanations   21
   2.2 The Political Dimensions of Labour and Trade Union Action   22
   2.3 Sources of Labour Power and Political Influence   25
   2.4 Collective Labour Action and Protest Waves   32
   2.5 Labour Political Strategies: Between Militancy and Moderation   35
   2.6 Conclusion   44
   Bibliography   53

3 Labour and the State: Corporatism and the Left, 1930–1977 — 59
3.1 Economic and Political Changes in the Early Twentieth Century — 61
3.2 Brazilian Workers and the Emergence of Corporatism — 64
3.3 Social and Political Polarization in the 1950s and 1960s — 70
3.4 The Military Coup and Labour Repression — 72
3.5 Conclusion — 75
Bibliography — 81

4 New Unionism: Protest, Mobilization, and Negotiating the Transition to Democracy, 1978–1988 — 85
4.1 "Multinationals Manufacture Misery": The Strike Movement, Labour Conflict, and Democratization, 1978–1982 — 87
4.2 Political Divisions and the Foundation of the PT — 95
4.3 Economic Crisis and the Consolidation of New Unionism: 1983–1985 — 99
4.4 Economic Decline, Direct Presidential Elections, and a New Constitution: 1985–1989 — 107
4.5 Conclusion — 112
Bibliography — 123

5 Economic Crisis, Reform, and the Pragmatic Left, 1989–2001 — 129
5.1 Political Strategies in Times of Economic Crisis: 1989–1992 — 131
5.2 Competition Within the Labour Movement and Relations with Social Movements — 137
5.3 Mobilization and Strikes in the Aftermath of the Real Plan — 141
5.4 The Struggle Against Privatization and the 1995 Oil Workers' Strike — 146
5.5 Conclusion — 154
Bibliography — 170

6 Labour Strategies and the Left in Power: Moderation, Division, and Renewed Militancy from Lula to Dilma — 177
6.1 Trade Unions, Lula's Election Victories, and the PT's Trajectory in Government — 179
6.2 Reluctance to Protest or Co-Optation? The Early Years of the Lula Government, 2003–2004 — 184

6.3	*Growing Discontent: Conflicts About Labour and Social Reform, 2005–2008*	193
6.4	*Resurgence of Protest, Revival of the Labour Movement, 2009–2016*	200
6.5	*Conclusion*	206
	Bibliography	218

7 Conclusion: Labour and the Ambiguities of Power   227

Index   235

Abbreviations

ABC region	Municipalities of Santo André, São Bernardo do Campo, São Caetano in Greater São Paulo.
AEPET	Associação de Engenheiros da Petrobras (Association of Petrobras Engineers)
APEOESP	Associação de Professores de Ensino Oficial do Estado de São Paulo (Teachers' Association of the State of São Paulo).
ARENA	Aliança Renovadora Nacional (National Renewal Alliance).
BNDES	Banco Nacional de Desenvolvimento Econômico e Social (National Economic and Social Development Bank).
CDES	Conselho de Desenvolvimento Econômico e Social (Socio-Economic Development Council).
CLT	Consolidação das Leis do Trabalho (Labour Code).
CMN	Conselho Monetário Nacional (National Monetary Council).
CMS	Coordenação dos Movimentos Sociais (Social Movement Coordination).
CNB	Confederação Nacional dos Bancários (National Bankworkers' Confederation).
CNI	Confederação Nacional das Indústrias (National Confederation of Industries).
CNM	Confederação Nacional dos Metalúrgicos (National Confederation of Metalworkers)

CNRT	Conselho Nacional de Relações de Trabalho (National Labour Relations Council).
CONCLAT	Congresso Nacional das Classes Trabalhadoras (National Congress of the Working Classes).
CONCUT	Congresso Nacional da CUT (CUT National Congress).
CONLUTAS	Coordenação Nacional de Lutas (National Struggle Coordination).
CONTAG	Confederação Nacional dos Trabalhadores na Agricultura (National Agricultural Workers' Confederation).
CSC	Corrente Sindical Classista (Class-based Union Movement).
CSN	Companhia Siderúrgica Nacional.
CTB	Central dos Trabalhadores e Trabalhadoras do Brasil (Brazilian Workers' Central).
CUT	Central Única dos Trabalhadores (Unified Workers' Central).
CVRD	Companhia Vale do Rio Doce.
DIEESE	Departamento Intersindical de Estatísticas e Estudos Socioeconômicos (Interunion Department of Statistics and Socio-Economic Studies).
DOS	Delegacia de Ordem Social (Social Order Delegation)
FIESP	Federação das Indústrias do Estado de São Paulo (Federation of Industries of the State of São Paulo).
FNT	Fórum Nacional do Trabalho (National Labour Forum, FNT).
FS	Força Sindical (Union Force).
FST	Fórum Sindical dos Trabalhadores (Union Labour Forum).
FTAA	Free Trade Area of the Americas
FUP	Federação Única dos Petroleiros (Unified Federation of Oil Workers).
IBASE	Instituto Brasileira de Análises Sociais e Econômicas (Brazilian Institute for Social and Economic Analyses).
IMF	International Monetary Fund.
MBL	Movimento Brasil Livre (Free Brazil Movement).
MDB	Movimento Democrático Brasileiro (Brazilian Democratic Movement).

MPL	Movimento Passe Livre (Free Fare Movement).
MST	Movimento dos Trabalhadores Rurais Sem Terra (Landless Workers' Movement).
MTST	Movimento dos Trabalhadores Sem Teto (Homeless Workers' Movement).
MVR	Movimento Vem Pra Rua (Come to the Streets Movement).
PAC	Plano de Aceleração do Crescimento (Growth Acceleration Plan).
PCB	Partido Comunista Brasileiro (Brazilian Communist Party).
PCdoB	Partido Comunista do Brasil (Communist Party of Brazil).
PLR	Participação nos Lucros e Resultados (Participation in Profits and Results).
PMDB	Partido do Movimento Democrático do Brasil (Brazilian Democratic Movement Party).
PSD	Partido Social Democrático (Social Democratic Party).
PSOL	Partido Socialismo e Liberdade (Socialism and Freedom Party).
PSTU	Partido Socialista dos Trabalhadores Unificado (Unified Socialist Workers' Party).
PT	Partido dos Trabalhadores (Workers' Party).
PTB	Partido Trabalhista Brasileiro (Brazilian Labour Party).
SBSP	Sindicato dos Bancários de São Paulo (Bankworkers' Union of São Paulo).
SINDIMINA	Sindicato dos Trabalhadores nas Indústrias de Prospecção, Pesquisa e Extração de Minérios (Union for Workers' in the Mineral Prospecting, Research and Extraction Industries).
SINDIPETRO-RJ	Sindicato dos Petroleiros de Rio de Janeiro (Petroleum Workers' Union of Rio de Janeiro)
SMABC	Sindicato dos Metalúrgicos do ABC (ABC Metalworkers' Union).
TST	Tribunal Superior de Trabalho (Supreme Labour Court).
UnS	Unidade Sindical (Union Unity).

List of Figures

Fig. 1.1　Public and private sector strikes in Brazil, 1984–2013. (Departamento Intersindical de Estatística e Estudos Socioeconômicos (DIEESE). "Balanço das greves em 2013." *Estudos e Pesquisas* 79, December 2015)　6

Fig. 4.1　Public and private sector strikes—1984–1991. (Public sector strikes include strikes in state-owned companies in this figure. Source: DIEESE, "Balanço das greves em 2013," *Estudos e Pesquisas* 79 (2015), 42)　109

Fig. 5.1　Public- and private-sector strikes—1989–2002. (DIEESE, "Balanço das greves em 2013", 42)　132

Fig. 6.1　Public- and private-sector strikes in Brazil, 2004–2013. (DIEESE, "Balanço das greves em 2013," *Estudos e Pesquisas* 79 (December 2015), 42)　192

CHAPTER 1

Introduction

Footage from early 1979 shows Lula pacing on a stage nervously, sweating in shirtsleeves, smoking a cigarette.[1] He was about to address 150,000 metalworkers who were on strike for fair wages while protesting against the impact of the military regime on ordinary Brazilians. There were too many people to fit in the metalworkers' union assembly hall, so the meeting had to be moved to the football stadium Vila Euclides in São Bernardo do Campo, Greater São Paulo. Tensions were rising as the police were readying themselves to intervene violently, while the union leadership had been forcibly removed from their posts with their civil and political rights annulled. In his speech Lula emphasized that the unions were exercising their legal right to strike and that they were not "radical". Meanwhile, and under the direct threat of repression, Lula and his fellow strike leaders tried to convince the strikers to accept a truce between the unions and the employers. After a turbulent meeting, the union assembly suspended the strike on May 1, 1979.

Back in São Bernardo, twenty-three years later and just months after he was inaugurated as Brazil's first working-class president in 2003, Lula spoke to an audience of trade unionists about the strike: "It was the most difficult meeting of my life; every time we tried to talk about an agreement, the workers booed. And I managed to convince my comrades to accept the agreement but they returned to the factories feeling that I had betrayed them. A feeling that a strike should go on to the bitter end. It was the

© The Author(s) 2019
M. Riethof, *Labour Mobilization, Politics and Globalization in Brazil*, Studies of the Americas,
https://doi.org/10.1007/978-3-319-60309-4_1

most difficult year of my union life." Despite the disappointing outcome, Lula himself saw the strike as the beginning of the labour movement's road to political power: "I thought with my feet: if the workers thought they could take the strike to the limits of the possible, they should. ... This was the strike in which we lost most economically, it was a strike in which we gained absolutely nothing." Yet, as Lula went on to observe, the strike had marked the first step on the road to political power, which would include the foundation of the Partido dos Trabalhadores (PT, the Workers' Party), the Central Única dos Trabalhadores (CUT, the Unified Workers' Central), and eventually "the election of this union leader to the presidency of the Republic".[2]

The 1979 strike marked a turning point in labour opposition to the dictatorship, transforming the union movement into a formidable opponent of the military regime. Lula's reflections on the 1979 strike as the country's president underlined the political importance of the strike movement that emerged in the late 1970s while also indicating that Brazil's famous labour militancy was not straightforward or uncontested, even during the heyday of the strikes of the late 1970s and early 1980s. The strike leaders had to consider the risks of a repressive backlash from the state, with employers threatening to fire the striking workers, all while attempting to balance the workers' wage demands with a wider agenda for political change. These difficult choices continued to shape the Brazilian union movement's strategies and tactics over the next decades.

Attempting to understand these strategic dilemmas, this book analyses the conflicts created by the union movement's active involvement in a changing political environment, particularly in the context of a centre-left party with such strong and defined roots in the union movement coming to power. Much of the literature on recent Brazilian politics has interpreted the union movement's political position as the PT's close ally as a move away from the political radicalism of the movement's early years, thus signalling a drift towards pragmatism and moderation. Although the trajectory of Brazilian unions cannot be analysed without reference to the changing political fortunes of the PT, to assume that its behaviour and agenda have been identical to the party's is to simplify a complex reality. Instead, this book's central argument is that the union movement's political ambitions have resulted in significant conflicts, given that labour activism experienced waves of militancy and moderation rather than a linear trajectory towards pragmatism and political co-optation. Through its study of the political trajectory of Brazilian trade unions, this book explores the conditions under which trade unionists developed moderate or militant strategies. The guiding questions of this analysis focus on the contexts which have shaped these political approaches: namely how the union movement came to an accommodation with the socio-political and economic structures in which it operates and how and why labour action acquired a political dimension, whether radical or not.

The academic literature on Brazil's recent political history has witnessed a great deal of polarized debate regarding the PT government's legacy and the party's relationship with civil society, including trade unions. On one side of the debate, the union movement's position is viewed primarily as having been subordinated to, or even willingly co-opted by, the PT government. Much of the literature on the Brazilian labour and the PT has emphasized the absorption of union leaders and other groups such as the landless workers' movement (MST) through their incorporation in government structures, reflecting the PT's own increasingly moderate political agenda while in government.[3] From this perspective, the union movement lost its voice as the legitimate representative of working people in Brazil by abandoning its critical stance towards the government. In his characteristically polemical style, Ricardo Antunes has referred to Lula as a "half-Bonaparte … politely effacing before the power of high finance while craftily managing his popular support".[4] Francisco de Oliveira characterized the relationship as a "hegemony in reverse": rather than pursuing a progressive agenda when finally in power, the CUT had become "a transmission belt for neoliberal policies", contributing to the fragmentation of the Brazilian working class.[5] According to Maria d'Araujo's study on union membership in government circles, the PT administrations had turned into "a confluence between government, the union movement, social movements and civil servants, ideologically mobilized and sociologically corporatist".[6] Moreover, David Samuels argues that due to the union movement's moderation in parallel with similar developments in the PT, after Lula's election to the presidency this created a dynamic whereby the government became less responsive to social pressure as the PT's leaders "no longer have to worry as much about a trade-off between adopting an electorally pragmatic approach and losing organized labor's support".[7] Meanwhile, Andréia Galvão[8] views the CUT's accommodation with the PT as a sign of weakness rather than a channel of political influence, having led to crippling divisions and fragmentation.[9]

For others, the improvements between 2003 and 2016 outweighed the negatives, focusing in particular on the improved legal position of trade unions, access to political influence, and social improvements such as reductions in poverty and inequality. Tonelli and Queiroz argue that the PT governments not only increased the number of formal jobs and redistributed income but also created a "permanent dialogue, initiating a process of cultural change".[10] Despite calling some of the first Lula government's labour reforms "piecemeal", Hall nevertheless views Lula's attempts to strengthen the legal position of unions as a positive departure from the Latin American trend towards deregulation.[11] French and Fortes point to the positive effects of economic growth on job creation and wages throughout most of the 2000s, the role of social policies in poverty reduction, as well as a more positive bargaining environment for trade unions.[12] In turn, Hochstetler has argued that co-optation was not as straightforward as often suggested, as civil society mobilized to move Lula to the left in the early years of the PT government and developed alternatives to the government's participatory mechanisms,[13] as well as proposing new policies such as the minimum wage.[14]

Despite the important parallels between the PT's and trade unions' respective trajectories, both sides of the debate tend to overemphasize the similarities between the political trajectory of the party and the unions, which can obscure the particular dynamics of labour mobilization. While these divergent evaluations suggest disillusionment on the one hand and recognition of moderate improvements on the other, the union movement's own position in this political scenario was equally conflicted. Indeed, although the CUT's trajectory undoubtedly became closely intertwined with the PT government, to reduce the union movement's position to one of co-optation and conservatism obscures the dilemmas this relationship generated. Therefore, this book explores the conflicts provoked by the union movement's political participation, particularly how unionists have attempted to reconcile their history of successful militancy with their decision to participate actively in politics, which often led to a degree of compromise and moderation.

1.1 Militancy, Moderation, and Political Strategies: Explaining the Political Dimensions of Labour Militancy

However we evaluate the failures and achievements of the PT during its time in government, the union movement's responses—both moderate and militant—should be understood as including strategies for political change beyond the workplace, which is particularly poignant in countries that have experienced democratic transitions. Union activists therefore not only translated militant strategies into strikes and demonstrations, but they also developed a proactive agenda for political change, both in the political arena and in the workplace. Moderation was reflected in reductions in the number of strikes and demonstrations, often resulting from a fear of job losses, and if industrial action did occur, unions focused on the defensive protection of existing rights, wage and employment levels, rather than proactive demands for workplace representation and wage increases. Lower levels of labour militancy did not preclude a political agenda, as evident in the mid- to late-1990s when the union movement struggled to sustain a high level of proactive strikes in the face of an economic downturn, shifting instead to organizing demonstrations in a largely unsuccessful attempt to challenge the government's neoliberal agenda. Another facet of moderation was evident during the governments of Lula and Dilma Rousseff, when unions became represented in the government apparatus and the economy began to recover.

The evolution of strikes from the early 1980s until 2013 allows significant insights into the relationship between political change and union militancy, while problematizing arguments about the straightforward relationship between labour militancy and economic conditions. Strikes have often been used as a proxy to measure labour militancy,[15] even though this particular form of action does not capture the full complexity of labour strategies. Indeed, labour militancy is not limited to strikes and can involve actions ranging from demonstrations, marches, and occupations, to sabotage and insubordination in the workplace as well as worker activism in communities, social movements,[16] and political participation. Some of these strategies have taken place outside of the institutionalized political sphere, such as marches, occupations, and sabotage, while others straddle the boundaries between the formal political arena and extra-institutional action. Nevertheless, the advantage of strike data is that researchers can use strike statistics as an approximation of how labour militancy changes over time while comparing these figures with different international contexts to detect certain trends.

In the Brazilian case, the changing character of strikes illustrates how this variation of collective labour action did not so much reflect a decline but peaks and troughs in response to political and economic change. Brazilian strike statistics have been collected systematically since 1984,[17] and although they do not capture the early years of the strike movement,[18] they illustrate how strikes responded both to changing economic conditions and political developments. This time span includes Brazil's democratization in the 1980s, the major economic crises of the 1980s and 1990s, as well as experiments with neoliberalism followed by a left-wing turn, which involved a return to state intervention in the 2000s. Most notably, as Fig. 1.1 illustrates, strikes peaked in the late 1980s and early 1990s in response to the government's failure to resolve the worsening economic crisis, Fernando Collor de Melo's (1990–1992) impeachment crisis in 1992, until Fernando Henrique Cardoso's 1994 stabilization plan reduced inflation to single digits. While the political and economic crisis unfolded, sharp divisions emerged, as the union movement considered whether to negotiate with the government or intensify the protests, favouring the latter in the first instance but struggling to maintain a high level of mobilization as economic conditions deteriorated.

From the mid-1990s until the late 2000s, the number of strikes stabilized at a relatively low level, at first due to the adverse economic conditions under the Cardoso government (1994–2002), continuing during the Lula administrations (2003–2010) when Brazil's economy began to boom. In the early 2010s, in the context of another economic downturn and the worsening political crisis under Dilma Rousseff, strikes began to

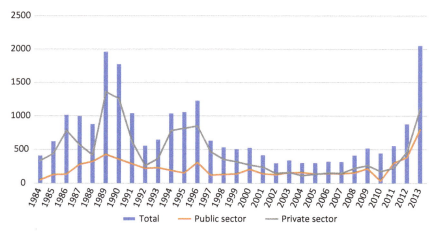

Fig. 1.1 Public and private sector strikes in Brazil, 1984–2013. (Departamento Intersindical de Estatística e Estudos Socioeconômicos (DIEESE). "Balanço das greves em 2013." *Estudos e Pesquisas* 79, December 2015)

increase in number again, peaking in 2013 with the highest number of strikes on record, also reflecting the mass demonstrations that erupted in June 2013 in Brazil's major cities. Although strike data for the period surrounding Dilma's impeachment are not yet available at the time of writing, the events suggest that grassroots labour militancy continued, while the union movement played a greater role in the protests against impeachment in 2015 and 2016 than it had for almost two decades. This brief overview of the turbulent Brazilian political context underlines that arguments about the decline of labour should be evaluated alongside the prevailing political dynamics, while treating labour militancy and moderation as a contingent factor rather than a fixed outcome. Therefore, the evolution of labour militancy in Brazil over the last three decades cannot be understood without considering both the political context to which the union movement responded and the internal political debates this union response generated.

1.2 Turbulent Political Trajectories: Understanding Cycles of Militancy and Moderation

This book contributes to theoretical and empirical debates about labour political strategies in Brazil, Latin America, and internationally by developing a nuanced argument about the union movement's political trajectories in contrast to the narrative of organized labour's inevitable decline in the face of globalization. The analysis of the Brazilian case puts the debate on globalization and labour in the context of developing countries with an emphasis on the exceptions to the dominant narratives of labour decline. Challenging generalizations about globalization's impact on workers, this book offers an explanation of Brazilian trade union strategies that is sensitive to Brazil's complex political history, while recognizing parallels to other experiences in developing countries. Another distinctive feature of this work is the focus on workers' active engagement with the political arena, which emphasizes their agency rather than treating labour as a passive subject of global political and economic change. While many studies on trade unions focus on workplace strategies, unions' political agendas and the role of political ideas in shaping these strategies have received relatively little attention. What this book offers instead is an analysis of some of the most contentious periods in recent Brazilian politics from the perspectives of workers and their unions while also engaging with unique empirical material from the 1980s and 1990s. Adopting this longer-term perspective on the evolution of labour strategies, this book explains not only under what conditions trade union strategies change but also their impact on Brazilian politics.

The Brazilian new unionist movement became one of the paradigmatic cases of trade unions that bucked the global trend of labour decline given that workers managed to successfully challenge the authoritarian regime and effectively promote labour rights. However, Brazilian unions have also faced major challenges in the various political and economic contexts examined in this book. Consequently, this book explains the dynamic evolution of labour political strategies using insights from labour and social movement theories, emphasizing that arguments about a linear trajectory from militancy to moderation fail to capture the cyclical and conflictive nature of these same strategies, which should instead be understood as being in a dialectical relationship. A teleological analysis in which all roads lead to decline risks underemphasizing the conflicts created by the changing context and shifting strategies, while also obscuring episodes of renewed militancy. Rejecting a narrow economic explanation of labour militancy and moderation—that organized labour inevitably declines in response to economic downturns and the pressures of globalization—this book shows that the rapidly changing political contexts, particularly during periods of heightened political change, sparked labour militancy, even in adverse economic conditions. In the Brazilian context, labour militancy in the late 1970s and early 1980s arose in response to the repression and political restrictions imposed on trade unions by the military dictatorship. Paradoxically, opportunities for political participation in the democratization process also raised questions about how the unions could maintain their radical agenda while participating in political and electoral processes. This dilemma could not be resolved without some degree of moderation. Analyses focused on the decline of the once powerful Brazilian union movement do not tell the full story of this dynamic; a gap which this book addresses through its focus not only on moderation but also on the resurgence of militant strategies, using an analytical framework that engages with internal and contextual factors to explain labour's political strategies.

Another contribution of this book is that its Latin American and Brazilian political analysis focuses on the responses of trade unions to political change. In a Latin American context, as the cycle of new left governments has come to a close in the second half of the 2010s, the book offers significant insights into the rise and fall of progressive governments, including the relationship with the latter's civil society supporters. While Brazil under Lula and Dilma is now generally considered as "mildly reformist"[19] compared to the more radical left in other countries in the region, the relationship between the PT and its supporters as well as the implications for their political agendas and strategies reflect similar dilemmas faced elsewhere. By focusing primarily on moderation, political analyses of this period have often lost sight of the waxing and waning of labour militancy, which rarely follows a linear trajectory. Instead, the explanation here focuses on why each period in Brazil's recent political history has witnessed the seesawing of social and political mobilization in response to changing economic and political contexts. The Brazilian case therefore functions as a microcosm of many of the political problems faced by the entire spectrum of the Latin American left, particularly in terms of how activists react when their political agenda is translated into their party allies' electoral victory. The case of Brazilian trade unions illustrates that when the left is in government, party supporters such as trade unionists have faced a number of strategic dilemmas when attempting to manage internal debates, often involving calls for a radical agenda, alongside the opportunity to influence or even participate in government. Progressive governments have faced another set of political pressures, including having to manage coalitions and their appeal to broad segments of the electorate while maintaining social movement support. Understanding the waves and legacies of militancy and moderation as well as the nature of union-party relations helps to explain how unions and social movements respond when progressive governments distance themselves from their own roots.

In sum, the evolution of labour political strategies and agendas is an inherently conflictive and complex process, shaped by trade unions' internal and external contexts. Reflecting this complexity, this book examines why such dynamics have sometimes constrained labour action, leading to pragmatism and moderation, while at other times they resulted in militant strategies and agendas. The analytical focus here concentrates on the interplay of strategies, ideas, and context, which includes the wider economic, social, and political circumstances in which trade unions and working people operate. Because of unions' complex political landscape, the union movement's trajectory cannot be reduced to a single factor, such as a specific institutional framework or, indeed, internal and external political dynamics. In light of this, this book examines how the Brazilian union movement pulled in two directions: one challenging the status quo, and the other concentrating on political participation. The resulting tensions and strains are key elements in the modern Latin American labour movement's story.

1.3 Approaching Brazilian Labour: Contexts and Outline

As outlined earlier, this book explores the debates and discourses surrounding the Brazilian unions' pursuit of an active political agenda, which was complicated by its representation of highly diverse groups of working people and attempts to maintain its autonomy in relation to the government and political parties. The trade-off between these objectives has shaped the union movement's ideas, agendas, and strategies over the years. To understand these conflicts and contradictions, each chapter analyses the unions' trajectory in relation to the following three factors: its relationship to the formal political arena, internal debates and conflicts about political strategies, and its reaction to a changing economic and political context in response to members' demands and interests.

Firstly, organized labour's relationship with the formal political arena directs our attention to the extent to which unions have acted as a protest force pressurizing the government from the outside as well as asking if its focus was on participating in formal decision- and policy-making procedures. One influential factor has been the unions' relationship with the PT, particularly in light of the party's growing electoral success. Their close relationship reinforced the tendency towards moderation and pragmatic electoral considerations, particularly in the second half of the 1990s and under the PT governments, given that a party organically linked to trade unions eventually became a significant national political force. Secondly, although the union movement's position outside the formal political arena resulted in militant strategies as witnessed in the late 1970s and early 1980s, electoral considerations provoked internal conflicts about the desirability and effectiveness of the latter, which led to a return to militant strategies in the early 1990s and 2010s while also contributing to organizational and political fragmentation. Thirdly, labour militancy and moderation evolved in a context in which the interests of union members and working people more generally were affected by economic and political change, which included regime change in the 1980s, questions about the distribution of the positive and negative effects of economic boom and bust, as well as controversial government proposals such as social and labour reforms.

Following a conceptual discussion of labour's political strategies and agency in the second chapter, each of the subsequent chapters focus on examples of negotiation, conflict, and protest to illustrate the relationship between labour political strategies and their respective contexts. All of these were relevant throughout the recent history of the union movement, which indicates that even the 1980s—known as the height of labour militancy— saw examples of negotiation and internal conflict, presaging future dilemmas. Similarly, while the years since Lula's election have often been seen as dominated by co-optation and pragmatism, this period also experienced significant levels of protest and challenges to the PT-led governments. In this discussion, negotiation refers to strategies focusing on government policies and agreements with employers. Protests refer not only to strike activity—just one indicator of trade union strength and power[20]—but also to other forms of contestation such as demonstrations, marches, sit-ins, work stoppages, and occupations. Following this book's argument that the conflicts and dilemmas generated by the left in power challenges assumptions about the Brazilian left as being overwhelmingly co-opted by the government, each chapter discusses debates about political strategies with reference to dynamics internal and external to organized labour. Conflict can arise from dilemmas about whether to negotiate, participate, or protest, leading to either militant or moderate strategies.

The second chapter discusses the theoretical question as to why there are variations in militancy and moderation in unions and how we can explain changes in political trajectories over time. This question is particularly salient with the PT's coming to power, which was also the ultimate objective of many participants in Brazilian unions; however, this led to significant political dilemmas about autonomy and cooperation. The theoretical framework is based on labour and social movement theories, beginning with a discussion concerning the inherently political nature of trade union strategies, including the significance of state-labour relations in developing countries such as Brazil. The debate on sources of labour power moves away from structural explanations of union behaviour by introducing the notion that collective labour action emerges in response to trade unionists' perceptions of their unions' strengths and weaknesses. Although social movement theories have often disregarded labour and trade unions in favour of identity-based movements, they provide significant insights into cycles of protests and the evolution of movement trajectories with reference to the political context and internal developments. Thereby, the chapter ends with a discussion about militancy and moderation as a framework to understand why trade union strategies change in response to given political and economic contexts.

From a historical perspective, Chap. 3 argues that the trajectory and development of the Brazilian union movement between 1930 and 1964 was closely intertwined with state development policies (developmentalism, neoliberalism, and more recently neo-developmentalism), creating an uneasy relationship between the government and organized labour, at times conflictive and at other moments cooperative. In the early to mid-twentieth century, working people—principally urban industrial workers—began to form an important source of political support and mobilization, however, conceding to workers' demands had the potential to jeopardize economic policies or alienate segments of the various alliances that supported the government, as evident in the years leading up to the 1964 military coup. Corporatism as the dominant organizational principle of both trade unions and state-labour relations also emerged in this era, an organizational mode that has continued to shape labour organization and political strategies to this day. After years of repression, trade unions re-emerged as a social and political actor towards the end of the military regime (1964–1985); indeed it strengthened during the dictatorship's final years. Despite the severe repression of trade unionists and the left, the authoritarian regime allowed the continued existence of trade unions in a corporatist framework, although their activities were initially highly restricted which sparked the mass pro-democracy protests of the late 1970s and early 1980s.

As examined in Chap. 4, unions in sectors that were strategically important for the Brazilian economy—particularly the automobile sector—managed to organize major strikes that turned into political protests against authoritarianism. Based on this militancy, the new unionist movement developed an explicitly political agenda, concentrating on the end of corporatism and state intervention, and the democratization of the workplace, and workers' significant role in the return to democracy. The strategies used to achieve these aims were intended to put pressure on the military regime by organizing strikes and actions in such a way that they circumvented repression and restrictions on militant labour action, such as sit-ins, work stoppages, marches, and demonstrations. These activities served to heighten workers' political awareness, eventually leading to the establishment of a new political party, the PT. Also discussed here is new unionists' development of strikes and mass mobilization as specific strategies. As more traditional forms of labour action, the purpose of the strikes and demonstrations was to protest against the regime's punitive labour and wage policies, which restricted the right to organize and mobilize. The protestors' awareness that wage policies restricted the adjustment of income levels to meet inflation led to the mobilization of many of those who had not been politicized previously. Throughout the early 1980s, questions about the opposition's role in the new democratic regime also emerged, leading to debates about electoral, the organizational, and political relationship between the PT and new unionism, and the negotiation of the new Constitution in 1988.

The 1990s form the backdrop for Chap. 5's discussion of the increasingly difficult context in which trade unions operated. The combination of democratization with neoliberal reforms resulted in organized labour attempting to reassert its role as the legitimate representative vehicle of workers' interests, both politically and in the workplace. Meanwhile, the union movement was paradoxically unable to define an effective alternative to economic reforms. Despite the political momentum that the democratic transition provided during the 1980s, the political space for organized labour's political activism became more restricted in the 1990s, with the devastating effects of hyperinflation and the financial crises increasing the threat of unemployment. Although economic problems provoked large-scale national strikes and protests, they also undermined many unions' capacity for effective collective bargaining at company level. In turn, the later success of the Plano Real stabilization programme (1994) in reducing inflation led to a decrease in the number of strikes and general mobilizations. The government's economic success undermined much of the justification for union opposition, as hyperinflation affected the poorest groups in society in particular. In this context, it became more difficult for trade unions to find an effective way to influence political and economic decision-making compared to the 1980s. Because the unions struggled to present a viable, alternative political project, and given the few institutionalized channels for political participation, unions and the left in general were strategically outmanoeuvred, often finding themselves in the position of defending the "old" system of state economic intervention. This position is illustrated by the protests against privatization, which initially provoked major demonstrations while in reality many individual unions ended up negotiating privatization terms on behalf of their members without much support from national labour organizations. In this context, rather than strike action putting pressure on the government's economic agenda, organized labour together with other social movements, campaigned against neoliberalism and in favour of a more generalized social and economic justice agenda, focusing on issues such as land reform and the reduction of the working week.

Turning to the 2000s, the relationship between trade unions and the PT in national government appeared to be based on participation, accommodation, and even co-optation. Chapter 6 analyses the involvement of union representatives in key reform proposals—such as labour, social security, and minimum-wage reform—which ended up being so controversial that they resulted in splits within both the union movement and the PT. In fact, protests against government policies, particularly the lack of progress compared to the PT's original agenda, also surfaced in the early days of Lula's presidency. The mass protests that took place between 2013 and 2016 focused popular anger on government spending priorities and corruption, receiving significant international attention, particularly in the context of similar protests taking place elsewhere in the world. However, these protests did not emerge out of a political vacuum and we can find examples of renewed labour militancy and conflicts throughout the Lula and Dilma years, particularly post-2009. Culminating in Dilma Rousseff's impeachment in August 2016, this period marked significant social and political polarization, in which labour militancy and moderation played a key but largely underappreciated role.

Notes

1. As featured in the documentary *ABC da Greve* (The ABC of Strike), directed by Leon Hirszman (1990).
2. The source for both quotes is a transcript of Lula's speech in Folha de Sao Paulo, "Leia íntegra do discurso de Lula em São Bernardo do Campo," *Folha de São Paulo*, May 1, 2003, http://www1.folha.uol.com.br/folha/brasil/ult96u48592.shtml
3. Apart from the authors quoted in here, see also Hernan B. Gómez, *Lula, the Workers' Party and the Governability Dilemma in Brazil* (New York: Routledge, 2013); Wendy Hunter, *The Transformation of the Workers' Party in Brazil, 1989–2009* (Cambridge: Cambridge University Press, 2010); André Singer, *Os sentidos do lulismo: Reforma gradual e pacto conservador* (São Paulo: Companhia das Letras, 2012).
4. Antunes also argues that Lula abandoned his traditional union and social movement support base, relying primarily on mobilizing the recipients of Bolsa Família social benefits. Ricardo Antunes, "Trade Unions, Social Conflict, and the Political Left in Present-Day Brazil: Between Breach and Compromise," in *The New Latin American Left: Cracks in the Empire*, ed. Jeffery R. Webber and Barry Carr (Lanham, MD: Rowman and Littlefield, 2013), 270. For other variations of the argument that the PT's electoral support base shifted away from the union movement to the poor, see Cesar Zucco, "The President's 'New' Constituency: Lula and the Pragmatic Vote

in Brazil's 2006 Presidential Elections," *Journal of Latin American Studies* 40 (2008), 29–49; Wendy Hunter and Timothy J. Power, "Rewarding Lula: Executive Power, Social Policy, and the Brazilian Elections of 2006," *Latin American Politics and Society* 49(1) (2007), 1–30; Singer, *Os Sentidos*. For a critical perspective on the electoral significance of social benefits recipients, see Simone R. Bohn, "Social Policy and Vote in Brazil: Bolsa Família and the Shifts in Lula's Electoral Base," *Latin American Research Review*, 46(1) (2011), 54–79.
5. Francisco de Oliveira, "Lula in the Labyrinth," *New Left Review* 42 (2006), 5 and 13.
6. Maria C. D'Araujo, *A elite dirigente do governo Lula* (Rio de Janeiro: FGV/CPDOC, 2009), 10.
7. David Samuels, "From Socialism to Social Democracy: Party Organization and the Transformation of the Workers' Party in Brazil," *Comparative Political Studies* 37 (9) (2004), 1007–8.
8. Andréia Galvão, "A reconfiguração do movimento sindical no governo Lula," *Revista Outubre* 18 (2009), 179–80.
9. See also Gómez, *Lula, the Workers' Party*, for a detailed analysis of how the divisions within the PT affected the party's relationship with social movements; Sluyter-Beltrão views the growing factionalism, political divisions, and fragmentation in the union movement in the late 1980s and early 1990s as a major factor in new unionism's political moderation, see Jeffrey Sluyter-Beltrão, *Rise and Decline of Brazil's New Unionism: The Politics of the Central Única dos Trabalhadores* (Oxford: Peter Lang, 2010).
10. Flávio Tonelli and Antônio A. Queiroz, "Trabalho e sindicalismo no governo Lula." In *Os anos Lula: Contribuições para um balanço crítico 2003–2010*, ed. João Paulo Almeida de Magalhães et al. (Rio de Janeiro: Garamond, 2010), 329.
11. Michael M. Hall, "The Labor Policies of the Lula Government," in *Brazil under Lula: Economy, Politics, and Society under the Worker-President*, ed. Joseph L. Love and Werner Baer (New York: Palgrave Macmillan, 2009), 161.
12. John D. French and Alexandre Fortes, "Nurturing Hope, Deepening Democracy, and Combating Inequalities in Brazil: Lula, the Workers' Party, and Dilma Rousseff's 2010 Election as President," *Labor* 9(1) (2012), 17.
13. Kathryn Hochstetler, "Organized Civil Society in Lula's Brazil," in *Democratic Brazil Revisited*, ed. Peter R. Kingstone and Timothy J. Power (Pittsburgh, PA: University of Pittsburgh Press, 2008), 33–4.
14. Reiner Radermacher and Waldeli Melleiro, "Mudanças no cenário sindical brasileiro sob o governo de Lula," *Nueva Sociedad* 211 (2007), 10.
15. While proxies of union strength, such as union density and strikes, are difficult to apply to complex political situations, they are among the few statistical measures available. John Kelly, *Rethinking Industrial Relations: Mobilisation, Collectivism and Long Waves* (London: Routledge, 1998), 9.

See also Franzosi's reflections on the use of quantitative and qualitative strike data, Roberto Franzosi, *The Puzzle of Strikes: Class and State Strategies in Postwar Italy* (Cambridge: Cambridge University Press, 1995), 21–5.
16. In his research on participatory democracy in Porto Alegre, Gianpaolo Baiocchi found that "'militancy' has evolved and merged with a conception of 'citizenship' borne of the 'new citizenship' social movements of the 1980s and 1990s". Baiocchi's conception of militancy emphasizes both participation in social struggles and community activism, see Gianpaolo Baiocchi, *Militants and Citizens: The Politics of Participatory Democracy in Porto Alegre* (Stanford, CA: Stanford University Press, 2005), 115.
17. The main source for Brazilian strike statistics is the Departamento Intersindical de Estatística e Estudos Socio-Econômicos's (DIEESE) strike database.
18. An overview can be found in Departamento Intersindical de Estatística e Estudos Socioeconômicos (DIEESE). "Balanço das greves em 2013." *Estudos e Pesquisas* 79, December 2015. Estimates of strike data between 1978 and 1984 can be found in Eduardo Noronha, "A explosão das greves na década de 80," in *O sindicalismo brasileiro nos anos 80*, ed. Armando Boito Jr. (Rio de Janeiro: Paz e Terra, 1990), 93–135; Maria H. Tavares de Almeida, "O sindicalismo brasileiro entre a conservação e a mudança," in *Sociedade política no Brasil pós-64*, edited by Bernardo Sorj and Maria H. Tavares de Almeida (São Paulo: Brasiliense, 1983), 279–312.
19. Jeffery R. Webber and Barry Carr, "Introduction: The Latin American Left in Theory and Practice," in *The New Latin American Left: Cracks in the Empire*, ed. Jeffery R. Webber and Barry Carr (Lanham, MD: Rowman and Littlefield, 2013), 4.
20. Mònica Clua-Losada and Laura Horn, "Analysing Labour and the Crisis: Challenges, Responses and New Avenues." *Global Labour Journal* 5(2) (2014), 105.

Bibliography

Almeida, Maria H. Tavares de. 1983. O sindicalismo brasileiro entre a conservação e a mudança. In *Sociedade política no Brasil pós-64*, ed. Bernardo Sorj and Maria H. Tavares de Almeida, 279–312. São Paulo: Brasiliense.

Antunes, Ricardo. 2013. Trade Unions, Social Conflict, and the Political Left in Present-Day Brazil: Between Breach and Compromise. In *The New Latin American Left: Cracks in the Empire*, ed. Jeffery R. Webber and Barry Carr, 255–276. Lanham: Rowman and Littlefield.

Baiocchi, Gianpaolo. 2005. *Militants and Citizens: The Politics of Participatory Democracy in Porto Alegre*. Stanford: Stanford University Press.

Bohn, Simone R. 2011. Social Policy and Vote in Brazil: Bolsa Família and the Shifts in Lula's Electoral Base. *Latin American Research Review* 46 (1): 54–79.

Clua-Losada, Mònica, and Laura Horn. 2014. Analysing Labour and the Crisis: Challenges, Responses and New Avenues. *Global Labour Journal* 5 (2): 102–113.

D'Araujo, Maria C. 2009. *A elite dirigente do governo Lula*. Rio de Janeiro: FGV/CPDOC.

DIEESE. 2015. Balanço das greves em 2013. *Estudos e Pesquisas* 79, December.

Folha de Sao Paulo. 2003. Leia íntegra do Discurso de Lula em São Bernardo do Campo. *Folha de São Paulo*, May 1. http://www1.folha.uol.com.br/folha/brasil/ult96u48592.shtml

Franzosi, Roberto. 1995. *The Puzzle of Strikes: Class and State Strategies in Postwar Italy*. Cambridge: Cambridge University Press.

French, John D., and Alexandre Fortes. 2012. Nurturing Hope, Deepening Democracy, and Combating Inequalities in Brazil: Lula, the Workers' Party, and Dilma Rousseff's 2010 Election as President. *Labor* 9 (1): 7–28.

Galvão, Andréia. 2009. A reconfiguração do movimento sindical no governo Lula. *Revista Outubro* 18: 177–200.

Gómez, Hernan B. 2013. *Lula, the Workers' Party and the Governability Dilemma in Brazil*. New York: Routledge.

Hall, Michael M. 2009. The Labor Policies of the Lula Government. In *Brazil Under Lula: Economy, Politics, and Society Under the Worker-President*, ed. Joseph L. Love and Werner Baer, 151–165. New York: Palgrave Macmillan.

Hochstetler, Kathryn. 2008. Organized Civil Society in Lula's Brazil. In *Democratic Brazil Revisited*, ed. Peter R. Kingstone and Timothy J. Power, 33–53. Pittsburgh: University of Pittsburgh Press.

Hunter, Wendy. 2010. *The Transformation of the Workers' Party in Brazil, 1989–2009*. Cambridge: Cambridge University Press.

Hunter, Wendy, and Timothy J. Power. 2007. Rewarding Lula: Executive Power, Social Policy, and the Brazilian Elections of 2006. *Latin American Politics and Society* 49 (1): 1–30.

Kelly, John. 1998. *Rethinking Industrial Relations: Mobilisation, Collectivism and Long Waves*. London: Routledge.

Noronha, Eduardo. 1990. A explosão das greves na década de 80. In *O sindicalismo brasileiro nos anos 80*, ed. Armando Boito Jr., 93–135. Rio de Janeiro: Paz e Terra.

Oliveira, Francisco de. 2006. Lula in the Labyrinth. *New Left Review* 42: 5–22.

Radermacher, Reiner, and Waldeli Melleiro. 2007. Mudanças no cenário sindical brasileiro sob o governo de Lula. *Nueva Sociedad* 211: 1–24.

Samuels, David. 2004. From Socialism to Social Democracy: Party Organization and the Transformation of the Workers' Party in Brazil. *Comparative Political Studies* 37 (9): 999–1024.

Singer, André. 2012. *Os sentidos do lulismo: Reforma gradual e pacto conservador.* São Paulo: Companhia das Letras.

Sluyter-Beltrão, Jeffrey. 2010. *Rise and Decline of Brazil's New Unionism: The Politics of the Central Única dos Trabalhadores.* Oxford: Peter Lang.

Tonelli, Flávio, and Antônio A. Queiroz. 2010. Trabalho e sindicalismo no governo Lula. In *Os anos Lula: Contribuições para um balanço crítico 2003–2010*, ed. João Paulo Almeida de Magalhães et al., 329–350. Rio de Janeiro: Garamond.

Webber, Jeffery R., and Barry Carr. 2013. Introduction: The Latin American Left in Theory and Practice. In *The New Latin American Left: Cracks in the Empire*, ed. Jeffery R. Webber and Barry Carr, 1–27. Lanham: Rowman and Littlefield.

Zucco, Cesar. 2008. The President's 'New' Constituency: Lula and the Pragmatic Vote in Brazil's 2006 Presidential Elections. *Journal of Latin American Studies* 40: 29–49.

CHAPTER 2

Labour Movements, Globalization, and the Dilemmas of Development

Trade unions in Latin America have faced a range of challenges affecting their ability to represent workers' interests while formulating an effective political agenda. In global terms, unions have struggled to respond to increasing globalization and economic integration, with workers competing globally for wages and improved labour conditions. Meanwhile, in a Latin American context, these constraints are compounded by the union movement's position in a highly diversified and heterogeneous labour market in which unionized workers have traditionally formed a minority of the working population. A common trope in the globalization debate is that workers have lost power as a result of the overwhelming and increasingly globalized power of capital. If unions have been organized primarily at a national level while capital operates globally, so the argument goes, workers can no longer bargain with employers in the same way they used to. Meanwhile, according to this narrative, workers also face the constant threat of job losses as companies relocate in search of lower labour costs.

This interpretation of globalization is problematic in several respects. It is an overly structural explanation that treats workers as passive victims of the faceless power of global capital. While there is no doubt that labour and capital relations are asymmetrical, this tells us little about what happens on the ground, particularly if we consider that labour conflicts continue to experience ebbs and flows, which cannot be explained by a focus on the linear trajectory of labour decline. To achieve a more nuanced understanding of how trade unions have fared, this chapter argues for a move away from narratives about decline and focuses instead on the dilemmas created by globalization, political change, and economic reforms. In particular, this chapter underlines the fundamentally political nature of the challenges facing trade unions, which requires an examination of how political dynamics shape trade union strategies.

Brazilian trade unions appeared to experience a different dynamic in the debate on globalization and labour, as trade unions based in the modern sectors of the economy and in multinational corporations played a key role in Brazil's democratization process and its aftermath. However, despite their significant political role, the union movement has also faced challenges associated with economic crisis and neoliberal reforms, pushing militant union activists towards defensive strategies. In the context of the increasing importance of progressive politics in Latin America since 1998, Brazilian trade unions have encountered new dilemmas after the left gained power, particularly regarding how to maintain a critical and autonomous stance towards its party ally while making full use of novel opportunities to influence the policy process. These dilemmas have often manifested themselves in debates about whether trade unionists should pursue militant or moderate strategies, providing significant insights into the union movement's response to political and economic change. In the Brazilian case, three dilemmas emerged from the democratization process: firstly, regarding the extent trade unionists needed to turn their opposition to military rule into a political agenda; secondly, how to address the impact of neoliberalism on labour and trade unions; and thirdly, what the effect would be on the union movement of a left-wing government.

To understand these dilemmas and their implications for labour politics in Brazil, the chapter begins with the argument that we should understand union strategies as inherently political, particularly if we consider organized labour's key role at various points in Latin America's political history. The discussion then turns to labour's opportunities to exert political influence, focusing on sources of labour power which unions have used to mobilize workers while also pressurizing employers and the state. A key element of this discussion is the notion of political power, including the ability to exert political influence both outside of and within the political arena. Because the interaction between these constraints and the union activists' response is not static, we need to take into consideration that the dynamics of political contention helps to explain the trajectories of union action, including how their strategies have evolved over time in interaction with the political and economic context as well as the influence of inherited strategies, ideas, and agendas. Using insights from the dialogue between labour and social movement theory, the argument proposed here is that debates about strategies do not represent a fixed or pre-set choice, rather they reflect the internal and external dynamics in which unions operate. Based on these insights, the chapter concludes by offering definitions of militancy and moderation, arguing that they are in fact relative terms whose meaning can change over time; therefore, they need to be understood with reference to the context in which these strategic and political debates have taken place.

2.1 Globalization and Labour: Beyond Structural Explanations

In order to explain the political position of trade unions, the literature on globalization and labour often refers to structural changes in capitalism and the labour market that have affected unions around the world.[1] Based on this argument, explanations for the loss of union political power refer to labour market changes resulting from industrial restructuring and factory relocation, thus eroding trade unions' affinity with and support from their traditional constituencies. In this scenario, unions have faced increasingly mobile capital, undermining their bargaining power as unions continue to be organized on a national basis, while workers now compete globally rather than nationally. In turn, as the scope for progressive demands has become increasingly constrained, organized labour's political strategies have turned to "defensive efforts to protect past gains",[2] making their political agenda effectively conservative, focused on protecting a narrow set of established union members' interests rather than a progressive agenda for political change, while failing to counter the forces of global capital.

As opposed to the arguments about a necessarily negative relationship between globalization and labour, this book argues that a focus on labour decline obscures the new conflicts created by intensified economic relations. Although there is no doubt that structural changes to the context in which unions operate have affected their political power and ability to shape political outcomes, in order to understand patterns of decline and renewed resistance, we also need to consider political factors, particularly in the context of developing countries, such as the role of the state in shaping labour relations, and the dynamics of authoritarianism and democratization, which have all had a long-lasting effect on labour's political strategies.

A focus on structural changes also struggles to explain national variations, political cultures, and changes in union action and agendas over time. This lack of explanatory power beyond general structural features is particularly true for developing countries, which tend to experience similar changes but in different circumstances which are not easily illuminated by these theories.[3]

To explain the Brazilian trajectory, we therefore need to analyse not only global trends but also the political and institutional context as well as the historical legacy of union strategies and organized labour's relationship with other actors, particularly the state, political parties, and other social movements. The active role of the state in shaping economic development through a "developmentalist" agenda[4] and state intervention in labour relations through corporatism is peculiar to many developing countries. Another key change shaping the Brazilian union movement's political trajectory was the end of authoritarianism, a transitionary moment in which organized labour played a crucial role and which lent it newfound legitimacy as a political actor. Furthermore, in countries such as Brazil, worker mobilization emerged in the modern, industrialized, and export-oriented sectors of the economy. Although only a relatively small proportion of the Brazilian population works in these sectors, they have had a disproportionate effect on political and union mobilization, providing an alternative to the argument that industrial unionism is inevitably in decline.

2.2 The Political Dimensions of Labour and Trade Union Action

Collective labour action, such as wage bargaining and strikes, is sometimes treated as primarily informed by economic and workplace considerations to achieve wage increases and improve working conditions. However, these actions cannot be understood without reference to their political dimensions in the sense that the political context shapes workers' strategies and determines the extent to which they can achieve their aims. To understand the evolution of labour politics in Brazil over the last four decades, it is necessary to analyse trade union strategies in political terms because collective labour action has often responded to political developments due to the nature of state-labour and, more recently, union-party relations. Working people and trade unions operate in a political arena characterized by unequal power relations, meaning that their demands have often challenged the existing political and economic order. For example, the political exclusion of trade unions and other parts of civil society in authoritarian Brazil politicized their members and actions, strengthening their role in the democratization process. Labour activism also has political implications because workers' demands can put democratic governments under pressure, particularly when striking employees implicitly or explicitly challenge government policy. Trade unions not only aim to increase wages but also focus on other factors that affect working conditions, welfare, and employment, such as social and macroeconomic policy.[5] Strikes can turn into a political problem if they disrupt public life, which trade unionists can use as leverage in negotiations with politicians to achieve their demands, as in the case of anti-privatization, public transport, or health sector strikes. To explain the reasons why labour activists and their unions have become politically involved, this section discusses why we should understand labour collective action as inherently political.

Many labour scholars recognize the political character of trade unions and labour movements in terms of the way wages and working conditions are shaped in the political arena, which makes trade union involvement in politics a logical next step. Trade union activists have also pursued political strategies because they are alert to the importance of influencing political decision-makers and the political nature of labour market institutions. For example, Seidman points out in her study of Brazilian and South African trade unions that it is difficult to disentangle their political and economic demands because "without access to state resources, without reforms in labor legislation and state policies, workers could not hope to improve either their working conditions or their general standard of living".[6] Similarly, according to Scherrer and Hachmann, the labour market does not operate exclusively in economic terms but is embedded in social and political structures so "[a] labour movement is bound to become involved in politics, because so many aspects of its own conditions of action, as well as of its members' lives are shaped by the prevailing laws and balance of forces in the political arena".[7] Furthermore, Candland and Sil emphasize the union movement's position as a major group in civil society, whose concerns and agendas transcend narrow demands: "workers and their formal and informal organizations represent an important collection of actors who are simultaneously political actors."[8] Although these studies recognize the political nature of union activism, how unions and labour activists turn this understanding into a political agenda and how this political engagement affects trade union strategies needs further discussion.

A significant explanation of labour's political involvement can be found in the literature on democratization in the historical sociology tradition. Explaining why the working class played a significant pro-democratic role in twentieth century Latin America is a key focus in this body of work.[9] For example, Collier and Collier posit that the existence of a strong working class was an essential determinant accounting for whether Latin American countries experienced democratization or a turn to authoritarian politics in the first half of the twentieth century.[10] A particularly important argument is that government responses to growing labour militancy in the early- to mid-twentieth century were a key factor in shaping both twentieth century Latin American politics and trade union political strategies. Collier and Collier's argument centres on how early twentieth century Latin American governments, faced with fundamental socio-economic changes resulting from the Great Depression, shifted from repression as their predominant response to labour militancy to attempting to either control or mobilize this new political group.[11] State strategies to control an increasingly militant working class resulted in corporatism while attempts to mobilize workers contributed to the rise of populism.[12] Both corporatism and populism left long political legacies for labour politics in Latin America today, contributing to an institutional framework that curtailed labour militancy.

The centrality of state-labour relations in Latin America draws our attention to the political, institutional, and cultural relations between trade unions, employers, and the state—structured through corporatism in the Latin American case—which helps explain political strategies and patterns of labour militancy and moderation. The political incorporation of workers through corporatism and populism proved to be problematic for unionists with radical political ambitions because corporatist regulations only recognized depoliticized unions while populist politicians tied workers to a political agenda focused on social order rather than radical political change.[13] The dual effect of corporatist labour laws was to constrain militancy by regulating and restricting union behaviour alongside creating organizational and financial resources which at times provided opportunities for radical action. This dynamic resulted in significant political dilemmas at the heart of the labour agenda or, according to Collier and Collier, helped to create "the tension between a conception of the political sphere as an essential arena for the defense of workers' interests and the concern that participation in politics will corrupt and co-opt unions and union leaders".[14] Thus, while trade unions obtained opportunities for political participation during this period, their political incorporation through corporatism and populism also sparked internal conflicts within unions about the best way to represent their members' interests, a question which was inextricably linked to their pursuit of a wider agenda for political change. The literature on sources of labour power helps explain how trade unions have turned their mobilizational power into political influence.

2.3 Sources of Labour Power and Political Influence

The debate on sources of labour power in the labour studies literature focuses on the ways in which trade unions can mobilize their membership and organizational structures to strengthen their position in collective bargaining processes and to achieve their political aims. In the context of this book, the significance of this debate lies in the development of a more nuanced argument about the decline of trade union power while including the political dimension of trade union action more explicitly in the sources of labour power debate. In turn, globalization and neoliberal reforms are often presumed to have led to the decline of labour in the face of global competition as the threat of company relocation has weakened workers' bargaining power, thereby pushing them towards accepting lower wages and inferior working conditions. Moreover, neoliberal reforms have led to deregulation and the erosion of social rights, contributing to the attrition of workers' previous rights and protections. However, while structural conditions such as inequality, corporatism, a repressive political climate, and globalization have often limited what unions can achieve, these same conditions shape but do not determine political change. According to Coe and Jordhus-Lier's argument, workers "constantly operate within complex and variable landscapes of opportunity and constraint: while for some their positionality within these structures will offer 'wiggle room' for reworking power relations, for others meaningful agency will be tightly circumscribed by the intersection of structural forces".[15] This notion of "constrained agency" focuses on the agency of workers and trade unions in what are often adverse economic and political circumstances, moving away from an overly structural explanation of collective labour action. To understand the interplay between the structure and labour's political agency, the debate on sources of labour power offers a powerful framework to understand how unions mobilize people and exert influence; the extent to which unionists can draw on these sources of power effectively depends on these structural constraints and the social balance of power. This section discusses structural and associational power as well as workers' and trade unions' symbolic, social, and political power resources that trade unions have employed to achieve their goals.

Theories of labour power emphasize the capacity of organized labour to both bargain (namely, structural power, linked to workers' position in the economy and the labour market) as well as to mobilize people (associational power, based on trade union organizational structures).[16] Structural power also refers to the location of unions and workers in the economy, for example, skilled workers in particular economic sectors have more bargaining power and leverage than others. Drawing on Erik Olin Wright's work, Beverly Silver distinguishes between two forms of structural power: power related to workers' position in the labour market ("marketplace bargaining power") and their position in the workplace ("workplace bargaining power").[17] The former is associated with the demand for labour, so factors such as low levels of unemployment and the scarcity of workers' skills can increase trade union leverage in collective bargaining. Tight labour markets make it more difficult for employers to replace workers during strikes, but the reverse situation of high unemployment can reduce workers' bargaining power. In turn, workplace bargaining power is associated with the role of workers in the production process when workers "are enmeshed in tightly integrated production processes, where a localized work stoppage in a key node can cause disruptions".[18] Meanwhile, structural labour power varies according to the economic sector in which a union is located as well as the wider economic conjuncture, which means that the extent to which trade unionists can mobilize this source of power depends on the time and location in which union action takes place.

Associational power refers to the organizational strengths of unions and other collective organizations, particularly their ability to mobilize people in order to put pressure on the government and employers through work stoppages and demonstrations.[19] Associational power has organizational and mobilizational dimensions; trade union organizational structures such as national federations or factory commissions can be used to gather information, communicate ideas, or circulate messages about upcoming strikes as well as to support striking workers. Trade union leaders have often used these structures to marshal large numbers of people to protest against employers or the government, which represents the mobilizational aspect of this form of power. As highlighted in the previous section, strikes and demonstrations often have a political impact in the sense that they put pressure on politicians, which is a manifestation of associational power in terms of the way union leaders use trade union organizational structures to organize people. The most common examples of workers' associational power are trade unions and their relationship with political parties[20] but this form of power can also manifest itself in networks and alliances with other civil society organizations, such as social movements.[21] The extent to which workers can deploy their associational power should be understood as shaped by national institutional and regulatory frameworks, as "historically, associational power has been embedded in state legal frameworks".[22] More specifically, in most of Latin America, institutions such as corporatism have circumscribed trade union associational power by, for example, banning trade unions from taking on political roles and limiting the geographical and sectoral scope of collective bargaining. These corporatist restrictions reflected government intentions to limit unions' associational power and leverage in collective bargaining processes. Despite these restrictions, trade union structures continued to exist and often became vehicles for pro-democracy mobilization in the 1970s and 1980s, illustrating how workers were able to operate within the constraints that they faced.

In addition to the capacity to bargain and organize, recent labour research has also engaged with symbolic, social or coalitional, and political power, which are particularly significant in explanations of organized labour's political trajectories. In her book on marginalized workers in the USA and South Korea, Jennifer Chun employs the concept of symbolic power, drawing on Pierre Bourdieu, in order to explain how struggles over moral and cultural understandings of justice and recognition have become important sites of contestation, not only for social movements but also for labour activists. Her understanding of symbolic power goes to the heart of the debate on segmented labour markets and increasingly precarious working conditions. She argues that a significant area of labour politics is about the recognition of workers who are marginalized from formal labour rights and trade union representation. Symbolic power therefore centres on "the ability to win recognition in the public arena as a legitimate political actor with the capacity to influence the distribution of power and resources in society".[23] Another distinct aspect of moral and symbolic power relevant to the examples analysed in this book is the legitimacy gained by the pro-democracy movement in their opposition to authoritarian politics,[24] which refers to the struggle for the recognition of citizenship, human and labour rights. Workers' central role in the opposition movement left a legacy of successful political contestation, emphasizing militancy, democratic union politics, and a rejection of state intervention. In the Brazilian context, the struggle regarding recognition and rights not only refers historically to formal workers achieving the right to organize under corporatism and the struggle for labour and citizenship rights in the democratic transition, but also to those who have fought for workers' rights outside of trade union representation.

In the Brazilian case, due to the high levels of repression the union movement experienced under the dictatorship, such non-traditional forms of labour militancy played a central role in effective pro-democracy activism. To sustain strike action in a hostile environment, Brazilian unions established networks with other social movements as well as community action campaigns. These networks had the capacity to translate into coalitional power,[25] when these alliances managed to weave together disparate grievances and protests into a strike or protest wave, as Brazil experienced in the late 1970s and 1980s. In her study of the South African and Brazilian unions, Gay Seidman refers to this symbiosis between unions and their communities as "social movement unionism": "strikes over factory issues receive strong community support; conversely, community campaigns for improved social services and full citizenship are supported by factory organizations as labor movements redefine their constituencies to include the broader working class."[26] Although several scholars have questioned the extent to which social movement unionism continued to exist after the transition to democracy, this book demonstrates that in Brazil it left a legacy of grassroots organizing and social movement networks.[27] The networks and alliances that trade unions formed with other social movements throughout the period analysed in this book have been a key factor in the union movement's political strategies. Apart from social and community movements, political parties are another key strategic ally for trade unions, allowing union activists to relate their political agenda to the formal political arena.

Political power refers to a complex mixture of political influence through both political participation and action not inside the formal political arena, involving relations with political parties and other civil society organizations. Workers' political influence has often taken place outside formal politics: the power to disrupt public life through "riots, mass demonstrations, or civil disobedience",[28] which can serve to pressurize the government and politicians. In the case of trade unions, the power to disrupt not only refers to the ability to organize or participate in demonstrations but also includes the disruptive effect of strike action in sectors such as public transport and education. Trade union involvement in formal politics is another key dimension of political power, providing labour activists with institutional influence, power which is "defined through the system of industrial relations, through mechanisms of participation in society, and through the institutional integration of the labor unions in government activities".[29] Indeed, Webster calls institutional power the missing link in the debate on power sources, stressing that "institutions shape the relationship between structural and associational/organisational power".[30] While political influence through formal institutions—such as governments, political parties, and participatory structures—have constituted a significant source of political power, this influence has also resulted in dilemmas about the extent to which unions should engage with these structures or challenge them. In addition, this predicament has proved to be a recurring theme in Brazilian labour politics, underlining the importance of considering labour sources of power in terms of how trade unionists have perceived and used them in practice.

The extent to which labour actors can exert political influence through political parties is another factor shaping militant and moderate strategies.[31] In a democratic context, the role of unions and labour-based parties has often been interdependent, even if they play different political roles: while trade unions can gain access to the state and decision-making through political parties, political parties can strengthen their electoral base through trade union support. Consequently, organized labour's influence in the political arena points to the significance of union-party relations for union political strategies. As Lee argues with reference to Taiwan and Korea, the extent to which unions were represented politically by parties or had political channels to voice their concerns, particularly through political parties, had a significant effect on labour militancy.[32] While in Korea unions were largely excluded from political influence and resorted to militant action, in Taiwan trade union moderation can be explained as a result of its incorporation in the government through the Kuomintang party. Lee's argument underlines the moderating role of close union-party relations, particularly when the party is in power, which we can also observe in the relationship between the PT and its support base in the unions.

Yet, conflicts have emerged due to the fact that these political parties represent wider interests beyond their union constituency. The need to compromise with other parties and groups—whether for electoral purposes, in coalitions or the formal political arena—can therefore distance labour-based parties from their union roots. Valenzuela summarizes this dilemma as follows: "[t]he more closely a party is identified only with unions, the greater will be its responsiveness to union demands, but the smaller will be its capacity to protect union interests. And the greater the political capabilities of the party, the lesser the possibility that the union will be able to subordinate it to its interests."[33] Because of this dynamic, the relationship between unions and labour-based parties not only has the potential to become conflictual but also affects unions when they face the question whether to protest or acquiesce when their party allies are in government.

One of the central dilemmas in union-party relations is what happens if labour-based parties are in power and the party's leaders decide to introduce policies that hurt their union constituency. Despite high expectations among their supporters, labour-backed parties in power have faced pressures to implement budget cuts while attempting to manage fragile coalitions, contributing to a sense that these parties had betrayed their principles. Contentious initiatives have ranged from specific policies that affect union members, such as labour and social security reform, to the treatment of the party's union allies—whether they gain greater access to political influence or whether the party distanced itself from the union movement—to disagreements about policy, such as budget cuts and public spending priorities. For a labour party's union supporters, these disagreements create a "loyalty dilemma": labour leaders "must choose between supporting the reforms, thereby remaining loyal to the party while behaving disloyally toward workers, or resisting the reforms, thereby remaining loyal to workers while behaving disloyally toward the party".[34] According to Burgess, whether unions decide to protest against their party allies depends on the extent to which the party punishes them for disloyalty by withholding access to political influence, which can lead to moderation, or if leaders face dissent among union members, which can provoke militant action.[35] Dissatisfaction with government reforms among rank-and-file members therefore has the capacity to increase labour militancy while also crippling the union movement, leading to splits and the emergence of competing union organizations[36] that offer alternatives to union members looking for either a more radical or moderate union to represent them.

In the Brazilian case, similar dynamics have characterized the relationship between the PT and the union movement. Roberts views the relationship among the PT, the unions, and social movements in the 1980s as symbiotic, bringing together formal politics and protest strategies:

Distinctions between the party and its constituent social organizations are deliberately blurred; indeed, the party may appear to be more of a movement than an apparatus for electoral contestation, as it is directly engaged in social struggles outside the sphere of institutional politics, and party members and leaders are drawn directly from social movements rather than from the ranks of a separate, professional political caste.[37]

Even in the early years of new unionism these relations were more conflictual than suggested by Roberts' description; however, they underline the significant overlap between the PT and social movements in terms of their membership, leaders, ideas, and agendas. PT-led municipal administrations faced conflicts with unions concerning strike action in the public sector while the MST increased land occupations in the immediate aftermath of Lula's inauguration. Amidst accusations that the PT administration would shift the government too far to the left, "civil society organizations tried to use their mobilizing power to support Lula and nudge him closer to their shared historic agenda".[38] In her study of urban protest in Brazil and Mexico, Bruhn argues that the reason why social and labour movements initially stepped up their protests against their party ally in government was that they expected the party to be more responsive to their demands.[39] However, labour-based parties like the PT have also experienced difficulties maintaining civil society support while appealing to the wider electorate and managing (often fractious) relations with coalition partners. In his study of the PT's relationship with civil society, Gómez found that as a result of these considerations, which he calls the "governability dilemma", both the party and its social movement allies became more moderate and pragmatic after the transition to democracy, shifting the focus of their political strategies from protests to the political arena.[40] Gómez demonstrates that the PT did not so much distance itself from its social movement allies but offered activists rewards, such as financial resources, political positions, and access to political decision-making, which often secured their loyalty.[41] These examples suggest that there is no straightforward causal relationship between the nature of union-party relations and labour militancy and even if parties and unions become more moderate, the seeds of militancy remain, as moderate agendas were strongly contested.

The sources of labour power discussed in this section help explain how and why trade unions engage in collective action, as the structural conditions in which workers operate shape what they can and cannot achieve. These different power resources are also linked to why trade unionists have used different strategies to achieve their aims based on what they perceive their strengths to be. Collective action among a skilled workforce in a key economic sector therefore displays a different dynamic than the collective action of street cleaners who are not members of formal trade unions and may need to rely on their ability to disrupt public life to get their point across to the authorities. Given the heterogeneity of working people and their organizations in Latin America, it is hard to treat these differential power resources as structural conditions that can be objectively measured in an analysis of collective labour action. Union membership, education and sectoral employment have sometimes been used as a proxy for labour power, but this approach is problematic in the diverse Brazilian context. Trade unions themselves are also internally diverse; as Barker and Lavalette have observed, unions "include complex networks and tendencies, which contend among themselves over the identity of the movement itself, its strategies and policies".[42] Moving beyond the most commonly cited sources of labour power—structural and associational power—to address symbolic, social, and political power means adding a subjective dimension to the debate, whereby the interaction between structural and subjective factors shapes collective labour action.[43] As Silver suggests, the crisis of organized labour may have resulted not so much from "transformations in the structural conditions facing workers' movements but [from] transformations in the discursive environment".[44] Recognizing the subjective dimension of labour power means treating sources of labour power as constructions that emerge from debates about politics and strategies within trade unions, not as objective conditions per se. This approach shifts the political analysis of labour strategies towards trade unionists' perceptions of their position in society as well as viewing these same perceptions as shaped by their experiences as a given worker and trade unionist, the legacies of past collective action, and political ideas.

2.4 Collective Labour Action and Protest Waves

The interplay of subjective and structural factors is an important addition to explanations of collective labour action, which requires us to understand the emergence of collective labour action, as well as how it evolves and changes in response to different political and economic contexts. Similarly, Silver has raised the possibility that "there is no strict correspondence between workers' bargaining power and the actual use by workers of that power to struggle for better working and living conditions".[45] To understand how workers draw on these power resources and to what effect, this section discusses the contributions of social movement research to an understanding of the reasons why grievances turn into collective action, bridging the gap between the potential for collective action and the actual outcomes. The dialogue between social and labour movement theories illustrates that trade unions have structures and strategies in common with social movements, meaning that social movement theory can provide useful insights into the evolution of labour politics. A major contribution of such theory is the focus on protests as a process rather than as singular events, showing that organizational structures and repertoires of collective action change as protest waves evolve and political opportunities emerge. A social movement approach also allows us to understand how internal characteristics of unions—such as the legacies or repertoires of past collective action—influence a movement's agenda. This perspective allows for a more dynamic view of strategic decisions and debates in relation to the union movement's changing context: "[c]ontention or moderation, protest or bargaining are not choices that are made once and for all."[46] This section starts with a brief overview of the connections between labour and social movements before discussing the contributions of social movement theory to the analysis of trade union political strategies, focusing on the impact of political opportunity and repression, and the role of ideas, the legacy of past experiences, and organizational structures.

Many labour and social movement scholars now recognize that aspects of social movement theory are relevant to the analysis of trade unions and labour movements.[47] However, a disadvantage of this theory is the tendency to neglect or even reject class as a relevant category based on the argument that identity rather than socio-economic conditions have come to shape collective action.[48] Indeed, many social movement theories have criticized the concept of class as a homogenizing and universal principle in relation to organization, mobilization, and interest formation.[49] Latin America-based research has also detected a move away from class politics to a "multiplicity of social actors" active in an increasingly "fragmented social and political space",[50] thereby leading to the marginalization of labour in academic research. However, new social movement studies have sometimes treated social movements as a *sui generis* phenomenon without considering the long historical roots of these "new" movements as well as the connections between identity and socio-economic factors. As Gledhill argues, because societies in the developing world are extraordinarily diverse, the new identity-based movements have operated alongside older interests and identities associated with class, poverty, and basic survival, both within and among social movements.[51] At times, new social movement arguments have ignored how these historical experiences and structures, such as populism and corporatism, shape present-day strategies and conflicts. Philip and Panizza also question the boundaries between old and new Latin American social movements, both of which use "transgressive and institutional mobilizing strategies and mix specific demands with broader political goals", thereby blurring the distinction "between identity-based movements and interest-based ones and that between social and political movements".[52] In reality, "[c]enturies-old types of protest, such as food riots and rural land seizures, appear alongside strikes, demonstrations, and protest meetings",[53] meaning that the separation of old and new forms of protest is essentially a futile exercise.

To understand the reasons why adverse conditions have led to labour militancy in some cases and to moderation in others, social movement theories help explain under what circumstances unions have been able to deploy the sources of labour power outlined previously in the course of a protest wave. An influential view in social movement theory is that protests increase when people perceive opportunities to demonstrate and if they feel that the risks—such as a repressive backlash—outweigh the benefits of what protestors hope to achieve.[54] In this view, the activities of social movements are shaped by "the broader set of political opportunities unique to the national context in which they are embedded",[55] or the political opportunity structure. This structure refers to the socio-political and economic context in which unions operate, particularly the trade-offs between opportunities and threats, such as state-sponsored repression and the undermining of livelihoods under neoliberalism and globalization.[56] Using this concept, the political process theory analyses how social movements emerge, consolidate, and decline over protest cycles. In the resulting political process model, external factors such as political opportunities as well as threats interact with internal characteristics of social movements to shape political outcomes.[57] This perspective allows for a dynamic view of movement strategies in response to changes in the political and economic context.[58]

As the democratic transitions in Latin America demonstrate, civil society organizations existed under authoritarian regimes and even flourished as activists had to identify alternative spaces for action outside of the political sphere, while traditional representative bodies such as political parties and unions were heavily repressed.⁵⁹ Both actual and threatened repression have therefore played a significant role in the evolution of labour politics in Latin America, as also recognized in the literature on twentieth century democratization discussed earlier in the chapter. Consequently, Almeida argues that social movement analysis should place more emphasis on threats, including repression and the constraining effects of economic crisis, in order to understand how protests evolve in developing countries.⁶⁰ These processes can trigger a protest wave, which Almeida defines as "periods of widespread protest activity across *multiple* collectivities that often encompass a sizeable portion of the national territory".⁶¹ Fragmented collective grievances and instances of unrest do not automatically turn into a wave of protests; rather they require networking and overlapping between social movements, using their associational and coalitional power to maximize their "political, ideological and economic power sources"⁶² to spread the protests beyond an initial sense of dissatisfaction. A key element of these protest waves is the movements' ability to translate disparate feelings of dissatisfaction into a powerful focus to unite disparate protests. In recent Brazilian history, protests developed into more widespread discontent at various times, often with significant trade union participation: the rise of grassroots and union opposition to the dictatorship from the early 1970s, which turned into the mass strikes of the late 1970s; the mass demonstrations for direct presidential elections in the mid-1980s; the anti-austerity protests in the 1980s and 1990s; since 2009, the new cycle of labour unrest and, from 2013 onwards, the anti-government protests leading to the impeachment of Dilma Rousseff in 2016. To understand Brazilian unions' significant role in these protests and the subsequent political change, the next section brings together the discussions on the political nature of trade union action, sources of labour power and protest waves, alongside a discussion on the relationship between labour militancy and moderation.

2.5 Labour Political Strategies: Between Militancy and Moderation

A useful way to connect political ideas to trade union strategies is to analyse trade union action on a spectrum of militancy to moderation. These concepts can be defined in terms of the range of strategies that unions use to achieve their aims, including strikes, negotiation, and political objectives.⁶³ The advantage of this approach is that militancy and moderation do not represent fixed political positions but depend on the context in which trade unionists operate, which provides a lens to analyse how and why trade union strategies change over time. A focus on militant and moderate strategies also allows us to explore both explicitly political dynamics and the workplace dimensions of collective labour action, with the latter emphasized more frequently in the labour studies literature. Before exploring definitions and explanations of labour militancy and moderation, the section briefly discusses the multiple meanings of militancy in the context of Brazilian unions.

The definition of militant and moderate labour strategies is not just a theoretical question but also an issue at the very centre of the political debates within the Brazilian left. A series of articles published in the PT magazine *Teoria e Debate* in the early 1990s discussed the future directions available to the left both in the aftermath of Brazil's democratization and the new realities of the post-Soviet world, framing the debate in terms of the prospects for militancy. These articles responded specifically to the challenges for left-wing politics posed by the fall of the Berlin Wall, which would redefine ideas about progressive politics among Brazilian activists. One article entitled "Metamorphoses of militancy" by José Corrêa Leite represented militancy as a "political activity which aims to achieve a profound transformation of the world",[64] combining a principled rejection of capitalist society with strategies such as developing effective movement action and establishing alliances with other social movements. A common theme in these articles was that continuing poverty and exclusion together with globalization and technological changes meant that certain models of militancy, such as "the Bolshevik, the anarchist agitator, the guerrilla fighter (in the image of Che), the communist party soldier" had become outdated.[65] An article written by João Rocha Sobrinho of the chemical workers' union in Bahia entitled "Militancy: Pleasure or sacrifice?"[66] added the orthodox Stalinist to this list. He lamented the lack of openness in political debates, particularly when the imperative of militancy overrode other priorities in life, such as family time, leisure, and education. Corrêa Leite also raised a set of key questions about the nature of political action as well as the relationship between social movements and left-wing parties: "Is political action restricted to parliament as the centre of gravity? Or, on the contrary, is the centre of transformative politics outside of this? Should a party militant defend their views in a union or movement? In case they are rejected, should they respect the entity's democratic decisions?"[67]

These quotes illustrate the various dimensions of militancy and moderation, including the nature of activism, activists, and the political agendas they pursue. In this debate, militancy and moderation did not just refer to protest strategies but also reflected the attributes of activists and their organizations as well as political agendas. As evident in Leite and Sobrinho's comments[68] about the prevailing "models" of militancy associated with—in their view—outdated ideologies, the terms *militante* and *militância* commonly refer to activists and activism engaged in a struggle for social justice and political change. In union circles, militant action is commonly referred to as *combativo* (combative), *confrontacional* (confrontational), *classista* or *de luta* (focused on class struggle), and *de base* (grassroots). Alternatively, moderate unionism is described as *sindicalismo de resultados* (results unionism), *negociador* (negotiating), and *pelego* (official, corporatist, state unionism). These terms have acted to delineate the difference between the militant new unionism that emerged in the late 1970s and 1980s as opposed to the official corporatist union movement and the emergence of the moderate "results unionism" of the early 1990s. Apart from the preferred focus of union action, another key division in labour militancy and moderation refers to the political agendas pursued by activists. As Leite's point highlights, this agenda was usually progressive in nature but contained significant disagreements about the extent to which unions should advocate for revolutionary change while continuing to represent their members' interests or aim to modify the worst excesses of capitalism while working within—and effectively accepting—existing political and economic constraints.

Indeed, the complexity of the Brazilian debate of the early 1990s shows that the differences between these two perspectives on union action are not as clear cut as suggested by the strict distinction between radical and pragmatic politics, particularly as militant unions have engaged in negotiations and moderate unions have organized strikes. In essence, militancy and moderation are to a large extent relative terms or, in other words, "what is radical at one time or in one place may not be radical later or elsewhere".[69] In a political sense, militant strategies are often linked to a generally progressive or even radical agenda, while moderation is associated with the acceptance of existing political and economic structures. In reality, the boundaries between these two approaches have often been blurred while changing in response to political and socio-economic transformations. Consequently, militancy and moderation are understood here as shaped by the given political context, including different political agendas, the strategies used to achieve these aims, as well as due to individual activists and leaders' attributes. In addition, how the union movement reacts to the influence of political dynamics underlines for us that the apparent poles of militancy and moderation frequently obscure the complexity of organized labour's reaction to the political arena.

Labour studies research has explored radical and pragmatic trade union strategies, leading to definitions that involve both workplace and political dimensions. John Kelly's starting point is the argument that the impact of structural conditions on trade union strategies varies over time and shapes the specific context, leading him to question narratives about the inevitable decline of labour.[70] His labour mobilization theory explains militant and moderate collective action as stemming from a collective "sense of injustice or illegitimacy amongst employees",[71] which the union leadership can deploy to persuade workers to participate in collective action. To explain how union leaders and members engage in collective action, Kelly uses the concept of "collective action frames [which emphasize] the importance of ideas in shaping people's behaviour and in particular their willingness to participate in collective action".[72] Closely related to the term "repertoires of collective action" used in the social movement literature, according to Johnston these ideas allow activists to make "strategic and tactical choices about how to pursue their cause, drawing on a mix of [available] protest forms".[73] Importantly, these repertoires build on "[m]emories of past situations" and activists' assessment of successful protests in the past, but also "present the established situation in a new light", thereby allowing protestors to link a new political context to the past, as Della Porta argues.[74] Meanwhile, Brazilian union activists have also ended up using particular organizational forms and strategies shaped by their assessment of past experiences, such as their criticism of corporatist unions as well as their experience as activists in other social movements, all of which has been reflected in their emphasis on grassroots mobilization and internal democracy. In other words, this political and organizational culture based on a history of effective militancy has become embedded in the movement's own assessment of its past successes and failures, which in turn has shaped subsequent strategic choices and debates.

The experiences, ideas, and debates that shape labour strategies are not predetermined by economically defined class interests but also reflect political ideologies, such as anarchism, socialism, and communism and the emergence of mass left-wing politics in the early twentieth century.[75] In Rueschemeyer, Stephens and Stephens' view, "the interests of labor inevitably involve a whole array of partly contradictory goals because labor is never simply a commodity and the whole human being cannot be eliminated from the factor of production that is labor".[76] This combination of ideas and interests is also reflected in the trade union debates and strategies analysed in this book. Indeed, for Barker and Lavalette, "[m]ovements are fields of argument, where the meaning of such apparently structuralist entities such as 'opportunities' are open to debate".[77] In this respect, the approach developed here suggests that we need to devote specific attention to the role of internal union debates on the vicissitudes of different political contexts, while being mindful of how frequently these debates and strategic dilemmas challenge overly polarized representations of militancy and moderation. On this issue, Kelly also stresses the role of debate and ideologies in connecting sources of labour power to collective action, remarking that "perceptions of power resources were critical in understanding power struggles, and ... such struggles involved not only an exchange of sanctions (strikes, etc.) but an exchange of arguments, designed to bolster the legitimacy of one side whilst undermining that of their opponents".[78]

The construction of these ideas and repertoires has often been subject to internal contestation, reflecting the union movement's own history and internal democratic structures.[79] In her study of urban protest in Mexico and Brazil, Bruhn has found that these protest repertoires shape a movement's identity, which often persisted when the context changed.[80] In addition, these ideas and values have been "inherited from the formative period of trade unions [and they shape] identities which cannot easily be altered"[81] without causing internal conflicts, which explains why debates about militancy and moderation can become so heated. Such debates have not only focused on employers but have also emerged within the union movement where "internal politics and in particular ... factional struggles"[82] along ideological lines have shaped how trade union leaders and activists framed labour conflicts and decided particular strategies. This subjective and ideational dimension reminds us that even though political opportunities and other structural conditions constrain the scope for action, their interpretation is subject to debate. The fact that structural conditions are contested means that there is no straightforward connection between structurally defined workers' interests and the actions trade unionists might decide to undertake. Instead, strategic decisions depend on considerations shaped by political ideas and past experiences with collective action. In the Brazilian case, trade unionists had significant successes with militant strike action in opposition to the dictatorship while new unionism's focus on democracy influenced strategic discussions, even when the political context changed.

Depending on the particular context, these political debates and strategic calculations have resulted in either militant or moderate union action, with Kelly characterizing the two poles as reflecting trade unions' willingness to engage in industrial action: such as strikes, or negotiation; the extent to which unions rely on mobilizing their membership; and whether unionists interpret their reality in terms of class conflict or partnership with employers and the state.[83] Similarly, for Dundon and Dobbins, militant and moderate orientations refer to the extent to which trade unionists consider their interests as fundamentally opposed to or reconcilable with those of employers:

> Both moderate and militant orientations relate to the formation of interests. *Moderation* is the accommodation between employees and managers based on understandings that respective interests are best fulfilled through cooperation… In contrast, *militancy* is frequently portrayed as eschewing accommodation and instead worker interests are deemed to be 'irreconcilable' with those of the managements.[84]

The authors connect militant strategies, particularly strikes, to an ideological position focused on class conflict, arguing that "Militant unions are typically regarded as those willing to invoke strike action *and* articulate an ideology of opposing interests".[85] As a result, as Darlington puts it, "trade unions are often the site of intense ideological struggles between different groups of activists about the definition of members' interests and the most appropriate means for their pursuit".[86] Thus, militant and moderate union strategies are shaped but not determined by political ideas and ideological perspectives, as well as trade unionists' perceptions of their environment, resources, and leverage. For example, in the context of the neoliberal reforms of the 1990s in Brazil, trade union debates continued to frame labour and political conflicts in terms of class struggle. Nevertheless, worsening economic conditions and the hostile political context pushed unions onto the defensive, demonstrating that their focus on opposing class interests did not necessarily translate into a confrontational approach.

Despite the different ideological perspectives that have often underpinned these debates, radical and pragmatic strategies are usually not fundamentally at odds but connected to each other.[87] A study by Bacon and Blyton has found that "a militant approach to mobilizing … secure[d] greater union involvement in management decision making whereas it was a militant approach to bargaining that was associated with stronger workplace trade unionism".[88] In the Brazilian context militant labour action, as exemplified by the strike waves of the late 1970s, often focused on strengthening a union's bargaining position and ensuring workplace union representation. Workplace representation through factory commissions opened up channels for direct bargaining with employers, which meant that union members felt they needed to maintain a climate conducive to negotiation by moderating their position. When economic conditions deteriorated and unionists faced reprisals, such as job losses, a return to strike action could strengthen the union's bargaining position by putting their employer under pressure to recognize the union's demands. Indeed, Kelly argues that we should contextualize these strategies and not treat them as static ideological choices, as they result "from an interaction between unions and their environments and cannot necessarily be regarded as a true measure of the preferences of the union and its constituent elements".[89] In addition, the dialectical nature of radicalism and pragmatism means that an analytical focus on changes in militant and moderate trade union strategies can tell us a considerable amount about the evolution of labour politics. The Brazilian strike movement of the late 1970s did not simply result from a strategic decision to engage in militant strike action but initially stemmed from workers' dissatisfaction with repression and the authoritarian nature of labour relations, which meant that strikes focused on strengthening the unions' collective bargaining position. The economically strategic position of industrial workers in the Brazilian southeast meant that they could leverage their structural power. Together with growing discontent with the dictatorship, these factors led to the escalation of strike action, which therefore cannot be reduced to either a commitment to militancy or moderation. Treating these types of strategies not as opposites but as interrelated allows for a move away from linear narratives of labour decline and moderation.

While most labour studies take trade unions' "constrained agency"[90] as a starting point in an analysis of labour strategies, scholars have developed different explanations of why workers adopt a militant or moderate approach. In particular, Beverly Silver's explanation focuses on the contradictions of global capitalism, arguing that labour militancy has resulted from the expansion of capitalism and struggles against the commodification of labour:

On the one hand, the expansion of capitalist production tends to strengthen labor and, therefore, brings capital (and states) recurrently face to face with strong labor movements. The concessions made to bring labor movements under control, in turn, tend to drive the system toward crises of profitability. On the other hand, efforts by capital (and states) to restore profits invariably involve breaking established social compacts and intensifying the commodification of labor, thereby producing crises of legitimacy and backlash resistance.[91]

Despite the asymmetrical relationship between labour and capital, Silver's argument that labour conflict follows the global expansion of capital suggests that the causal relationship between globalization and labour decline requires rethinking. Her study demonstrates that labour mobilization emerged in response to global capitalism's search for a "spatial fix", as exemplified by multinational corporations' relocation to countries with lower wages, such as Brazil, South Korea, and South Africa. In Silver's argument, it is not a coincidence that these conflicts have also contributed to significant political changes.[92]

Silver's Polanyian explanation of the repeated struggles against the commodification of labour also helps us shift our focus from linear explanations of labour decline to studying the conditions under which labour militancy re-emerges. Several labour and social movement scholars have adopted a similar Polanyian approach to recent protest waves, moving away from a focus on militancy at the point of production to resistance to the reproduction of labour, involving communities, livelihoods, and land. For example, Silva views the contestation of neoliberalism in Latin America in the 1990s as "defensive reactions to the imposition of market society or the threat of doing so".[93] The spike in Brazilian labour militancy at the end of the 1970s and early 1980s can then be interpreted as a response from workers with high levels of structural and associational power to the expansion of capitalist production in an authoritarian context.

Social movement theorists have also analysed how the evolution of protests affects pragmatic and radical movement strategies, positing that the ebb and flow of protests also influences internal debates about strategies, leading to radicalization in some cases and moderation in others.[94] For example, threats of repression or other negative repercussions can turn moderates into radicals, as evident in Brazil in the late 1970s and 1980s. As the strike movement evolved, union leaders were aware that high levels of state-led repression meant that workers were not necessarily prepared to protest directly against the military regime. The strike organizers found that they could mobilize workers to contest wages and working conditions, which started to include demands for political change as the strike movement grew in scope and impact.

Another insight is that union activists can radicalize as protests decline, with activists reaching back to a more militant past to inform debates about a new context. For example, the return to civilian rule in Brazil in the mid-1980s meant that trade union leaders had to rethink their political approach in the newly democratic context, while capitalizing on their learned ability to rally large numbers of people. However, their mass mobilization strategies were not always successful in the early years of the democratic government, leading to internal debates about the extent to which trade unionists should call for radical change. From this perspective, the legacy of successful militancy could compensate internally for the "loss of novelty" in protests; however, this same legacy has also had the capacity to divide moderate and radical groups as they experience changing circumstances.[95] In addition, the complicated legacy of successful militancy was also evident in the debates of the 1990s and 2000s, when union documents often referred to strategic successes of the past, without being able to replicate them in the new circumstances. However, in other cases, a tapering off of mobilization together with public recognition of movement demands can lead to activists pursuing participation in state institutions, often requiring activists' professionalization and a moderation of their demands.[96]

Moreover, organizational aspects of trade unions such as their bureaucratic nature has created an ambiguity within the union movement, which pushes labour activists towards both militancy and moderation, as Fantasia and Stepan-Norris have argued:

> Part of the difficulty in analysing the labor movement as a social movement has to do with the heavily institutionalized character of certain of its dimensions and practices. The organizations that constitute a labor movement are not simply (or even frequently) organizations mobilized to engage in direct action or social combat. Unions also bargain and negotiate with employers, they help to regulate economic activity ... In these ways unions restrain social combat and collective action, and thus a significant part of the labor movement can be seen as not only institutionalized, but institutionalizing.[97]

Union action is then "shaped by practices of deal making, bureaucratic wrangling and institutional administration",[98] which is a scenario familiar in unions around the world. In countries such as Brazil, the corporatist labour framework constitutes another institutionalizing—and moderating—influence on trade unions, one designed to limit the scope of collective bargaining and trade union political strategies. Although the new unionists rejected the bureaucratic nature of corporatist unions, viewing it as stifling union militancy, their aspiration to develop democratic unions that represented their members directly was never fully realized, underlining the power of a corporatist regulatory framework in pushing union strategies in a moderate direction.

In order to explain union militancy, many labour studies scholars have concentrated on the crucial role of the union leadership in mobilizing their membership. For example, Darlington has emphasized the tendency in labour militancy for left-wing union leaders to frame labour disputes in terms of class conflict and left-wing politics.[99] However, in Brazil, while many trade union debates were framed in class terms, the political context meant that trade unionists did not always do so explicitly while still engaging in militant action. For example, due to the high levels of repression under the dictatorship alongside corporatist restrictions on political activity, union leaders did not necessarily frame strikes in terms of class struggle. Instead, they had to operate more subtly to persuade workers to take the risk to strike while the leadership also began to frame their strategic actions as part of the struggle for democratization. In addition to the role of the union leadership, Upchurch and Mathers have underlined the importance of internal democratic structures in facilitating radicalism, arguing that a union leadership with a democratic, rather than a bureaucratic, approach tends to lead to strategies focused on the mobilization of union members.[100] While the stress on the interplay of structural conditions, union leadership, and subjective factors found in trade union research provides a useful explanation of union militancy, what is missing is a consideration of how political ideas and debates react to a changing political context, an issue which the remainder of this book addresses.

2.6 Conclusion

The repressive and authoritarian context of the Brazilian dictatorship led to a strong commitment among trade unionists to grassroots organizing and internal democracy, which allowed union leaders to engage workers in strike action. However, during the 1990s when new unionists continued to pursue a broadly progressive agenda in the workplace and in the political arena, they also faced adverse economic conditions and a government unresponsive to union demands. Although strikes managed to tap into the wider dissatisfaction with austerity politics until the mid-1990s, unionists could not maintain this level of strike action in the face of job losses. After Lula's election to the presidency, the context changed from a relatively hostile political environment to one in which union activists and other PT supporters had high expectations of the new government's responsiveness to their demands. The unionists' reluctance to challenge the PT in government out of a fear of destabilizing it inspired a moderate approach, leading to a stagnation of strike activity. Nevertheless, when government policies hurt the interests of core union constituencies and Brazilians began to question the distribution of the costs and benefits of the government's economic development plans, workers returned to militancy, as exemplified by the increase in strike activity from 2009 onwards.

The impact of these rapidly changing political dynamics on union action demonstrates the complexity of collective labour action beyond the strategic considerations of union leaders. These strategic calculations have been extensively discussed in research on union militancy while the Latin American historical sociology tradition and the literature on sources of labour power have also debated the impact of structural conditions. However, the influence of the wider political context on union strategies—in particular what happens when trade unionists develop political strategies and participate in politics—has received relatively little attention within labour studies research. While social movement theory rightly establishes a link between the evolution of protests and strategic debates, the Brazilian case underlines how this debate also responds to the changing political context. Despite the attention devoted to political ideas and ideologies in studies of union militancy, more research is needed to determine the ways in which these ideas translate into strategies that influence political change. Although the influence trade unionists had on the democratic transition in Brazil and their later close relations with the PT before and after the party assumed power is relatively unusual, even in a Latin American context, it demonstrates that this political participation had significant repercussions. As this book argues, the interaction between the union movement and the changing political context constitutes an important additional explanation of the types of action that unions undertake and their political impact.

The complex wavering between militant and moderate union action discussed here have been closely linked to political developments in Brazil, particularly as evidenced in the struggle against authoritarianism and neoliberalism that lasted from the 1970s until the mid-1990s. The evolution of trade union political strategies has involved the translation of workers' demands and interests into a specific political agenda, a programme which was then promoted through a range of conflictive and contested strategies: these have ranged from workplace action with political implications, pressure on the government through demonstrations and mobilization, to lobbying and participation in government. This political agenda has been fraught with contradictory interests and strategies, often reflecting the way workers are embedded in socio-political and economic contexts. By focusing on the conflicts which have emerged from trade union responses to rapid political and economic change, we can analyse labour political trajectories as shaped but not determined by structural conditions, rejecting discourses about the inevitable decline of labour as a political actor. Most importantly, the Brazilian case shows that political engagement should be understood as a double-edged sword: on the one hand, disengaging from politics can leave actors such as trade unions withoutvoice; on the other hand, political influence can also change unions' political demands, leading to conflicts between moderate and radical agendas.

NOTES

1. For a comprehensive review of the debate about globalization and labour since the 1980s, see Verity Burgmann, *Globalization and Labour in the Twenty-First Century* (Abingdon: Routledge, 2016), loc. 951–1125. For other recent critical literature in this field see also Ronaldo Munck, *Globalisation and Labour: The New 'Great Transformation'* (London: Zed, 2002); Stephanie Luce, *Labor Movements: Global Perspectives* (Cambridge: Polity, 2014); Edward Webster, Rob Lambert and Andries Bezuidenhout, *Grounding Globalization: Labour in the Age of Insecurity* (Oxford: Wiley-Blackwell, 2008).
2. Lowell Turner, "A Future for the Labour Movement?" In *The International Handbook of Labour Unions: Responses to Neo-liberalism*, edited by Gregor Gall, Richard Hurd, and Adrian Wilkinson, 311–27. Cheltenham: Edward Elgar, 2011: 321.
3. José R. Ramalho and Roberto Véras de Oliveira. "A atualidade do debate sobre trabalho e desenvolvimento." *Cadernos CRH*, 26(68) (2013): 211–5. For related arguments in the Asian context, see Kevin Gray, *Labour and Development in East Asia: Social Forces and Passive Revolution* (New York: Routledge, 2015) and Yoonkyung Lee, *Militants or Partisans:*

Labor Unions and Democratic Politics in Korea and Taiwan (Stanford, CA: Stanford University Press, 2011).
4. See also Kathryn Sikkink, *Ideas and Institutions: Developmentalism in Brazil and Argentina* (Ithaca, NY: Cornell University Press, 1991) and Christopher Wylde, *Latin America after Neoliberalism: Developmental Regimes in Post-Crisis States* (Basingstoke: Palgrave Macmillan, 2012).
5. Erik Olin Wright, "Working-Class Power, Capitalist-Class Interests, and Class Compromise," *American Journal of Sociology* 105(4) (2000), 963.
6. Gay W. Seidman, *Manufacturing Militance: Workers' Movements in Brazil and South Africa, 1970–1985* (Berkeley: University of California Press, 1994), 165.
7. Christoph Scherrer and Luciana Hachmann, "Can a Labour-Friendly Government be Friendly to Labour? A Hegemonic Analysis of Brazilian, German and South African Experiences," in *Labour in the Global South: Challenges and Alternatives for Workers*, ed. Sarah Mosoetsa and Michelle Williams (Geneva: ILO, 2012), 141.
8. Christopher Candland and Rudra Sil, "The Politics of Labor in Late-industrializing and Post-socialist Economies: New Challenges in a Global Age," in *The Politics of Labor in a Global Age: Continuity and Change in Late-Industrializing and Post-Socialist Economies*, ed. Christopher Candland and Rudra Sil (Oxford: Oxford University Press, 2001), 7–8.
9. Ruth Berins Collier and David Collier, *Shaping the Political Arena: Critical Junctures, the Labor Movement, and Regime Dynamics in Latin America* (Princeton: Princeton University Press, 1991); Dietrich Rueschemeyer, Evelyne Huber Stephens and John D. Stephens, *Capitalist Development and Democracy* (Cambridge: Polity Press, 1992).
10. Collier and Collier argue that the working class in Latin America was relatively weak and therefore not as powerful a democratic force as in other parts of the world. This perspective is mirrored in Brazilian labour studies in the argument that the heterogeneous society and labour market together with corporatist labour relations constrained not only labour militancy but also labour's democratic potential. For a critical perspective on this argument, see Oliver J. Dinius, *Brazil's Steel City: Developmentalism, Strategic Power, and Industrial Relations in Volta Redonda, 1941–1964* (Stanford, CA: Stanford University Press, 2011), 5–7; José Welmowicki, *Cidadania ou classe? O movimento operário da década de 80* (São Paulo: Editora Instituto José Luís e Rosa Sundermann, 2004), 83–9.
11. Collier and Collier, *Shaping the Political Arena*, 40–1.
12. Maria V. Murillo, *Labor Unions, Partisan Coalitions, and Market Reforms in Latin America* (Cambridge: Cambridge University Press, 2001), 50–1.

13. Corporatist state–labour relations can also be found in other developing countries, for example Lee, *Militants or Partisans*, 39–42; Gray, *Labour and Development in East Asia*.
14. Collier and Collier, *Shaping the Political Arena*, 49.
15. Neil M. Coe and David C. Jordhus-Lier, "Constrained Agency? Re-Evaluating the Geographies of Labour," *Progress in Human Geography* 35(2) (2010), 229.
16. Wright, "Working-Class Power," 962.
17. Beverly J. Silver, *Forces of Labor: Workers' Movements and Globalization Since 1870* (Cambridge: Cambridge University Press, 2003), 13.
18. Silver, *Forces of Labor*, 13.
19. Silver, *Forces of Labor*, 13.
20. Silver, *Forces of Labor*, 13.
21. Waldeli Melleiro and Jochen Steinhilber, "Brothers in Arms? Trade Union Politics under the Workers' Party Governments," in *The Political System of Brazil*, ed. Dana de la Fontaine and Thomas Stehnken (Berlin: Springer, 2016), 204.
22. Silver, *Forces of Labor*, 14.
23. Jennifer J. Chun, *Organizing at the Margins: The Symbolic Politics of Labor in South Korea and the United States* (Ithaca: Cornell University Press, 2009), 14.
24. On the moral power of protests and the question of regime legitimacy in Eastern Europe, see Anthony Oberschall, "Opportunities and Framing in the Eastern European Revolts of 1989," in *Comparative Perspectives on Social Movements: Political Opportunities, Mobilizing Structures, and Cultural Framings*, ed. Doug McAdam et al. (Cambridge: Cambridge University Press, 1996), 94.
25. Eduardo Silva, *Challenging Neoliberalism in Latin America* (Cambridge: Cambridge University Press, 2009), 48.
26. Seidman, *Manufacturing Militance*, 2–3.
27. For example, Seidman argues that the term "social movement unionism" is "used rather vaguely, often idiosyncratically". While her use of the term refers to new union practices in a specific historical context in South Africa, she argues that the term has also been used to contest the neglect of labour within social movement theory and more practically to develop new labour agendas to counter union decline, see Gay Seidman, "Social Movement Unionism: From Description to Exhortation," *South African Review of Sociology* 42(3) (2011), 94. See also Martin Upchurch and Andy Mathers, "Neoliberal Globalization and Trade Unionism: Toward Radical Political Unionism?" *Critical Sociology* 38(2) (2011), 265–80; Kevin Gray, *Korean Workers and Neoliberal Globalization* (London: Routledge: 2007).

28. Steve Jenkins, "Organizing, Advocacy, and Member Power: A Critical Reflection," *WorkingUSA* 6(2) (2002), 56–89, cited in Luce, *Labor Movements*, 63.
29. Melleiro and Steinhilber, "Brothers in Arms?" 203.
30. Edward Webster, "Labour after Globalisation: Old and New Sources of Power," Institute of Social and Economic Research, Rhodes University. ISER Working Paper no. 2015/1, 9.
31. Francisco Zapata explicitly includes political power along with associational power in his analysis of Latin American trade unionism, see Francisco Zapata, *História minima del sindicalismo latinoamericano* (México, DF: El Colegio de México, 2013), loc. 131.
32. Lee, *Militants or Partisans*.
33. J. Samuel Valenzuela, "Labor Movements and Political Systems: Some Variations," In *The Future of Labor Movements*, ed. Mario Regini (London: Sage, 1992), 65.
34. Katrina Burgess, *Parties and Unions in the New Global Economy* (Pittsburgh, PA: University of Pittsburgh Press, 2004), 9.
35. Burgess, *Parties and Unions*, 13.
36. Murillo, *Labor Unions, Partisan Coalitions*, 12–17.
37. Kenneth M. Roberts, *Deepening Democracy? The Modern Left and Social Movements in Chile and Peru* (Stanford, CA: Stanford University Press, 1998), 75.
38. Kathryn Hochstetler, "Organized Civil Society in Lula's Brazil," in *Democratic Brazil Revisited*, ed. Peter R. Kingstone and Timothy J. Power (Pittsburgh, PA: University of Pittsburgh Press, 2008), 33–4.
39. Kathleen Bruhn, *Urban Protest in Mexico and Brazil* (Cambridge: Cambridge University Press, 2008), 166.
40. Hernan B. Gomez, *Lula, the Workers' Party and the Governability Dilemma in Brazil* (New York: Routledge, 2013), loc. 1194.
41. Gómez, *Lula, the Workers' Party*, loc. 1344–1422.
42. Colin Barker and Michael Lavalette, "Strategizing and the Sense of Context: Reflections on the First Two Weeks of the Liverpool Docks Lockout, September-October 1995," in *Social Movements: Identity, Culture, and the State*, ed. David S. Meyer and Nancy Whittier (Oxford: Oxford University Press, 2002), 153.
43. Heather Connolly and Ralph Darlington, "Radical Political Unionism in France and Britain: A Comparative Study of SUD-Rail and RMT," *European Journal of Industrial Relations* 18(3) (2012), 241–2.
44. Silver, 2003, 16.
45. Silver, 2003, 15.
46. Donatella della Porta, *Mobilizing for Democracy: Comparing 1989 and 2011* (Oxford: Oxford University Press, 2014), 200.

47. For example, John Kelly, "Theories of Collective Action and Union Power," in *International Handbook on Labour Unions: Responses to Neo-Liberalism*, ed. G. Gall, R. Hurd and A. Wilkinson (Cheltenham: Edward Elgar, 2011); Peter Gahan and Andreas Pekarek, "Social Movement Theory, Collective Action Frames and Union Theory: A Critique and Extension," *British Journal of Industrial Relations*, 51 (4) (2013), 754–76; Donatella della Porta, "From Corporatist Unions to Protest Unions? On the (Difficult) Relations Between Organized Labour and New Social Movements," in *The Diversity of Democracy: Corporatism, Social Order and Political Conflict*, ed. Colin Crouch and Wolfgang Streeck (Cheltenham: Edward Elgar, 2006).
48. Upchurch and Mathers, "Neoliberal Globalization," 268. Social movement scholar Donatella della Porta has also called for renewed attention to class and capitalism in social movement analysis to explain the anti-austerity movements that emerged since the turn of the twentieth century, see Donatella della Porta, *Social Movements in Times of Austerity: Bringing Capitalism back into Protest Analysis* (Cambridge: Polity, 2015), 3–11.
49. Ernesto Laclau, "New Social Movements and the Plurality of the Social," In *New Social Movements and the State in Latin America*, ed. David Slater (Amsterdam: CEDLA, 1985), 28–9.
50. Sonia E. Alvarez, Evelina Dagnino and Arturo Escobar, "Introduction: The Cultural and the Political in Latin American Social Movements," in *Cultures of Politics, Politics of Culture: Re-visioning Latin American Social Movements*, ed. Sonia Alvarez, Evelina Dagnino and Arturo Escobar (Boulder, CO: Westview Press, 1998), 3.
51. John Gledhill, *Power and its Disguises: Anthropological Perspectives on Politics* (London: Pluto, 2000), 185–7.
52. George Philip and Francisco Panizza, *The Triumph of Politics: The Return of the Left in Venezuela, Bolivia and Ecuador* (Cambridge: Polity, 2011), 50.
53. Susan Eckstein, "Power and Popular Protest in Latin America," in *Power and Popular Protest: Latin American Social Movements*, ed. Susan Eckstein (Berkeley and London: University of California Press, 1989), 10.
54. Sydney Tarrow, *Power in Movement: Social Movements and Contentious Politics* (Cambridge: Cambridge University Press, 2011, 3rd edition), loc. 4227.
55. Doug McAdam, John D. McCarthy, and Mayer N. Zald, "Introduction: Opportunities, Mobilizing Structures, and Framing Processes – Toward a Synthetic, Comparative Perspective on Social Movements," in *Comparative Perspectives on Social Movements: Political Opportunities, Mobilizing Structures, and Cultural Framings*, ed. Doug McAdam, John D. McCarthy, and Mayer N. Zald (Cambridge: Cambridge University Press, 1996), 3.

56. Paul Almeida, *Waves of Protest: Popular Struggle in El Salvador, 1925–2005* (Minneapolis, University of Minnesota Press, 2008), 13–4; David S. Meyer and Lindsey Lupo, "Assessing the Politics of Protest: Political Science and the Study of Social Movements," in *Handbook of Social Movements across Disciplines*, edited by Bert Klandermans and Conny Roggeband (New York: Springer, 2007), 135–8.
57. Meyer and Lupo, "Assessing the Politics", 124.
58. Patricia L. Hipsher, "Democratic Transitions as Protest Cycles: Social Movement Dynamics in Democratizing Latin America," in *The Social Movement Society: Contentious Politics for a New Century*, ed. David S. Meyer and Sidney Tarrow (Lanham, MD: Rowman and Littlefield, 1998), 163–6.
59. Silva, *Challenging Neoliberalism*, 30.
60. Almeida, *Waves of Protest*, 13.
61. Almeida, *Waves of Protest*, 12.
62. Silva, *Challenging Neoliberalism*, 30.
63. See John Kelly, *Rethinking Industrial Relations: Mobilisation, Collectivism and Long Waves* (London: Routledge, 1998), 61.
64. José Corrêa Leite, "Metamorfoses de militância," *Teoria e Debate* 32 (1996).
65. Corrêa Leite, "Metamorfoses de militância".
66. João Rocha Sobrinho, "Militância: Prazer ou sacrifício?" *Teoria e Debate* 26 (1994).
67. Corrêa Leite, "Metamorphoses of militancy".
68. Corrêa Leite, "Metamorfoses de militância"; João Rocha Sobrinho, "Militância: Prazer ou sacrifício?"
69. Colin J. Beck, *Radicals, Revolutionaries, and Terrorists* (Cambridge: Polity Press, 2015), 26.
70. Kelly, *Rethinking Industrial Relations*, 10–12.
71. Kelly, *Rethinking Industrial Relations*, 44. See also Ralph Darlington, "The Interplay of Structure and Agency in Strike Activity," *Employee Relations* 34(5) (2012), 520.
72. Kelly, "Theories of Collective Action", 26. See also McAdam et al. "Introduction: Opportunities," 5.
73. Hank Johnston, *States & Social Movements* (Cambridge: Polity, 2011), 53–4.
74. Della Porta, *Mobilizing for Democracy*, 112–3.
75. Collier and Collier, *Shaping the Political Arena*, 60–3.
76. Rueschemeyer, Huber Stephens and Stephens, *Capitalist Development*, 54.
77. Barker and Lavalette, "Strategizing and the Sense", 143.
78. Kelly, *Rethinking Industrial Relations*, 52.
79. Kelly, "Theories of Collective Action", 23; Bruhn, *Urban Protest*, 6; Rueschemeyer, Huber Stephens and Stephens, *Capitalist Development*, 53.

80. Bruhn, *Urban Protest*, 9.
81. Richard Hyman and Rebecca Gumbrell-McCormick, "Trade Unions, Politics and Parties: Is a New Configuration Possible?" *Transfer* 16(3) (2010), 317.
82. Kelly, *Rethinking Industrial Relations*, 54.
83. Kelly, *Rethinking Industrial Relations*, 61.
84. Tony Dundon and Tony Dobbins, "Militant Partnership: A Radical Pluralist Analysis of Workforce Dialectics," *Work, Employment and Society*, 29(6) (2015), 2. Italics in the original.
85. Dundon and Dobbins, "Militant Partnership," 5.
86. Ralph Darlington, "Union Militancy and Leftwing Leadership on London Underground," *Industrial Relations Journal*, 32(1) (2001), 3.
87. Dundon and Dobbins, "Militant Partnership," 16.
88. Nicolas Bacon and Paul Blyton, "Militant and Moderate Trade Union Orientations: What are the Effects on Workplace Trade Unionism, Union-Management Relations and Employee Gains?" *International Journal of Human Resource Management*, 13(2) (2002), 312.
89. Kelly, *Rethinking Industrial Relations*, 61.
90. Coe and Jordhus-Lier, "Constrained Agency?", 229.
91. Silver, *Forces of Labor*, 20.
92. Silver, *Forces of Labor*, 5–6.
93. Silva, *Challenging Neoliberalism*, 18. See also Webster, Lambert and Bezuidenhout, *Grounding Globalization*; Sahan Savas Karatasli, Sefika Kumral, Ben Scully and Smriti Upadhyay, "Class, Crisis, and the 2011 Protest Wave: Cyclical and Secular Trends in Global Labor Unrest," in *Overcoming Global Inequalities*, ed. Immanuel Wallerstein, Christopher Chase-Dunn and Christian Suter (London: Paradigm, 2015).
94. Hanspeter Kriesi, Ruud Koopmans, Jan Willem Duyvendak and Marco G. Giugni, *New Social Movements in Western Europe: A Comparative Analysis* (London: UCL Press, 1995), 138–9.
95. Kriesi, Koopmans, Duyvendak and Giugni, *New Social Movements*, 138–9.
96. Rebecca Abers, Lizandra Serafim and Luciana Tatagiba, "Changing Repertoires of State-Society Interaction under Lula," in *Brazil under the Workers' Party: Continuity and Change from Lula to Dilma*, ed. Fábio de Castro, Kees Koonings and Marianne Wiesebron (Basingstoke and New York: Palgrave Macmillan, 2014); Brian K. Grodsky, *Social Movements and the New State: The Fate of Pro-Democracy Organizations when Democracy is Won* (Stanford: Stanford University Press, 2012); Rick Fantasia and Kim Voss, *Hard Work: Remaking the American Labor Movement* (Berkeley: University of California Press, 2004); Hank Johnston, *States & Social Movements* (Cambridge: Polity, 2011), 68–73.

97. Rick Fantasia and Judith Stepan-Norris, "The Labor Movement in Motion," in *The Blackwell Companion to Social Movements*, ed. David A. Snow, Sarah A. Soule and Hanspeter Kriesi (Oxford: Blackwell, 2004), 557.
98. Fantasia and Voss, *Hard Work*, 81.
99. Darlington, "Union Militancy and Left-wing Leadership".
100. Upchurch and Mathers, "Neoliberal Globalization," 270.

Bibliography

Abers, Rebecca, Lizandra Serafim, and Luciana Tatagiba. 2014. Changing Repertoires of State-Society Interaction under Lula. In *Brazil under the Workers' Party: Continuity and Change from Lula to Dilma*, ed. Fábio de Castro, Kees Koonings, and Marianne Wiesebron, 36–61. Basingstoke/New York: Palgrave Macmillan.

Almeida, Paul. 2008. *Waves of Protest: Popular Struggle in El Salvador, 1925–2005.* Minneapolis: University of Minnesota Press.

Alvarez, Sonia E., Evelina Dagnino, and Arturo Escobar. 1998. Introduction: The Cultural and the Political in Latin American Social Movements. In *Cultures of Politics, Politics of Culture: Re-visioning Latin American Social Movements*, ed. Sonia Alvarez, Evelina Dagnino, and Arturo Escobar, 1–32. Boulder: Westview Press.

Bacon, Nicolas, and Paul Blyton. 2002. Militant and Moderate Trade Union Orientations: What are the Effects on Workplace Trade Unionism, Union-Management Relations and Employee Gains? *International Journal of Human Resource Management* 13 (2): 302–319.

Barker, Colin, and Michael Lavalette. 2002. Strategizing and the Sense of Context: Reflections on the First Two Weeks of the Liverpool Docks Lockout, September-October 1995. In *Social Movements: Identity, Culture, and the State*, ed. David S. Meyer and Nancy Whittier, 140–156. Oxford: Oxford University Press.

Beck, Colin J. 2015. *Radicals, Revolutionaries, and Terrorists.* Cambridge: Polity Press.

Bruhn, Kathleen. 2008. *Urban Protest in Mexico and Brazil.* Cambridge: Cambridge University Press.

Burgess, Katrina. 2004. *Parties and Unions in the New Global Economy.* Pittsburgh: University of Pittsburgh Press.

Burgmann, Verity. 2016. *Globalization and Labour in the Twenty-First Century.* Abingdon: Routledge.

Candland, Christopher, and Rudra Sil. 2001. The Politics of Labor in Late-industrializing and Post-socialist Economies: New Challenges in a Global Age. In *The Politics of Labor in a Global Age: Continuity and Change in Late-Industrializing and Post-Socialist Economies*, ed. Christopher Candland and Rudra Sil, 3–28. Oxford: Oxford University Press.

Chun, Jennifer J. 2009. *Organizing at the Margins: The Symbolic Politics of Labor in South Korea and the United States*. Ithaca: Cornell University Press.

Coe, Neil M., and David C. Jordhus-Lier. 2010. Constrained Agency? Re-Evaluating the Geographies of Labour. *Progress in Human Geography* 35 (2): 211–233.

Collier, Ruth Berins, and David Collier. 1991. *Shaping the Political Arena: Critical Junctures, the Labor Movement, and Regime Dynamics in Latin America*. Princeton: Princeton University Press.

Connolly, Heather, and Ralph Darlington. 2012. Radical Political Unionism in France and Britain: A Comparative Study of SUD-Rail and RMT. *European Journal of Industrial Relations* 18 (3): 235–250.

Corrêa Leite, José. 1996. Metamorfoses de Militância. *Teoria e Debate* 32.

Darlington, Ralph. 2001. Union Militancy and Leftwing Leadership on London Underground. *Industrial Relations Journal* 32 (1): 2–21.

———. 2012. The Interplay of Structure and Agency in Strike Activity. *Employee Relations* 34 (5): 518–533.

Dinius, Oliver J. 2011. *Brazil's Steel City: Developmentalism, Strategic Power, and Industrial Relations in Volta Redonda, 1941–1964*. Stanford: Stanford University Press.

Della Porta, Donatella. 2006. From Corporatist Unions to Protest Unions? On the (Difficult) Relations Between Organized Labour and New Social Movements. In *The Diversity of Democracy: Corporatism, Social Order and Political Conflict*, ed. Colin Crouch and Wolfgang Streeck, 71–95. Cheltenham: Edward Elgar.

———. 2014. *Mobilizing for Democracy: Comparing 1989 and 2011*. Oxford: Oxford University Press.

———. 2015. *Social Movements in Times of Austerity: Bringing Capitalism Back into Protest Analysis*. Cambridge: Polity.

Dundon, Tony, and Tony Dobbins. 2015. Militant Partnership: A Radical Pluralist Analysis of Workforce Dialectics. *Work, Employment and Society* 29 (6): 1–20.

Eckstein, Susan. 1989. Power and Popular Protest in Latin America. In *Power and Popular Protest: Latin American Social Movements*, ed. Susan Eckstein, 1–60. Berkeley: University of California Press.

Fantasia, Rick, and Judith Stepan-Norris. 2004. The Labor Movement in Motion. In *The Blackwell Companion to Social Movements*, ed. David A. Snow, Sarah A. Soule, and Hanspeter Kriesi, 555–575. Oxford: Blackwell.

Fantasia, Rick, and Kim Voss. 2004. *Hard Work: Remaking the American Labor Movement*. Berkeley: University of California Press.

Gahan, Peter, and Andreas Pekarek. 2013. Social Movement Theory, Collective Action Frames and Union Theory: A Critique and Extension. *British Journal of Industrial Relations* 51 (4): 754–776.

Gledhill, John. 2000. *Power and Its Disguises: Anthropological Perspectives on Politics.* London: Pluto.
Gómez, Hernan B. 2013. *Lula, the Workers' Party and the Governability Dilemma in Brazil.* New York: Routledge.
Gray, Kevin. 2007. *Korean Workers and Neoliberal Globalization.* London: Routledge.
———. 2015. *Labour and Development in East Asia: Social Forces and Passive Revolution.* New York: Routledge.
Grodsky, Brian K. 2012. *Social Movements and the New State: The Fate of Pro-Democracy Organizations when Democracy is Won.* Stanford: Stanford University Press.
Hipsher, Patricia L. 1998. Democratic Transitions as Protest Cycles: Social Movement Dynamics in Democratizing Latin America. In *The Social Movement Society: Contentious Politics for a New Century*, ed. David S. Meyer and Sidney Tarrow, 153–172. Lanham: Rowman and Littlefield.
Hochstetler, Kathryn. 2008. Organized Civil Society in Lula's Brazil. In *Democratic Brazil Revisited*, ed. Peter R. Kingstone and Timothy J. Power, 33–53. Pittsburgh: University of Pittsburgh Press.
Hyman, Richard, and Rebecca Gumbrell-McCormick. 2010. Trade Unions, Politics and Parties: Is a New Configuration Possible? *Transfer* 16 (3): 315–331.
Jenkins, Steve. 2002. Organizing, Advocacy, and Member Power: A Critical Reflection. *Working USA* 6 (2): 56–89.
Johnston, Hank. 2011. *States & Social Movements.* Cambridge: Polity.
Karatasli, Sahan Savas, Sefika Kumral, Ben Scully, and Smriti Upadhyay. 2015. Class, Crisis, and the 2011 Protest Wave: Cyclical and Secular Trends in Global Labor Unrest. In *Overcoming Global Inequalities*, ed. Immanuel Wallerstein, Christopher Chase-Dunn, and Christian Suter, 184–200. London: Paradigm.
Kelly, John. 1998. *Rethinking Industrial Relations: Mobilisation, Collectivism and Long Waves.* London: Routledge.
———. 2011. Theories of Collective Action and Union Power. In *International Handbook on Labour Unions: Responses to Neo-Liberalism*, ed. Gregor Gall, Richard Hurd, and Adrian Wilkinson, 13–28. Cheltenham: Edward Elgar.
Kriesi, Hanspeter, Ruud Koopmans, Jan Willem Duyvendak, and Marco G. Giugni. 1995. *New Social Movements in Western Europe: A Comparative Analysis.* London: UCL Press.
Laclau, Ernesto. 1985. New Social Movements and the Plurality of the Social. In *New Social Movements and the State in Latin America*, ed. David Slater, 27–42. Amsterdam: CEDLA.
Lee, Yoonkyung. 2011. *Militants or Partisans: Labor Unions and Democratic Politics in Korea and Taiwan.* Stanford: Stanford University Press.
Luce, Stephanie. 2014. *Labor Movements: Global Perspectives.* Cambridge: Polity.

McAdam, Doug, John D. McCarthy, and Mayer N. Zald. 1996. Introduction: Opportunities, Mobilizing Structures, and Framing Processes – Toward a Synthetic, Comparative Perspective on Social Movements. In *Comparative Perspectives on Social Movements: Political Opportunities, Mobilizing Structures, and Cultural Framings*, ed. Doug McAdam, John D. McCarthy, and Mayer N. Zald, 1–20. Cambridge: Cambridge University Press.

Melleiro, Waldeli, and Jochen Steinhilber. 2016. Brothers in Arms? Trade Union Politics under the Workers' Party Governments. In *The Political System of Brazil*, ed. Dana de la Fontaine and Thomas Stehnken, 201–227. Berlin: Springer.

Meyer, David S., and Lindsey Lupo. 2007. Assessing the Politics of Protest: Political Science and the Study of Social Movements. In *Handbook of Social Movements Across Disciplines*, ed. Bert Klandermans and Conny Roggeband, 111–154. New York: Springer.

Munck, Ronaldo. 2002. *Globalisation and Labour: The New 'Great Transformation'*. London: Zed.

Murillo, Maria V. 2001. *Labor Unions, Partisan Coalitions, and Market Reforms in Latin America*. Cambridge: Cambridge University Press.

Oberschall, Anthony. 1996. Opportunities and Framing in the Eastern European Revolts of 1989. In *Comparative Perspectives on Social Movements: Political Opportunities, Mobilizing Structures, and Cultural Framings*, ed. Doug McAdam, John D. McCarthy, and Mayer N. Zald, 93–121. Cambridge: Cambridge University Press.

Philip, George, and Francisco Panizza. 2011. *The Triumph of Politics: The Return of the Left in Venezuela, Bolivia and Ecuador*. Cambridge: Polity.

Ramalho, José R., and Roberto Véras de Oliveira. 2013. A atualidade do debate sobre trabalho e desenvolvimento. *Cadernos CRH* 26 (68): 211–215.

Roberts, Kenneth M. 1998. *Deepening Democracy? The Modern Left and Social Movements in Chile and Peru*. Stanford: Stanford University Press.

Rocha Sobrinho, João. 1994. Militância: Prazer ou sacrifício? *Teoria e Debate* 26.

Rueschemeyer, Dietrich, Evelyne Huber Stephens, and John D. Stephens. 1992. *Capitalist Development and Democracy*. Cambridge: Polity Press.

Scherrer, Christoph, and Luciana Hachmann. 2012. Can a Labour-Friendly Government be Friendly to Labour? A Hegemonic Analysis of Brazilian, German and South African Experiences. In *Labour in the Global South: Challenges and Alternatives for Workers*, ed. Sarah Mosoetsa and Michelle Williams, 141–158. Geneva: International Labour Organization.

Seidman, Gay W. 1994. *Manufacturing Militance: Workers' Movements in Brazil and South Africa, 1970–1985*. Berkeley: University of California Press.

———. 2011. Social Movement Unionism: From Description to Exhortation. *South African Review of Sociology* 42 (3): 94–102.

Sikkink, Kathryn. 1991. *Ideas and Institutions: Developmentalism in Brazil and Argentina*. Ithaca: Cornell University Press.

Silva, Eduardo. 2009. *Challenging Neoliberalism in Latin America*. Cambridge: Cambridge University Press.

Silver, Beverly J. 2003. *Forces of Labor: Workers' Movements and Globalization Since 1870*. Cambridge: Cambridge University Press.

Tarrow, Sydney. 2011. *Power in Movement: Social Movements and Contentious Politics*. 3rd ed. Cambridge: Cambridge University Press.

Turner, Lowell. 2011. A Future for the Labour Movement? In *The International Handbook of Labour Unions: Responses to Neo-liberalism*, ed. Gregor Gall, Richard Hurd, and Adrian Wilkinson, 311–327. Cheltenham: Edward Elgar.

Upchurch, Martin, and Andy Mathers. 2011. Neoliberal Globalization and Trade Unionism: Toward Radical Political Unionism? *Critical Sociology* 38 (2): 265–280.

Valenzuela, J. Samuel. 1992. Labor Movements and Political Systems: Some Variations. In *The Future of Labor Movements*, ed. Mario Regini, 53–101. London: Sage.

Webster, Edward. 2015. Labour after Globalisation: Old and New Sources of Power. Institute of Social and Economic Research, Rhodes University. ISER Working Paper no. 2015/1.

Webster, Edward, Rob Lambert, and Andries Bezuidenhout. 2008. *Grounding Globalization: Labour in the Age of Insecurity*. Oxford: Wiley-Blackwell.

Welmowicki, José. 2004. *Cidadania ou classe? O movimento operário da década de 80*. São Paulo: Editora Instituto José Luís e Rosa Sundermann.

Wright, Erik Olin. 2000. Working-Class Power, Capitalist-Class Interests, and Class Compromise. *American Journal of Sociology* 105 (4): 957–1002.

Wylde, Christopher. 2012. *Latin America after Neoliberalism: Developmental Regimes in Post-crisis States*. Basingstoke: Palgrave Macmillan.

Zapata, Francisco. 2013. *História mínima del sindicalismo latinoamericano*. México: El Colegio de México.

CHAPTER 3

Labour and the State: Corporatism and the Left, 1930–1977

The Brazilian government's interventionist industrialization policies during the 1950s and 1960s contributed to the emergence of a large urban working class whose militancy opened a space for organized labour's political role. In order to understand the position of the Brazilian union movement during the late twentieth and early twenty-first centuries, this chapter argues that the historical relationship between labour and the state left a legacy for labour politics that has lasted to the present day. This legacy lies in particular in the legal and political nature of state-labour relations and the position of organized labour in Brazil's national development agenda, which pushed the union movement towards both resistance and collaboration. In response to the rise of labour militancy and mass political participation, as elsewhere in Latin America, the Brazilian government under Getúlio Vargas introduced corporatist state-labour relations to control the labour movement. Taking place in the context of state-led industrialization, corporatist laws were accompanied by Vargas' politically moderate ideology of *trabalhismo* ("labourism"), which focused on class harmony rather than conflict, with the intention to depoliticize and weaken the Brazilian left.

Vargas' legacy therefore bequeathed the union movement with a particular state-labour relationship which, while intended to constrain labour militancy, at significant times in Brazilian history created opportunities for labour political action. Although the corporatist unions often lacked a

© The Author(s) 2019
M. Riethof, *Labour Mobilization, Politics and Globalization in Brazil*, Studies of the Americas,
https://doi.org/10.1007/978-3-319-60309-4_3

radical agenda, the roots of militancy and radicalism remained, leading to political turbulence at various points in Brazil's political history. Meanwhile, a combination of changes in the socio-economic structure of Brazilian society and a grassroots political mobilization triggered by economic problems radicalized the union movement in the early 1960s. Populist politicians attempted to simultaneously contain and mobilize these radical demands, creating highly unstable political and economic conditions, which culminated in the 1964 military coup. Although the military regime (1964–1985) directly repressed its opponents, including labour activists, it also continued to employ corporatist labour laws to undermine trade unions and ban their political activity, which ultimately led to escalating labour militancy in the 1970s.

This chapter discusses how this unique state-labour relationship shaped the labour movement's political trajectory at various points in time, as significant elements of the socio-economic and political relations that emerged in the first half of the twentieth century had survived. The connections between the national development agenda, *trabalhismo*, and corporatism that first emerged in the 1930s and 1940s remained largely in place until 1964. When the military took over, they strengthened the repressive aspects of corporatism while deepening national developmentalism, abandoning the idea of common interests between workers, the state, and employers. While the democratic governments in power between 1945 and 1964 focused their development agenda on attempts to establish a compromise between various sectors of society, after 1964 the military subordinated labour through direct repression and control using corporatist labour legislation to achieve their development goals. After the transition to civilian rule in 1985, the social impact of the government's development objectives continued to be an area of political concern for organized labour, sparking resistance in some cases and acquiescence in others, while creating tensions among union activists about whether to respond with militant action or moderate political strategies. This chapter begins with an analysis of how economic and political changes in the early twentieth century, particularly the government's response to the crisis of the 1930s, together with increasing political participation created the conditions for state-led industrialization (also known as national developmentalism or import-substitution industrialization). Another central element of this arrangement was the political incorporation of workers through corporatist labour legislation but this set-up was also exceedingly volatile, leading to high levels of social and political polarization and a military coup in 1964. In conclusion, together with the military regime's reconfiguration of state-society relations and economic development, the political arrangements that emerged in the first half of the twentieth century contained the seeds of both resistance and accommodation, while shaping labour politics far into the future.

3.1 Economic and Political Changes in the Early Twentieth Century

The 1920s and 1930s saw important developments in Brazilian economic and politics, which would shape the Brazilian union movement for decades to come, particularly in terms of the effects on labour militancy of the inclusion of formal workers in the post-war political compromise. In their study on the driving forces of political change in Latin America, Collier and Collier argue that the early decades of the twentieth century constitute a critical juncture in the region's political history,[1] as this period saw the emergence of new political forces challenging the existing balance of power. The rise of organized labour increased social pressure for the widening of political participation, with some political figures discovering that workers could be mobilized as a political force for electoral purposes. Political parties also widened political participation to emerging socio-economic groups, while mobilizing and channelling popular pressure for inclusion in the political system, through parliamentary representation rather than revolution. By channelling political pressure, political parties played a crucial role in mediating elite perceptions of the threat of the working class, leading to the gradual political incorporation of emerging socio-economic groups such as working people.[2] Before demonstrating how this situation shaped labour politics, the argument developed here is that political unrest in this crucial period in Brazilian history helped create a new development agenda focused on state-led industrialization.

Following intensifying political protests in the aftermath of the First World War, the country experienced political turbulence leading to a series of political reforms in the 1930s, which developed a new framework for development policies and political contestation. The key figure in this period was Getúlio Vargas, who recognized not only the threat but also the political potential of Brazil's growing working class. Coming to power in the midst of a political crisis when military rebels had forced President Washington Luís Pereira de Souza (1926–1930) to leave office, Vargas became president in an episode known as "the Revolution of 1930". Vargas' vision was supported by a coalition whose project "was one of social, political, and administrative reform, which would change the nature of the state and displace the hegemony of the oligarchy, but would not attack the economic position of the oligarchy nor leave it without substantial political power".[3]

After he came to power, Vargas continued to face instability, with unrest and armed revolt spreading from the mid-1930s onwards. The elite perception was that the Communist Party was planning to take over, so Vargas managed to pass a state of emergency in Congress and reacted to opposition with increasing levels of repression. As a result of the cycle of repression and instability, Vargas and his supporters became convinced that the country needed someone who could prevent both the extreme left and the extreme right from taking over political power. On November 10, 1937, a coup d'état resulted in a Vargas-led dictatorship that would last until 1945. Under the influence of Vargas-supporting military officers, the belief that a liberal-democratic state could not perform this function or promote economic development became widespread.[4] Instead, social and economic reforms would be pursued under a nationalist authoritarian regime—the Estado Nôvo (1937–1945)—which laid the basis for new institutional structures and state-led economic development. Reflecting the coalition that supported Vargas' agenda, the Estado Nôvo therefore formed the basis for a political compromise between traditional conservative forces and reformists, and between the military and civilians. The Estado Nôvo was not only fundamental for the introduction of national developmentalism but would also decisively shape the union movement's political position by introducing a corporatist framework which linked trade unions to the state and incorporated them into the new developmental project.

During the same period in Brazil, the Wall Street Crash and the Great Depression manifested themselves politically in a shift towards nationalism and national developmentalism, particularly as the international economy had proven to be an unpredictable source of growth.[5] The turn towards state-led development not only increased the urban working class, a major source of labour strength, but also raised concerns among the political class because of the potentially disruptive role of workers' strikes in strategic sectors of the economy. Labour militancy therefore emerged at the intersection of global and national economic change, while national developmentalism evolved in response to the devastating impact of the global recession on Brazil. The Brazilian export sector was seriously affected by the fall in global commodity prices, which also brought the inflow of foreign capital to a halt.

For instance, Brazil's economy depended heavily on coffee exports, which constituted 73% of the country's exports between 1924 and 1929.[6] As a result of the crisis, coffee prices dropped to a third of pre-crisis levels, which resulted in a decline in the volume of coffee exports to the order of 48%.[7] When the international coffee market collapsed, the Brazilian government decided to buy all coffee supplies and to destroy portions of it, known as the "Coffee Support Programme". This ad hoc measure increased prices on the world market, as Brazilian exports dominated the world coffee market. Functioning as a form of Keynesianism *avant la lettre*, this policy resulted in the maintenance of domestic income levels and national demand. It also formed a counterbalance to the decline in investment, partially replaced by growing public investment and the emergence of more profitable opportunities for investors in the domestic industrial sector. The example of the coffee sector showed politicians that coping with fluctuating global prices through short-term solutions for trade imbalances such as the coffee programme could also boost industrial production, as the rising prices of imported manufactured goods opened new opportunities for domestic producers. Because short-term policies were insufficient in themselves to produce recovery, the Vargas government expanded state intervention, economic planning, and monetary policy.[8]

The introduction of new economic policies with a greater state role led to the subsequent centralization of political power at a federal level as the state assumed a more active role in the economy. The expanded bureaucracy was needed to administer and unify a large, developing country, simultaneously creating strong clientelist relations that formed a basis for political alliances. The federal state took control of policy areas which could influence economic performance and industrialization, such as taxes, exchange rate policy, labour, and educational policy. A multiple exchange rate control system was introduced alongside the establishment of state agencies to stimulate national economic development, particularly industrial development, and to regulate imports.[9] Reduced imports in the aftermath of the Great Depression also led to declining customs duties and an increasing fiscal deficit, which in turn led to the restructuring of the tax system, further strengthening the role of the state, as it broadened its tax base and powers of control.[10] The decline in primary exports stimulated economic planning by identifying strategic sectors of the domestic economy,[11] supported by the establishment of state-owned enterprises in the steel and mining sector in the 1940s and 1950s. The federal state also expanded public investment into new areas, particularly in infrastructure, utilities, and mixed private-public ownership of basic industries. Furthermore, the government centralized social welfare, and the settlement of the minimum wage became the exclusive task of the federal state.[12] These initiatives not only paved the way to systematic state intervention but also began to shape state-labour relations as politicians were aware that strikes and demonstrations could destabilize Brazil's as yet fragile economy. The social counterpart of expanding state intervention therefore focused on constraining labour militancy through corporatist control of trade unions.

3.2 Brazilian Workers and the Emergence of Corporatism

The labour policies that emerged in the 1930s and 1940s can be considered the societal counterpart of the emerging interventionist state in Brazil, as the government intended to minimize conflicts between labour and capital in order to promote accelerated industrialization. Guillermo O'Donnell has defined corporatism in a Latin American context in terms of the state-controlled political representation of socio-economically defined sectors of society, whereby

> those structures through which functional, nonterritorially based organizations officially represent "private" interests before the state, formally subject for their existence and their right of representation to authorization or acceptance by the state, and where such right is reserved to the formal leaders of those organizations, forbidding and excluding other legitimate channels of access to the state for the rest of its members.[13]

The basic principle of Brazilian corporatism was that the state organized and controlled interest groups (both workers and employers) from above, which effectively limited political participation outside of political parties to corporatist interaction mediated by the state.[14] According to Erickson, the "symmetrical hierarchies of associations for employers and workers, assured institutional contact between the two at all levels, and established the state as arbiter between them".[15] In the corporatist system, interest groups such as trade unions became integrated vertically in the state's bureaucracy which, as Schmitter argues, not only in strengthened state control but also suggested a degree of mutual interest: "The social groups are linked vertically to the upper strata, or at least the governing authorities, who in turn have a special asymmetrical responsibility for the well being of those below them."[16] Brazil's corporatist policies had three core elements: the idea of class harmony directed by the state, also known as *trabalhismo*; the political and legal regulation of trade unions; and the expansion of social welfare. Another key component of corporatist state-society relations was the principle that government structures had to be relatively autonomous from the pressures of social and economic groups, or at least from the demands of those groups that threatened to destabilize the government through excessive wage demands or political unrest.[17] At its core, the corporatist labour laws and policies introduced during the Vargas regime represented an attempt to control and regulate the increasingly militant urban working class. In this respect, the corporatist arrangement's purpose was to contain political radicalism and labour militancy, not only through legal provisions and social policies but also through a new politics of progress and class harmony.

Getúlio Vargas introduced the idea of *trabalhismo* as a paternalistic ideology that not only appealed to the loyalty of workers but also allowed Vargas to mobilize them for electoral purposes.[18] The leading motivation was Vargas' emphasis on his paternalistic role as the benefactor of the working classes, a role enabled by the new labour laws and extended social welfare provision. The linking of corporatism and populism was based on the argument that peace, harmony, and the national interest would replace class conflict, aided and abetted by the depoliticization of trade unions through repressive and legal means, and their separation from radical political ideologies and political parties. Trade unions were therefore restructured so as to make them "instruments of social integration in the nation-building process",[19] resulting in the creation of an official union movement led by *pelegos*, or union leaders co-opted by the state. The second part of this "ideology" was the attempt to turn the labour movement into a political support base by setting up no less than two populist parties in 1945, the Partido Trabalhista Brasileiro (Brazilian Labour Party, PTB) based on the official trade unions and other groups that supported Vargas, and the Partido Social Democrático (Social-Democratic Party, PSD), for which he was a presidential candidate in 1951.[20] Although Vargas' legacy for Brazilian politics is perhaps not quite as far reaching as that of his contemporary Juan Perón in Argentina, from the perspective of labour politics, the official trade unions and their *pelego* leaders continued to form a significant force within the union movement up to the present day, while corporatist labour laws have continued to shape industrial relations and trade union behaviour under both authoritarian and democratic regimes.

To administer the new labour laws, Getúlio Vargas established a Labour Ministry in 1930 and a new labour law (Consolidação das Leis do Trabalho, CLT, or Labour Code) in 1931. The CLT had a significant impact on trade union strategies, encouraging moderate rather than militant action by regulating the functions and scope of trade union action, encouraging judicial mediation in labour conflicts, and social welfare provision. According to the new Labour Code trade unions (*sindicatos*) could only exist at the municipal (*município*)[21] level, representing workers of a given occupational category as defined by the state in the 1940s.[22] The enormous impact of the CLT can be illustrated by the fact that despite the many economic changes that Brazil has experienced since the 1940s, trade unions continue to be organized along the same functional lines today. The functional and territorial restrictions forced unions to organize and represent a particular category of workers within one municipality, often leaving companies divided between several unions, thereby making it more difficult to organize workers across occupational categories within the same workplace. All workers in a particular locality had to pay a compulsory union tax (*impôsto sindical*) of one day's pay a year, collected by the Labour Ministry and channelled towards their union, which they dispensed as welfare benefits to their members. As a result of this arrangement unions not only had significant financial resources at their disposal but also offered services ranging from insurance to holidays and haircuts. Another well-known effect of the law was that many unions existed exclusively to collect their share of the union tax while their leaders did little to represent their members. Illustrating the long-lasting impact of this law, decades later a trade unionist in the food-processing industry explained to me that trade union activists not only referred to these unions as *pelego* but also as *sindicatos de carimbo* ("rubber stamp unions"), with reference to the fact that when they were officially recognized—that is, once their form was stamped—by the Labour Ministry, they only needed to exist on paper to collect their dues.[23] Unions therefore benefited from guaranteed financial support and the right to represent a given occupational category,[24] making it all but impossible for competing unions or for union activists with an alternative agenda to challenge the official union structure.

The Labour Code also introduced a system of labour courts with extensive powers to mediate in disputes between workers and employers, which meant that judicial mediation often replaced strike action in the collective bargaining process. The labour courts had a broad mandate to intervene in labour conflicts, which discouraged the use of strikes to achieve collective goals, making legal mediation more attractive than organizing a strike.

The right to strike was also highly regulated and only allowed in the period of annual collective bargaining (known as the *data-base*).[25] By holding collective negotiations in sectors with strong unions at different times of the year, the Labour Ministry arranged the collective bargaining cycle in such a way that strong unions could never negotiate at the same time, thereby avoiding the escalation of strikes. If a collective agreement proved impossible to reach, an absolute majority of a union's membership with a quorum of two-thirds of the membership had to vote in favour of going on strike. Although the state's official role was to mediate in collective conflicts, the labour law also allowed intervention in the financial and political affairs of unions.[26] (This provision was only removed in the 1988 Constitution.) In cases where a strike was declared illegal by the labour court—either for procedural reasons or because the strike did not take place within the framework of collective bargaining—the state could intervene in the union by removing its leaders from their posts and holding new union elections to replace the recalcitrant leaders.[27] The leadership of trade unions was also effectively co-opted by the prospect of benefits and jobs provided by the Labour Ministry. For example, apart from legal professionals, a proportion of labour court judges were representatives of employers and unions, or *juizes classistas* ("class judges").[28] A job as a labour court judge entailed few working hours and high wages, offering a popular employment opportunity for some union leaders.[29]

Another purpose of the Labour Code was to promote social harmony through the distribution of welfare payments to workers, turning trade unions away from militancy to service provision. Corporatism's welfare dimension functioned as an important instrument of corporatist regulation, as workers were subject of state control in exchange for their inclusion in social security legislation. Crucially, the social security system excluded those without a stable income, stable employment, or those in the informal sector,[30] creating a segmented labour market and "providing overprotection to core workers in the modern sector at the expense of the underprotection of labor in general".[31] These policies primarily targeted the urban working class working in the formal sector but excluded rural workers, while the middle class benefited from increased public employment in the expanding state bureaucracy.

Scholars have drawn attention to how these policies shaped citizenship practices in Brazil, effectively creating differentiated citizenship rights, as a result of which people outside of the formal labour market—often migrants living in illegal and precarious conditions in Brazil's growing cities—were citizens in the formal sense but lacked the substantive rights that the urban working class had received under Vargas.[32] This system not only marginalized significant parts of the urban and rural population but also depoliticized the trade unions: "the state constituted urban workers as special citizens by bestowing social rights they had never had and celebrating a dignity of labor it had never recognized. However, it did so as the means to absorb them into its legal and administrative orders. Vargas reformulated the citizenship of workers precisely to eviscerate any alternative public sphere of autonomous working-class organization."[33] Despite these limitations, national social security legislation and the trade union provision of social services still functioned as a redistributive mechanism in a highly unequal society[34] but only for a limited proportion of the population.

In sum, the corporatist framework allowed the state to limit labour militancy in several ways: it could shape the outcome of union elections by controlling who could run for elected posts, usually on the basis of the candidates' political agendas, and it could ensure that the unions focused on non-political and non-militant activities by limiting their use of funds to welfare rather than political activities. The political impact on the union movement was that representatives of the official trade unions thought they would benefit more from bargaining with the state, often via non-working class politicians, than from strikes and direct collective bargaining with employers, particularly as access to the government became more rewarding than strikes. Corporatism therefore consolidated the union movement's subordinate relationship to the state as "official trade unionism derived its strength not from its membership but from its relationship to the elites holding state power".[35] This effect was also visible in the forced separation of union action in the economic sphere from the political activity of the new mass parties as unionists tended to focus trade union activity on the state and the judicial system as the crucial mediators in industrial relations, instead of on employers.[36]

Corporatism's long-lasting impact on Brazilian labour politics has raised the question whether such high levels of state control quashed labour militancy in the twentieth century, thereby weakening Brazil's union movement for decades to come. Paradoxically, while corporatist regulation functioned to constrain militancy in many cases, it also created organizational resources for labour opposition, as seen in the strike wave in the late 1970s which radicalized a new generation of workers. Underlying this question is the dynamic analysed above, which simultaneously subordinated the unions and offered benefits such as legal recognition and financial resources[37] while excluding significant sectors of society. A related argument is that the demographic changes that Brazil experienced in this period weakened unions' structural power by creating a labour surplus due to high levels of rural-urban migration[38] that resulted from poverty and "the more or less intact persistence of traditional modes of production and authority in rural areas".[39] However, the reality in the first half of the twentieth century was more complicated as political developments and demographic changes pulled the union movement both towards militancy and moderate political strategies. For example, while rural-urban migration helped to moderate trade union strategies, John French interprets the rise of worker militancy as due to a shift in the labour market from artisanal, skilled workers, to semi-skilled industrial workers in large cities.[40] At the beginning of the twentieth century, artisanal workers (and particularly the anarcho-syndicalists among them) played a formative role in the labour movement. Their strong position was undermined by the emergence of large-scale factory production and work organization, which facilitated the rise of modern trade unions. Through immigration from Europe to Latin America, socialism, communism, and anarcho-syndicalism became widely known, which inspired the emergence of more politically engaged trade unionism and the rise of major left-wing parties.

Trade unions were therefore not just the passive victims of government control, as some unions had radical leaders willing to challenge state intervention and employers. For example, in his study of the Communist Party (Partido Comunista Brasileiro, PCB) and organized labour, Santana argues that while the party leadership focused on parliamentary strategies and alliances, many of its affiliated unions continued to engage in militant strike action.[41] Economic development and the rise of urban manufacturing activity in particular led to an increase in trade union attempts to assert workers' demands, while factory commissions involved in wage bargaining existed in many companies in the state of São Paulo from the 1950s onwards.[42] Many unionists also recognized the potentially positive aspects of government control, as regulation of the union movement implied that unions could have a legally recognized position in society.[43] Although the effects of corporatism and the characteristics of the Brazilian labour market certainly affected labour militancy, it did not eradicate political radicalism as evident in the 1950s and 1960s when Brazilian politics became increasingly turbulent and polarized.

3.3 Social and Political Polarization in the 1950s and 1960s

Despite the moderating effects of corporatism, the period from 1945 to 1964 in Brazil was characterized by substantial political polarization and social conflict. Because of the size of the urban working class and their increasing capacity to strike and demonstrate, politicians' ability to appeal politically to workers became increasingly important.[44] Many politicians simultaneously wanted to contain the militant trade unions and use this new force for electoral purposes, which further increased political conflicts in this period. For example, Vargas continued to appeal to workers and used them as a political base after he became president in 1951. In exchange for their support, Vargas flexibilized some of the Labour Code requirements, such as the Labour Ministry's control over union elections, which meant that communist union leaders increased their influence within the unions.[45] Despite these developments, Vargas "vacillated and was never willing to take the risk of really mobilizing labor support by the kinds of concessions needed to make a realistic appeal or to take the risk of strengthening working-class political organizations necessary for building an effective support base".[46] In combination with discontent with declining real wages and rising inflation in the early 1950s, these measures contributed to renewed radicalization and militancy among unions. These contradictions led to increasing political turbulence in the 1950s and early 1960s in the run-up to the 1964 military coup.

After Vargas' suicide in 1954, Juscelino Kubitschek (1956–61) came to power with João Goulart as vice-president. Some elements of the opposition and the military claimed that Kubitschek's victory was illegal because he did not receive the majority of votes while there were rumours that the military would stage a coup to prevent Kubitschek from taking office. The Minister of War then decided to stage a preventive or counter-coup after which Kubitschek could finally take office.[47] As the 2014 National Truth Commission report found, this turbulent situation led to a growing sense among the armed forces that a military intervention would be legitimate.[48] Nevertheless, the Kubitschek government accelerated development planning—culminating in the construction of Brasília as the new capital, a symbol of Brazil's progress towards modernity—and attracted foreign capital and private investors through a new foreign investment regime that involved mutual benefits for foreign investors and the Brazilian economy. The large Brazilian market, heavily protected by tariffs and other trade barriers, was an attractive one, leading to high levels of growth in the industrial sector, particularly the automobile industry which would become the centre of labour opposition to the military in the late 1970s. Despite the problematic political context, the perception among many union leaders therefore was that the effects of Kubitschek's policies on the position of workers in Brazil were largely positive, as employment rose while the minimum wage helped increase living standards,[49] even though inflation rates averaged 22.6% per year between 1957 and 1961.[50] Despite Kubitschek's attempts to alleviate the negative effects of economic stabilization, this radicalization led the government to repress protests and threatened to limit the right to strike.

Both Kubitschek and Goulart, who became president in 1961, therefore held an ambivalent position towards organized labour. João Goulart himself was a controversial politician because as a candidate of the PTB and a supporter of the pro-Vargas movement, many suspected him of having Peronist or even Communist sympathies.[51] Within this context, Goulart continued developmentalist policies while being torn between nationalistic and internationalist positions, while making concessions to the left by introducing structural reforms in controversial areas such as land ownership, taxes, and education. Goulart was faced with similar dilemmas to his predecessors as he had to prove that he was not a radical to ensure the support of centre-right forces, while simultaneously having to deal with a divided left that he could not fully control. On the left, some groups advocated using the political instability to destabilize the regime for revolutionary purposes, while many communists supported developmentalism, arguing that the country was not yet ready for a revolution.[52] The political fault lines that emerged in this period illustrate the complex relationship between political change and labour militancy in the mid-twentieth century. On the one hand, the working-class electorate could no longer be ignored and merely mobilized to support the president at appropriate moments. Because of their ability to destabilize politics and the linked importance of wage demands for the functioning of the economy, passive or active support was needed to ensure political and economic success. On the other hand, concessions to the working class in the form of wage increases and social policy improvements also aroused the suspicion of various forces opposed to the Goulart government, such as the military. The political tensions already evident under Kubitschek's government would eventually result in 1964's military coup.

3.4 The Military Coup and Labour Repression

In the eyes of the military the political and economic turmoil and the pressure of popular demands, including those of the union movement, threatened Brazil's political and economic stability. Many in the military believed that the coup had protected the country from a communist takeover as the Cuban Revolution inspired the idea that the main threat to order and stability came from within. Soon after 1964, the military began to rule as an institution through a hierarchical bureaucracy controlled by national security agencies and military commanders.[53] They saw the state as "rising 'above' its society, with technocrats and military ruling in the best interests of the nominally unrepresented social sectors",[54] depoliticizing decision-making and insulating the state from destabilizing societal demands. The military's core reforms were consolidated in the Institutional Act of April 1964, which strengthened and centralized the executive, the latter acquiring the power to suspend political rights and to shut down legislative organs at all levels.[55] Maintaining a semblance of representation, the regime abolished all existing political parties, replacing the previous multi-party system with two new parties: the pro-government party, Aliança Renovadora Nacional (ARENA, National Renewal Alliance), and the opposition party, Movimento Democrático Brasileiro (MDB, Brazilian Democratic Movement).[56] These changes formed the basis of a new constitution in 1967,[57] while in December 1968, the notorious fifth Institutional Act extended censorship and suspended habeas corpus. On the basis of the national security doctrine and the belief that the left had created much of the economic turmoil that took place during the democratic governments, the military government used these new institutional provisions alongside the security apparatus to severely repress and deplete the opposition on several fronts.

During the years after 1964, the government arrested communist union leaders, reinforced by a pattern of repression, arrests, and torture of alleged opposition forces. The military government used the repressive features of the Labour Code to replace the leadership of militant unions and to curtail any political or opposition activities within trade unions.[58] Although trade unions continued to exist, union leaders had few incentives to maintain an organized and militant base in their unions,[59] which suited the military's goal of constraining any hint of opposition. Using the existing labour legislation, the new regime also tightened government control over wage determination in 1964 to help promote economic and political stability.

Due to the centralization of wage policy and the repression of trade unions, collective bargaining became effectively meaningless, as the decision to increase wages was transferred to the federal government. The military presidents used their power to limit union action and wage demands as part of their overall objective to deepen industrialization, which they saw as essential to national security.

During the first years of the military regime, economic stabilization dominated the government's development agenda, resulting in a long-term negative impact on real wages and the income distribution. The regime also intervened heavily in the economy and established new state-owned enterprises,[60] while the second National Development Plan (for the years 1974–1979) promoted further state intervention and state ownership in sectors such as steel, oil, and petrochemicals.[61] In addition, the government inaugurated massive infrastructural and industrial projects, including the Trans-Amazon highway, which it viewed as necessary for the country's integration; hydroelectric dams (e.g., the Itaipu dam in southern Brazil); and industrial projects such as a national aeronautical industry to produce light passenger and military aircrafts. This economic agenda, together with the diversification of exports and Brazil's improving terms of trade at the end of the 1960s, contributed to the "Brazilian miracle" between 1968 and 1973, with average annual growth rates of 11.3%. One of the most important engines of economic growth during the miracle years was the automobile sector dominated by multinational corporations,[62] which helped create the roots of militant labour opposition to the military regime in the late 1970s. The growing workforce in these industries and the sector's strategic importance for the Brazilian economy provided the workers with a significant source of structural power, which turned them into a central actor in the opposition to the military regime.

In political terms, the military's approach to a potential return to civilian rule planted the seeds for opposition, which unintentionally created political spaces for grassroots movements to oppose authoritarianism. The military envisioned a return to a civilian regime or a form of electoral democracy at some stage in the future, which created a fundamental contradiction between the military's pursuit of political legitimacy and their attempt to keep control over the political liberalization process.[63] The military leadership initially defined legitimacy in terms of the regime's "success" in returning the country to order but as renewed opposition emerged in the early 1970s, the military looked for alternative sources of legitimacy by initiating a controlled political liberalization process. The regime's drive to institutionalize a new political order after the coup led to experiments with limited political representation, such as the two-party system, which was intended to lend legitimacy to a highly repressive regime. When President Ernesto Geisel (1974–1979) initiated the *abertura* (opening) process of political liberalization, grassroots mobilization and other civil-society movements began to gain political space, leading to what Juan Linz called the "explosion of civil society" in the early 1970s.[64] As the military began to permit limited political participation in the early 1970s, this initiative inadvertently strengthened the opposition, which in turn sparked internal conflicts in the military between the soft-liners, who supported liberalization, and hard-liners, who believed that repression remained necessary: "The outcome is an impossible game that confronts the military rulers with the increasingly difficult-to-control experiments at liberalization that are likely to lead to important schisms within the governing elite."[65]

For the opposition, the dilemma was whether or not it would operate within the limits of the transition established by the military government in order to avoid confrontation or repression, or if they should challenge and reject all aspects of the democratization initiative from above.[66] The gradual political liberalization process in Brazil therefore increased the opportunities for political opposition outside of political parties but also meant that the opposition faced a cycle of liberalization and repression as a result of the military's ambiguous attitude to the transition. However, repressing channels of political influence and dissidence such as trade unions and political parties led to the emergence of non-traditional opposition forces. Social movements, such as human rights groups, and community- and church-based organizations came to play an important role in raising consciousness, providing political space for discussion and dissent, which was not available to them in the militarized public sphere. It is within this dialectical relationship between the authoritarian regime, the opposition, and the political conflicts created by the *abertura* that the labour opposition emerged in full force.

The birth of what became known as the "new unionism" movement at the close of the 1970s took place in a highly repressive political context and an urban industrial environment characterized by rapid change associated with technological development and workers' increasing skill levels,[67] illustrating how they linked their structural power to the organizational roots in the corporatist unions. The military regime's own rapid state-led industrialization process had produced the conditions for politically significant changes in the Brazilian workforce: groups of semi-skilled industrial workers were geographically concentrated in the state of São Paulo, particularly in the multinational industries which were crucial for the country's economic growth.[68] Although Brazilian industrial workers constituted a minority of the working population, their relatively privileged position in terms of wages and skill levels, combined with an escalation of workers' demands due to repression and a lack of wage adjustment to economic gains,[69] produced new types of union action, representing a rupture both with the regime's repressive labour policies and corporatist unionism. Despite the high levels of repression experienced by labour activists during most of the 1960s and 1970s, the continued existence of the corporatist union structure and its associated financial resources created an organizational and financial basis for mobilization and protests. Inspired and often supported by social movement strategies in this period, the new unionists moved beyond the boundaries of the official union structure to focus on direct action.[70] The wave of strikes that hit the industrial suburbs of São Paulo at the end of the 1970s was therefore not only a protest against the wage losses, but also it contained an attack on the authoritarian system of labour relations, which resulted in trade union activists joining other oppositional forces. By 1979, workers' participation in the opposition to the military regime had become a reality that could no longer be avoided.

3.5 Conclusion

The analysis of the transformation of the labour movement in the early- to mid-twentieth century illustrates the interconnections between the emerging working class, corporatism, and state-led development. The government's ability to regulate and control labour became a central feature of the Brazilian state's interventionist strategies in this period. This process stimulated industrialization while simultaneously contributing to the emergence of a large working class, whose militancy would open up spaces for organized labour's political role. Nevertheless, the political and economic turmoil of the late 1950s and early 1960s, including the pressure of popular demands for wage increases and social reforms, threatened the country's stability in the eyes of the military. The new regime tightened its control over unions and wage determination in 1964, using the existing labour legislation to promote stability and economic growth. As the following chapters discuss in more detail, the institutional, ideational, and political framework for labour relations constructed between 1930 and 1964 continued to play a significant role in the formation of trade union strategies during the military dictatorship and afterwards, both by constraining labour militancy and creating opportunities for labour political action. As the next chapter discusses, the contradictions between rapid economic growth and growing dissatisfaction with authoritarian labour politics sparked unprecedented labour militancy in the late 1970s, shaping both the democratization process and the political role of the trade unions.

Notes

1. Ruth Berins Collier and David Collier, *Shaping the Political Arena: Critical Junctures, the Labor Movement, and Regime Dynamics in Latin America* (Princeton, NJ: Princeton University Press, 1991) 29.
2. Dietrich Rueschemeyer, Evelyne Huber Stephens and John D. Stephens, *Capitalist Development and Democracy* (Cambridge: Polity Press, 1992), 156.
3. Collier and Collier, *Shaping the Political Arena*, 171.
4. Kenneth P. Erickson, *The Brazilian Corporative State and Working Class Politics* (Berkeley: University of California Press, 1977), 17.
5. Kathryn Sikkink, *Ideas and Institutions: Developmentalism in Brazil and Argentina* (Ithaca, NY: Cornell University Press, 1991), 246.
6. The fate of the coffee export economy illustrates the continuing role of primary exports before and during the introduction of import-substitution policies, although the product became less significant towards the end of the twentieth century: the share of coffee exports in total exports declined from 62.9% in 1930 to 56.1% in 1950 and 12.3% in 1980; however, the share of manufactured products increased from 13.5% in 1940 to 44.8% in 1980. See Marcelo P. de Abreu, Afonso S. Bevilacqua, and Demosthenes M. Pinho, "Import Substitution and Growth in Brazil, 1890s–1970s," in *An Economic History of Twentieth-Century Latin America*, Vol. 3, ed. Enrique Cárdenas, José A. Ocampo, and Rosemary Thorp (London: Palgrave, 2000), 169.
7. Peter Evans, *Dependent Development: The Alliance of Multinational, State, and Local Capital in Brazil* (Princeton: Princeton University Press, 1979), 66–7.
8. Victor Bulmer-Thomas, *The Economic History of Latin America since Independence* (Cambridge: Cambridge University Press, 1994), 209, 228.
9. Werner Baer, *The Brazilian Economy: Growth and Development* (Westport: Praeger, 1995), 36–7; Bulmer-Thomas, *Economic History*, 221; Thomas E. Skidmore, *Politics in Brazil 1930–1964: An Experiment in Democracy* (Oxford: Oxford University Press, 1967), 43.
10. Bulmer-Thomas, *Economic History*, 239–7, 252–8.

11. Enrique Cárdenas, José A. Ocampo, and Rosemary Thorp, "Introduction," in *An Economic History of Twentieth-Century Latin America*, Vol. 3, ed. Enrique Cárdenas et al. (London: Palgrave, 2000), 9–10.
12. Skidmore, *Politics in Brazil*, 42.
13. Guillermo O'Donnell, "Corporatism and the Question of the State," in *Authoritarianism and Corporatism in Latin America*, ed. James M. Malloy (Pittsburgh: University of Pittsburgh Press, 1977), 49.
14. For a classic studies of corporatist associations in Brazil, see Philippe C. Schmitter, *Interest Conflict and Political Change in Brazil* (Stanford: Stanford University Press, 1971); Phillipe C. Schmitter, "Still the Century of Corporatism?" in *Trends Towards Corporatist Intermediation*, ed. Philippe C. Schmitter and Gerhard Lehmbruch (Beverly Hills: Sage, 1979); Kenneth S. Mericle, "Conflict Regulation in the Brazilian Industrial Relations System." Ph.D. thesis, University of Wisconsin, 1974; and Erickson, *Brazilian Corporative State*. For a discussion on the long-term effects of the corporatist system on collective action in general, see Manuel A. Garretón, "Social and Economic Transformations in Latin America: The Emergence of a New Political Matrix," in *Markets and Democracy in Latin America: Conflict or Convergence*, ed. Pamela K. Starr and Philip Oxhorn (Boulder: Lynne Rienner, 1999).
15. Erickson, *Brazilian Corporative State*, 2.
16. Schmitter, *Interest Conflict*, 95.
17. James M. Malloy, "Authoritarianism and Corporatism in Latin America: The Modal Pattern," in *Authoritarianism and Corporatism in Latin America*, ed. James M. Malloy (Pittsburgh, University of Pittsburgh Press, 1977), 4.
18. Oliver J. Dinius, *Brazil's Steel City: Developmentalism, Strategic Power, and Industrial Relations in Volta Redonda, 1941–1964* (Stanford, CA: Stanford University Press, 2010), 3–4.
19. Erickson, *Brazilian Corporative State*, 28.
20. Collier and Collier, *Shaping the Political Arena*, 146; Skidmore, *Politics in Brazil*, 39–40.
21. *Município* refers to a municipal territorial unit. The size of a municipality can range from the city of São Paulo to small towns in the interior of Brazil. The variation in size affects the number of workers a local union can organize, as, for example, a metalworkers' union in the state of São Paulo has a very large constituency compared to a much smaller city.
22. Mericle, "Conflict Regulation", 78.
23. Interview with participant at the Seminário Internacional da Cargill and member of the CONTACS trade union, São Paulo, August 14, 2006.
24. Maurício Rands Barros, *Labour Relations and the New Unionism in Contemporary Brazil* (New York: St. Martin's Press; London: Macmillan, 1999), 17–8; Collier and Collier, *Shaping the Political Arena*, 187–8; Schmitter, *Interest Conflict*, 115–6.

25. Adalberto Moreira Cardoso, *Sindicatos, trabalhadores e a coqueluche neoliberal: A era Vargas acabou?* (Rio de Janeiro: Fundação Getúlio Vargas, 1999), 31.
26. Mericle, "Conflict Regulation", 111.
27. Cardoso, *Sindicatos, trabalhadores*, 31–2.
28. Barros, *Labour Relations*, 20; Collier and Collier, *Shaping the Political Arena*, 188; Erickson, *Brazilian Corporative State*, 29–36.
29. The system of corporatist representation in the labour courts was only abolished in 1999, with a transitional period of three years, see Rubens Penha Cysne, "Aspectos macro e microeconômicos das reformas," in *Brasil: Uma década em transição*, ed. Renato Baumann (Rio de Janeiro: Editora Campus/CEPAL, 2000), 97.
30. Kurt Weyland, *Democracy Without Equity: Failures of Reform in Brazil* (Pittsburgh: University of Pittsburgh Press, 1996), 89.
31. Amaury de Souza, "Redressing Inequalities: Brazil's Social Agenda at Century's End," in *Brazil under Cardoso*, ed. Susan Kaufman Purcell and Riordan Roett (Boulder: Lynne Rienner, 1997), 69. See also Bolivar Lamounier, "Brazil: Inequality against Democracy," in *Politics in Developing Countries: Comparing Experiences with Democracy*, ed. Larry Diamond, Juan J. Linz, and Seymour M. Lipset (Boulder and London: Lynne Rienner, 1995), 144.
32. Many authors also emphasize the continuities of these citizenship practices as the citizen rights agenda became a focal point for the pro-democratic opposition in the 1970s and 1980s. At the same time, the return to democracy left many inegalitarian citizenship practices in place. See for example, James Holston, *Insurgent Citizenship: Disjunctions of Democracy and Modernity in Brazil* (Princeton, NJ: Princeton University Press, 2008); Janice E. Perlman, "Redemocratization Viewed from Below: Urban Poverty and Politics in Rio de Janeiro, 1968–2005," in *Democratic Brazil Revisited*, ed. Peter R. Kingstone and Timothy J. Power (Pittsburgh: University of Pittsburgh Press, 2008), 259; Peter P. Houtzager and A.K. Acharya, "Associations, Active Citizenship, and the Quality of Democracy in Brazil and Mexico," *Theory & Society*, 40(1) (2011), 4–5; Philip Oxhorn, *Sustaining Civil Society: Economic Change, Democracy, and the Social Construction of Citizenship in Latin America* (University Park, PA: Pennsylvania State University Press, 2011); Evelina Dagnino, "Meanings of Citizenship in Latin America," IDS Working Paper 258 (Brighton: Institute of Development Studies, 2005), 5–7. Camille Goirand, "Citizenship and Poverty in Brazil," *Latin American Perspectives*, 30(2) (2003), 229–30.
33. Holston, *Insurgent Citizenship*, 186.
34. Evelyne Huber, "Options for Social Policy in Latin America: Neo-Liberal versus Social-Democratic Models," Discussion Paper no. 66, Geneva: UNRISD, 1995, 7–8.

35. John D. French, *The Brazilian Workers' ABC: Class Conflict and Alliances in Modern São Paulo* (Chapel Hill: University of North Carolina Press, 1992), 5.
36. Collier and Collier, *Shaping the Political Arena*, 187; French, *Brazilian Workers' ABC*, 253–4; Schmitter, *Interest Conflict*, 122.
37. French, *Brazilian Workers' ABC*, 137–9.
38. Charles Bergquist, *Labor in Latin America: Comparative Essays on Chile, Argentina, Venezuela and Colombia* (Stanford, CA: Stanford University Press, 1986); Collier and Collier, *Shaping the Political Arena*, 63–73.
39. Schmitter, *Interest Conflict*, 372.
40. French, *Brazilian Workers' ABC*.
41. Marco Aurélio Santana, *Homens partidos: Comunistas e sindicatos no Brasil* (São Paulo: Boitempo, 2001); Collier and Collier, *Shaping the Political Arena*, 388.
42. The state of São Paulo concentrated the majority of industrial workers in Brazil: the percentage of industrial workers in São Paulo compared to the whole of Brazil increased from 38% in 1939, to 41% in 1949 and 46.6% in 1959. See Renato Colistete, *Labour Relations and Industrial Performance in Brazil: Greater São Paulo, 1945–60* (London: Palgrave, 2001), 4.
43. French, *Brazilian Workers' ABC*. Barros, *Labour Relations*.
44. Collier and Collier, *Shaping the Political Arena*, 507–9, 513; Paulo Rabello de Castro and Marcio Ronci, "Sixty Years of Populism in Brazil," in *The Macroeconomics of Populism in Latin America*, ed. Rudiger Dornbusch and Sebastian Edwards (Chicago: University of Chicago Press, 1991), 158–61.
45. Collier and Collier, *Shaping the Political Arena*, 380–1.
46. Collier and Collier, *Shaping the Political Arena*, 382.
47. Sikkink, *Ideas and Institutions*, 132–3.
48. Comissão Nacional da Verdade, *Relatório final da Comissão Nacional da Verdade*, Vol. I (Brasília: CNV, 2014), 91.
49. Sikkink, *Ideas and Institutions*, 158; Skidmore, *Politics in Brazil*, 169.
50. Luiz Orenstein and Antonio C. Sochaczewski, "Democracia com desenvolvimento: 1956–1961," in *A ordem do progresso: Cem anos de política econômica republicana, 1889–1989*, ed. Marcelo de Paiva Abreu (Rio de Janeiro: Editora Campus, 1990), 179.
51. Sikkink, *Ideas and Institutions*, 211.
52. Skidmore, *Politics in Brazil*, 225–226; Sikkink, *Ideas and Institutions*, 157.
53. O'Donnell, "Corporatism and the Question"; Fernando H. Cardoso, (1979) "On the Characterization of Authoritarian Regimes in Latin America," in *The New Authoritarianism in Latin America*, ed. David Collier (Princeton: Princeton University Press, 1979), 41–3; David Collier, "Overview of the Bureaucratic-Authoritarian Model," in *The New Authoritarianism in Latin America*, ed. David Collier (Princeton: Princeton

University Press, 1979), 24; Gerardo L. Munck, *Authoritarianism and Democratization: Soldiers and Workers in Argentina, 1976–1983* (University Park, PA: Pennsylvania State University Press, 1998), 26–8.
54. Thomas E. Skidmore, *The Politics of Military Rule in Brazil, 1964–1985* (Oxford: Oxford University Press, 1988), 106.
55. Skidmore, *Politics of Military Rule*, 20, 112–7.
56. Skidmore, *Politics of Military Rule*, 46–8.
57. Skidmore, *Politics of Military Rule*, 56–7.
58. Mericle, "Conflict Regulation", 104.
59. Mericle, "Conflict Regulation", 301–2.
60. Thomas J. Trebat, *Brazil's State-Owned Enterprises: A Case Study of the State as Entrepreneur* (Cambridge: Cambridge University Press, 1983), 36–7.
61. Luiz C. Bresser Pereira, *Development and Crisis in Brazil, 1930–1983* (Boulder, CO: Westview Press, 1984), 45.
62. Baer, *The Brazilian Economy*, 77–9; Skidmore, *Politics of Military Rule*, 139; Helen Shapiro, *Engines of growth: The State and Transnational Auto Companies in Brazil* (Cambridge: Cambridge University Press, 1994).
63. Consequently, authors such as Lamounier and Linz emphasized the gradual character of the transition and the central importance of legitimacy for both the regime and the opposition, see Bolivar Lamounier, "*Authoritarian Brazil* Revisited: The Impact of Elections on the *Abertura*," in *Democratizing Brazil: Problems of Transition and Consolidation*, ed. Alfred Stepan (New York and Oxford: Oxford University Press, 1989), 69; Juan J. Linz, "The Future of an Authoritarian Situation or the Institutionalization of an Authoritarian Regime: The Case of Brazil," in *Authoritarian Brazil: Origins, Policies, and Future*, ed. Alfred Stepan (Princeton: Princeton University Press, 1973).
64. Two important large-scale strikes occurred in 1968, in Contagem (Minas Gerais) and Osasco (São Paulo). The strikes started as a result of wage demands, soon spreading to other workers in the region and taking on a wider political meaning as a result of the workers' rejection of military oppression, see Skidmore, *Politics of Military Rule*, 76–8.
65. Munck, *Authoritarianism and Democratization*, 40.
66. Lamounier, "Brazil: Inequality", 123–5.
67. Gay W. Seidman, *Manufacturing Militance: Workers' Movements in Brazil and South Africa, 1970–1985* (Berkeley, CA: University of California Press, 1994), 6; Susan Eckstein, "Power and Popular Protest in Latin America," in *Power and Popular Protest: Latin American Social Movements*, ed. Susan Eckstein (Berkeley, CA: University of California Press, 1989), 4.
68. Paul W. Drake, *Labor Movements and Dictatorships: The Southern Cone in Comparative Perspective* (Baltimore and London: Johns Hopkins University Press, 1996), 71–77; Seidman, *Manufacturing Militance*, 143–8.

69. Eckstein, "Power and Popular Protests", 10–1; Seidman, *Manufacturing Militance*.
70. Skidmore, *Politics of Military Rule*, 204.

Bibliography

Abreu, Marcelo de P, Afonso S. Bevilacqua, and Demosthenes M. Pinho. 2000. Import Substitution and Growth in Brazil, 1890s–1970s. In *An Economic History of Twentieth-Century Latin America*, ed. Enrique Cárdenas, José A. Ocampo, and Rosemary Thorp, vol. 3, 154–175. London: Palgrave.

Baer, Werner. 1995. *The Brazilian Economy: Growth and Development*. Westport: Praeger.

Barros, Maurício Rands. 1999. *Labour Relations and the New Unionism in Contemporary Brazil*. New York/London: St. Martin's Press/Macmillan.

Bergquist, Charles. 1986. *Labor in Latin America: Comparative Essays on Chile, Argentina, Venezuela and Colombia*. Stanford: Stanford University Press.

Bresser Pereira, Luiz C. 1984. *Development and Crisis in Brazil, 1930–1983*. Boulder: Westview Press.

Bulmer-Thomas, Victor. 1994. *The Economic History of Latin America Since Independence*. Cambridge: Cambridge University Press.

Cárdenas, Enrique, José A. Ocampo, and Rosemary Thorp. 2000. Introduction. In *An Economic History of Twentieth-Century Latin America*, ed. Enrique Cárdenas, José A. Ocampo, and Rosemary Thorp, vol. 3, 1–35. London: Palgrave.

Cardoso, Fernando H. 1979. On the Characterization of Authoritarian Regimes in Latin America. In *The New Authoritarianism in Latin America*, ed. David Collier, 33–57. Princeton: Princeton University Press.

Cardoso, Adalberto Moreira. 1999. *Sindicatos, trabalhadores e a coqueluche neoliberal: A era Vargas acabou?* Rio de Janeiro: Fundação Getúlio Vargas.

Colistete, Renato. 2001. *Labour Relations and Industrial Performance in Brazil: Greater São Paulo, 1945–60*. London: Palgrave.

Collier, David. 1979. Overview of the Bureaucratic-Authoritarian Model. In *The New Authoritarianism in Latin America*, ed. David Collier, 19–32. Princeton: Princeton University Press.

Collier, Ruth Berins, and David Collier. 1991. *Shaping the Political Arena: Critical Junctures, the Labor Movement, and Regime Dynamics in Latin America*. Princeton: Princeton University Press.

Comissão Nacional da Verdade. 2014. *Relatório final da Comissão Nacional da Verdade*. Brasília: CNV.

Cysne, Rubens Penha. 2000. Aspectos macro e microeconômicos das reformas. In *Brasil: Uma década em transição*, ed. Renato Baumann, 56–99. Rio de Janeiro: Editora Campus/CEPAL.

Dagnino, Evelina. 2005. Meanings of Citizenship in Latin America. IDS Working Paper 258, Brighton: Institute of Development Studies.

Dinius, Oliver J. 2010. *Brazil's Steel City: Developmentalism, Strategic Power, and Industrial Relations in Volta Redonda, 1941–1964*. Stanford: Stanford University Press.

Drake, Paul W. 1996. *Labor Movements and Dictatorships: The Southern Cone in Comparative Perspective*. Baltimore: Johns Hopkins University Press.

Eckstein, Susan. 1989. Power and Popular Protest in Latin America. In *Power and Popular Protest: Latin American Social Movements*, ed. Susan Eckstein, 1–60. Berkeley: University of California Press.

Erickson, Kenneth P. 1977. *The Brazilian Corporative State and Working Class Politics*. Berkeley: University of California Press.

Evans, Peter. 1979. *Dependent Development: The Alliance of Multinational, State, and Local Capital in Brazil*. Princeton: Princeton University Press.

French, John D. 1992. *The Brazilian Workers' ABC: Class Conflict and Alliances in Modern São Paulo*. Chapel Hill: University of North Carolina Press.

Garretón, Manuel A. 1999. Social and Economic Transformations in Latin America: The Emergence of a New Political Matrix. In *Markets and Democracy in Latin America: Conflict or Convergence*, ed. Pamela K. Starr and Philip Oxhorn, 61–78. Boulder: Lynne Rienner.

Goirand, Camille. 2003. Citizenship and Poverty in Brazil. *Latin American Perspectives* 30 (2): 18–40.

Holston, James. 2008. *Insurgent Citizenship: Disjunctions of Democracy and Modernity in Brazil*. Princeton: Princeton University Press.

Houtzager, Peter P., and A.K. Acharya. 2011. Associations, Active Citizenship, and the Quality of Democracy in Brazil and Mexico. *Theory and Society* 40 (1): 1–36.

Huber, Evelyne. 1995. Options for Social Policy in Latin America: Neo-Liberal Versus Social-Democratic Models. Discussion Paper no. 66, Geneva: UNRISD.

Lamounier, Bolivar. 1989. *Authoritarian Brazil* Revisited: The Impact of Elections on the *Abertura*. In *Democratizing Brazil: Problems of Transition and Consolidation*, ed. Alfred Stepan, 43–79. New York: Oxford University Press.

———. 1995. Brazil: Inequality Against Democracy. In *Politics in Developing Countries: Comparing Experiences with Democracy*, ed. Larry Diamond, Juan J. Linz, and Seymour M. Lipset, 119–169. Boulder: Lynne Rienner.

Linz, Juan J. 1973. The Future of an Authoritarian Situation or the Institutionalization of an Authoritarian Regime: The Case of Brazil. In *Authoritarian Brazil: Origins, Policies, and Future*, ed. Alfred Stepan, 233–254. Princeton: Princeton University Press.

Malloy, James M. 1977. Authoritarianism and Corporatism in Latin America: The Modal Pattern. In *Authoritarianism and Corporatism in Latin America*, ed. James M. Malloy, 3–19. Pittsburg: University of Pittsburgh Press.

Mericle, Kenneth S. 1974. Coneflict Regulation in the Brazilian Industrial Relations System. Ph.D. thesis, University of Wisconsin.
Munck, Gerardo L. 1998. *Authoritarianism and Democratization: Soldiers and Workers in Argentina, 1976–1983.* University Park: Pennsylvania State University Press.
O'Donnell, Guillermo. 1977. Corporatism and the Question of the State. In *Authoritarianism and Corporatism in Latin America*, ed. James M. Malloy, 47–87. Pittsburgh: University of Pittsburgh Press.
Orenstein, Luiz, and Antonio C. Sochaczewski. 1990. Democracia com desenvolvimento: 1956–1961. In *A ordem do progresso: Cem anos de política econômica republicana, 1889–1989*, ed. Marcelo de Paiva Abreu, 171–195. Rio de Janeiro: Editora Campus.
Oxhorn, Philip. 2011. *Sustaining Civil Society: Economic Change, Democracy, and the Social Construction of Citizenship in Latin America.* University Park: Pennsylvania State University Press.
Perlman, Janice E. 2008. Redemocratization Viewed from Below: Urban Poverty and Politics in Rio de Janeiro, 1968–2005. In *Democratic Brazil Revisited*, ed. Peter R. Kingstone and Timothy J. Power, 257–280. Pittsburgh: University of Pittsburgh Press.
Rabello de Castro, Paulo, and Marcio Ronci. 1991. Sixty Years of Populism in Brazil. In *The Macroeconomics of Populism in Latin America*, ed. Rudiger Dornbusch and Sebastian Edwards, 151–173. Chicago: University of Chicago Press.
Rueschemeyer, Dietrich, Evelyne Huber Stephens, and John D. Stephens. 1992. *Capitalist Development and Democracy.* Cambridge: Polity Press.
Santana, Marco A. 2001. *Homens partidos: Comunistas e sindicatos no Brasil.* São Paulo: Boitempo.
Schmitter, Philippe C. 1971. *Interest Conflict and Political Change in Brazil.* Stanford: Stanford University Press.
———. 1979. Still the Century of Corporatism? In *Trends Towards Corporatist Intermediation*, ed. Philippe C. Schmitter and Gerhard Lehmbruch, 7–52. Beverly Hills: Sage.
Seidman, Gay W. 1994. *Manufacturing Militance: Workers' Movements in Brazil and South Africa, 1970–1985.* Berkeley: University of California Press.
Shapiro, Helen. 1994. *Engines of Growth: The State and Transnational Auto Companies in Brazil.* Cambridge: Cambridge University Press.
Sikkink, Kathryn. 1991. *Ideas and Institutions: Developmentalism in Brazil and Argentina.* Ithaca: Cornell University Press.
Skidmore, Thomas E. 1967. *Politics in Brazil 1930–1964: An Experiment in Democracy.* Oxford: Oxford University Press.
———. 1988. *The Politics of Military Rule in Brazil, 1964–1985.* Oxford: Oxford University Press.

Souza, Amaury de. 1997. Redressing Inequalities: Brazil's Social Agenda at Century's End. In *Brazil under Cardoso*, ed. Susan Kaufman Purcell and Riordan Roett, 63–88. Boulder: Lynne Rienner.

Trebat, Thomas J. 1983. *Brazil's State-Owned Enterprises: A Case Study of the State as Entrepreneur*. Cambridge: Cambridge University Press.

Weyland, Kurt. 1996. *Democracy Without Equity: Failures of Reform in Brazil*. Pittsburgh: University of Pittsburgh Press.

CHAPTER 4

New Unionism: Protest, Mobilization, and Negotiating the Transition to Democracy, 1978–1988

The strike movement that emerged in the late 1970s challenged state intervention in labour relations, thereby linking wage demands with the struggle for democratization. Its focus on worker mobilization and militancy, both in the workplace and in its engagement with national and local politics, created the new unionist movement. Where this movement differed from the unionism that had developed before the 1964 coup was in its pursuit of democratic workplace relations, autonomy from the state, and stronger connections with social movements, working-class communities, and the PT. New unionism's history of militancy also became a history of political success, which trade unionists continued to reference as a benchmark for successful labour action. For example, according to Herbert de Souza (Betinho),[1] one of the leading figures of the pro-democracy movement,

> The CUT has a history of rebellion, courage and strength. It was born from and fed by the experience of struggle. It grew, widening its bases, learning to struggle and to create dialogues, occupy spaces, make proposals and valorise the freedom of expression, organization and autonomy in relation to the state.

However, as this chapter argues, the struggle to become both a legitimate political actor and a genuine representative of workers created internal tensions between militant strategies and political participation, even during a time marked by intense labour mobilization. Although the new unionists identified values such as political autonomy together with action both within and outside the formal political arena as essential to improve the conditions of working people, combining these aims also produced the seeds for internal divisions and strategic dilemmas.

This chapter's central argument is that despite the successes resulting from militant strategies in the late 1970s, the economic and political conditions of the 1980s sparked intense debates about the union movement's participation in political negotiations as well as heightened conflicts about how labour militancy translated into a political agenda. To explain the origins of these conflicts, this chapter posits that trade union strategies became politicized in the initially highly restrictive political and economic context of the late 1970s. The examples of politicized labour strategies in this period illustrate why arguments about a linear trajectory from militancy to moderation only capture part of new unionism's story. Instead, the rapidly changing political dynamic in the 1980s shows that both the militant and moderate strategies that emerged in this period were shaped by the following factors: the union movement's relationship to the formal political arena; the evolving connections between the PT and the union movement; and the unions' ability to mobilize large numbers around key issues on the labour agenda, as demonstrated by the key importance of wage demands and the unions' bargaining position in the late 1970s. In relation to the book's overall argument, this chapter contends that a combination of exclusion from formal channels of political influence, together with repression and participation in the emerging pro-democracy movement, sparked unprecedented levels of labour militancy. The dynamics of the democratic transition itself shaped labour action, underlining the union movement's claim to have turned into a legitimate political actor capable of representing working people all over Brazil. However, other political developments during the 1980s, such as the foundation of the PT, the introduction of democratic elections, and the constitutional process, also called for political participation, which in turn led to the moderation of some of the union movement's strategies and demands.

The chapter begins by arguing why the restrictive economic and political context of the late 1970s and early 1980s sparked a pro-democracy movement in Brazilian society, a development reflected in a large-scale, militant strike movement that began in São Paulo. The unions' position outside the political arena, and thereby excluded from effective democratic representation, contributed to the decision to use the most powerful form of action available, namely strikes, thereby linking wage demands to democratization. Organized labour's moral claim that workers should benefit from economic growth also contributed to the movement's increasingly significant role as an effective critic of government economic policy. Secondly, from 1983 onwards the pro-democracy momentum began to shift from grassroots social movements to the formal political arena and negotiations about the new democratic rules, while union activists planned to institutionalize new unionist organizational principles at a national level. Strikes and mass mobilization continued to put pressure on the political process, as evident in the campaign for direct presidential elections in 1984–5, while internal conflicts were also heightened as labour activists faced concrete questions about their political participation in a democratic society. Thirdly, internal debates about the new unionist political agenda continued as labour activists and leaders reconsidered militant strategies in light of opportunities for political participation, including Lula's decision to run for president in 1989.

4.1 "Multinationals Manufacture Misery"[2]: The Strike Movement, Labour Conflict, and Democratization, 1978–1982

Between the first strike wave in 1978 and the foundation of the CUT in 1983, labour militancy peaked in response to the dynamics of political liberalization, state repression, and regressive wage policies. The process of gradual political liberalization combined with growing societal dissatisfaction with government policies in this period explains how trade unionists translated their protests against centralized wage policies into a challenge to authoritarianism and repression. It can be argued that the dynamics of the military regime's relationship with civil society politicized labour action in the late 1970s as wage demands became connected to the union activists' realization that effective union action could only develop in a democratic context. During this period labour militancy increased despite and often in response to violent repression and state intervention in union affairs. This repression forced unionists to engage in grassroots mobilizing in the workplace and neighbourhoods, which became one of the hallmarks of new unionism. Through their protests, trade unions established themselves as a crucial actor in the democratization process, constructing a democratization agenda spurred by mass mobilization and labour militancy but also rooted in grassroots democracy in the workplace and community activism.

Paradoxically, the military government's gradual political liberalization policy and ambivalent attitude to the opposition ended up strengthening the pro-democracy opposition, reflected in the government simultaneously conceding to democratic demands while repressing protests when they challenged government control of the liberalization process. For example, the military government extended the *abertura* process to dealing with workers' movements by entering into centralized wage negotiations, while continuing to intervene in union affairs and violently repressing demonstrations, as shown when the police used teargas to disperse participants in a Metalworkers' Union assembly in the ABC region of greater São Paulo and imprisoned the union's leaders in 1979.[3] In line with the book's argument about the union movement's relationship to the formal political arena, workers' exclusion from "political-governmental and institutional-entrepreneurial negotiation channels"[4] turned strikes into the preferred strategy, despite the risk of state repression. Although the immediate focus of the new unionists was on wages and working conditions, their strikes gained a broader political significance by challenging the political restrictions imposed by the military regime and the corporatist structures that regulated the unions' political behaviour. As a result, the strike movement's successes in achieving wage adjustments in the late 1970s set the scene for a political agenda focused on democratization, which posited that respect for labour rights, such as effective union representation in the workplace, formed an essential element of the return to democratic rule.[5] Trade unionists, predominantly in urban settings,[6] politicized not only everyday labour conflicts but also the existing organizational trade union structures by organizing strikes and demonstrations with an increasingly political focus. Unions also began articulating new aims as the striking workers put pressure on employers to negotiate wages and working conditions directly with the unions, rejecting the military government's centralized wage policy. Through these strategies, the striking workers managed to challenge the state's central role in labour relations, turning the workplace into the main site of their struggle, as depicted by the evolution of the strike movement in 1978 and 1979.

One of the key triggers of the strike movement during the late 1970s was the campaign for fair wages, underlining the argument developed here regarding the significance of immediate workers' interests in explaining labour militancy in an adverse political context. The unions involved in the early strike movement also benefitted from high levels of structural and associational power, while supported by community and social movement solidarity. Wage policy had become a crucial element of economic policy under the military, depoliticizing unions by pre-empting and prohibiting attempts to bargain collectively or go on strike to increase wages and improve working conditions. This policy also functioned to depress wage demands which, according to the military government, contributed to reducing inflation and to economic stability.[7] At the end of the 1970s, the union research institute DIEESE played a crucial role in the campaign promoting wage demands based on an inflation index different from the one used by the government,[8] arguing that the latter had obscured the real extent of inflation during the years of economic prosperity (1968–1973). Trade unions in the industrial sector used DIEESE's criticisms of the government's wage policies to impose direct wage bargaining with employers, demanding a fair adjustment of salaries relative to inflation.[9] Based on the discrepancy between inflation rates and real wage increases, the metalworkers' union in São Paulo's ABC region under Lula's leadership attempted to negotiate a 34.1% wage increase and agree union reforms with the Labour Ministry in 1977,[10] supported by assemblies attended by thousands of workers[11] and grassroots factory commissions (*comissões de fábrica*), which often operated clandestinely.[12] The failure to reach an agreement contributed directly to the strike wave in 1978 as union activists realized that wage bargaining within the highly restrictive political framework did not result in the desired outcomes. When union leaders began to recognize that the protests against the military's wage policy and the lack of respect for labour rights could be connected in order to mobilize workers, the strikes for wage adjustment developed into explicit demands for democratization.

The 1978–1979 strikes illustrate how union action had changed since the 1950s and 1960s, with a new generation of union leaders demanding political autonomy while circumventing the political limitations on militant action by organizing large numbers of workers[13] in highly repressive conditions. The strike movement mobilized a working class that was "new in size and experience",[14] rooted in the generally young workforce's "strategies to deal with factory and state repression".[15] The strike cycle began in May 1978 when 1800 workers stopped work in the Saab-Scania truck factory in São Bernardo do Campo in Greater São Paulo, following tensions between workers and management, ongoing since the previous year.[16] The workers in this factory circumvented the military's limitations on strikes by entering the workplace but refusing to switch on their machines. The local press reported that the strike started in the tool room at 7.00 am, before the managers arrived, thus "paralyzing the company's entire production system within minutes"; the reporter also noted the unusual silence in the factory.[17] Because it was not a normal strike in accordance with the 1964 strike law, with picket lines that the police could forcibly remove, the authorities were unable to repress this "crossed-arms" protest as the workers were present but decided not to operate their machines.[18] One of the leaders of the Saab-Scania strike, Gilson Menezes, explained that due to the repressive climate in the factory and the country more generally the decision to protest could not be taken in a union assembly: "we used word of mouth, hiding in the bathroom, it was very difficult."[19] Reflecting on the relationship between wage bargaining and political demands, Menezes also pointed out that given the high levels of repression, workers were more likely to mobilize for wage demands than for a challenge to the military regime: "I knew [the strike] had a political nature, but the workforce as a whole did not know this yet. They participated in a wage dispute. If we had said that the strike was against the dictatorship … then they would not have gone on strike."[20] This comment illustrates that while the strikes had clear political implications, fear of repression and intervention meant that union leaders often cited wage demands and democratic representation in the workplace rather than their opposition to authoritarianism.[21] The Saab-Scania strike became a symbol of labour opposition, sparking similar actions in other factories, marking the beginning of a major strike wave which simultaneously challenged authoritarian politics and reshaped the union movement's political strategies.

The 1978 strike wave illustrates the strategic importance of the industrial sector for Brazil's economy while the authoritarian nature of labour-management relations in individual companies explains the intensity of the strike movement. Ford's decision to start charging employees for transport to work in 1974, followed by wage cuts and the introduction of a shorter working week in 1978 contributed to its workforce becoming "the most politicized and well-organized" in the region.[22] In the case of Volkswagen, the company's "close government relationship and antiunion positions contributed to its designation as the key target" of the strike movement.[23] Mario dos Santos Barbosa, a union leader who worked for Volkswagen at the time the strike movement started, also cites the company's repressive climate, describing how when a number of Volkswagen toolmakers decided to stop work in May 1978, the security guards managed to isolate them, barring them from the workplace. When they were eventually allowed back to work, they decided to continue their strike and were subsequently fired. According to Barbosa, unionists then began informing and mobilizing the workforce outside the factory gates, while communicating their ideas through clandestine pamphlets stuck on the wall, close to where workers clocked in every day, including a marionette dressed in a Volkswagen uniform, mocking the idea of the complacent worker.[24] Barbosa's account of union action in Volkswagen is testament to the effects of the restrictive political climate, which provoked rather than stifled militancy, also resulting in the growing significance of grassroots union organizing in opposition to state corporatism.

Reflecting widespread dissatisfaction with repression and the lack of wage adjustment to inflation, the strikes soon spread to other factories in Greater São Paulo as well as other economic sectors and regions. Within two months of the Saab-Scania strike—by mid-July 1978—245,935 workers were on strike in companies such as Ford, Mercedes-Benz, and Volkswagen.[25] These strikes set the scene for the 1979 metalworkers' strike introduced at the start of this book, exemplifying both the strategic dilemmas the new unionists faced and the impact of state repression on the strike movement's escalation. Based on their experience in 1978 and having obtained government support, the employers refused to bargain in 1979, leading to the moderate São Paulo Metalworkers' Federation calling off the strike, a decision which many of the strike's participants, including Lula, opposed. Government repression and intervention in the participating unions—removing the strike leaders from their posts and imprisoning them—initially bolstered the protests but the impetus behind the strike waned when employers produced a 63% pay offer and the government allowed the strike leaders to return to the union. Despite the union members' controversial collective decision to finally end the strike,[26] the protests nevertheless marked the transformation of the union movement into a successful political force as politicized labour conflicts began to spread.

The workers' dissatisfaction with repression and social conditions led to the subsequent escalation of labour conflicts beyond the numbers seen in 1978, spreading quickly beyond the industrial sector and to other regions. According to strike data collected by María Helena Moreira Alves, 1979 saw a total of 113 strikes with almost a million striking workers, with some of the largest ones occurring in urban transport and education.[27] Not only were the numbers the unions managed to mobilize impressive, but they also managed to negotiate new wage deals. According to a 1985 union document, the strike movement resulted in 103 wage agreements in São Paulo in 1979, the majority of which were negotiated not by the unions but by factory commissions, which "not only took on the negotiations as a result of the [official] union leaders' impotence and the lack of confidence in these leaders among workers but many commissions also ended up being recognized by the companies".[28] Even though the unions had joined the pro-democracy opposition relatively late compared to other parts of civil society, the scale and success of the 1978–1979 strikes turned labour militancy into a particularly powerful form of political protest as the strikes affected the Brazilian economy's core. The strikes also took place in a context of growing cooperation between opposition forces, which helped sustain prolonged strikes and reinforce the impact of the strike movement.

During the strikes, financial, logistical, and moral support from social movements and the church played a significant role.[29] Up until the late 1970s, the repression of labour militancy in any form contributed to the decision by many trade unionists to focus on community work instead, not only strengthening relations with grassroots movements but also inspiring the new unionists' focus on workplace organization.[30] As one of the key opposition organizations, the Catholic Church provided meeting places, sanctuary, official statements, and material support for striking workers as well as human rights advocacy.[31] For example, workers' pastoral commissions[32] (*pastorais operárias*) created spaces for union activism to develop outside of the official union structures which simultaneously restricted political activism and were subject to repression if union leaders stepped out of line. The intensifying repression also drove union activists away from the "militarized public sphere" towards social movements, "developing a sphere of independence ... organized around the social life of residence, beyond immediate state, party, and employer sanction, [where] new spaces of civic participation and collective evaluation emerged".[33]

Particularly in the regions where new unionism first emerged, community and labour activists living in the same neighbourhoods came to view "wages and living conditions as socially and historically defined"[34] rather than static, viewing both as an object of social and political contestation. As a result of this convergence, workers, who were often also community activists, introduced new ideas into union activism, including "grassroots democracy, union autonomy, and organization at the level of communities and workplaces,"[35] which became central features of the new unionism movement. Based on these extensive cooperative relations, during the 1970s and 1980s trade unions developed a strong grassroots focus which supported labour militancy in the repressive climate that prevailed at the end of the dictatorship while disagreements about strategies and agendas also became apparent at this point.

Reflecting political and strategic differences, the strike movement gave rise to several political groupings (referred to as *tendências* or *correntes* in Portuguese), each with different organizational and political demands. The most moderate and pragmatic group that emerged during this period was called Unidade Sindical ("Union Unity", or UnS) which, though emphasizing unified opposition to military rule, did not reject the corporatist system. While UnS proposed union autonomy from the state, unlike the new unionists they supported corporatist principles such as a single union representing each category of workers and the union tax administered by the state,[36] both of which provided union leaders with organizational and financial resources. Based on UnS' support for corporatism and its emphasis on political action through institutional channels rather than direct action, this grouping became associated with the union movement's moderate sectors.[37] Unidade Sindical avoided direct confrontation with government authorities, rejecting general strikes because they could provoke an unwanted confrontation with the military regime.[38] By contrast, the two groups that became the cornerstone of the new unionism movement—the "Union Oppositions" (*oposições sindicais*), who rejected corporatism entirely, and the "Authentics" (*autênticos*)—preferred to reform the system from within the existing unions. Although these two groups differed primarily in the extent of their rejection of corporatism, they also represented different political strategies, with the Authentics developing more pragmatic views and strategies, and the Union Oppositions a more radical agenda.[39] The political positions of these groups therefore exemplify the political forcefield that shaped the evolution of militant and moderate strategies within the union movement in the 1980s.

For the Union Oppositions the grassroots focus that had emerged from the strike movement translated into their complete rejection of the prevailing corporatist union leadership and organizational structures. Dissatisfied with the official corporatist unions, opposition unionists set up alternative structures alongside the existing unions, which challenged the corporatist leadership in union elections.[40] Instead, the opposition leadership argued that corporatist industrial relations had to be abolished in favour of autonomous factory commissions, allowing direct negotiation with employers without state interference.[41] In their view, the role of unions was to support grassroots organizations, not to replace them.[42] By using these alternative union structures to mobilize workers, strike leaders politicized labour action in open defiance of the highly restrictive strike laws,[43] circumventing the strict conditions that unions had to meet to go on strike. For example, the Union Opposition leader Waldemar Rossi moved to São Paulo in 1960 to work with the Juventude Operária Católica (Catholic Workers' Youth), also becoming actively involved in the metalworkers' union. As a union leader, he criticized corporatism as divisive and weakening the union movement, preferring to mobilize his colleagues directly through "conversations, discussing ideas about unions, organization and our struggle, starting with small problems within the company".[44] These strategies led to the establishment of direct worker representation through a factory commission in the company where Rossi worked in the early 1960s, and he stood as an opposition candidate in the 1981 union elections. While this strong belief in grassroots strategies among leaders such as Rossi became an essential feature of the new unionism movement, the Authentic leaders took a more pragmatic stance regarding corporatist organizational structures.

The Authentic group consisted of union leaders who, instead of rejecting the official unions, had taken over leadership positions from their conservative predecessors. In one of the most famous examples of this approach, Lula won the metalworkers' union elections in 1975 while standing against the official leadership and was re-elected in 1978. These union leaders worked with the existing structures in their attempt to transform the corporatist system, supported by the grassroots modes of organizing that had evolved during the strike wave. They were usually young workers who had migrated from the northeast of Brazil to find work in São Paulo,[45] generally rejecting not only corporatism but also populism and other pre-1964 political views.[46] Authentic union activists used both direct action and negotiations to achieve their political goals, promoting direct struggle against the authoritarian regime, principally through general strikes and manifestations and using their ability to mobilize large numbers of workers to challenge the regime. They valued negotiation based on the principle that workers should be represented in their workplace and should be allowed to bargain directly with employers through factory commissions.[47]

Although some Union Opposition leaders feared that the Authentics would move away from their roots in the factory,[48] the choice between grassroots mobilization and the existing union structures was not mutually exclusive and often turned into a pragmatic response to changing economic and political circumstances. For example, a 1985 union report on factory commissions detailed how repression and dismissals in the aftermath of the strikes in late 1978 had weakened the factory commissions.[49]

This dynamic also shifted the strikes from the shop floor to the streets, changing the organizational characteristics of new unionism, moving away, to some extent, from the personal conversations cited by the union leaders Rossi, Bargas, and Barbosa, to more strongly coordinated action, decision-making in large assemblies, *comandos de greve* (strike commandos), pickets in factories and neighbourhoods. In the case of the 1980 metalworkers' strike, Barbosa de Macedo shows how the strikes had "spilled into the streets of São Bernardo do Campo", turning the working-class neighbourhoods in Greater São Paulo, where most of the strike leaders lived, into a site of struggle.[50] Due to the high levels of repression, the strike organizers relied not only on their union to disseminate information but also on their social networks, family, and friendships to mobilize people. During this strike, as Barbosa de Macedo describes, picketing shifted from the factory gates to bus stops, bars, and the door step, thereby mobilizing people and maintaining their morale over the course of the strike, which contributed "to an increasing politicization of the spaces and relationships within the workers' everyday lives".[51] These examples underline that while the striking workers occupied a structurally powerful position in strategic sectors of the economy, due to the repressive and economically difficult context they often relied on community and other social networks to sustain their actions. While these networks and social movement support helped sustain strike action despite the threat of repression, thus turning into a central aspect of the pro-democracy movement more generally, union organizers also became concerned about their position in the country's political future as the military government began to introduce democratic elections, leading to internal debates about the PT's electoral involvement and the best way to achieve workers' demands in a new political arena.

4.2 Political Divisions and the Foundation of the PT

The differences and similarities between the political groupings present in the trade unions of the early 1980s should not obscure their intense discussions about political participation, particularly in light of questions about the left's electoral strategies. The Union Opposition groups were the most sceptical about the new unionists' pursuit of political power and about the party-political influences of union activists. For example, although political and strategic differences had already started to emerge in the late

1970s, Rossi believed that the Union Oppositions in Greater São Paulo were neither divided into political factions nor dictated by political parties. He nevertheless noticed a shift from union activism to party politics, which began to spark debates about the desirability of electoral participation and the political goals that workers should pursue. Rossi viewed the struggle for political power as divisive, resulting in the left arguing mainly with itself rather than getting on with the workers' struggle, but he hoped that union activists would return to union action soon after participating in the elections.[52] Others wanted to establish a new party that reflected the principles of new unionism, allowing unionists to extend their political agenda from the workplace and the communities to the formal political arena, resulting in the PT's foundation in February 1980. Due to these differing expectations of what a workers' party could achieve, the foundation of the PT not only raised questions about the relationship between the unions and the party in organizational, strategic, and political terms but also came to encapsulate many of the political and strategic dilemmas faced by the new unionists in the 1980s.

As a new party on Brazil's political scene, the PT reflected the social movement opposition of the 1970s, including groups such as the new unionists, the student movement, progressive Catholics, and academics. The idea to found a workers' party first emerged in metalworkers' conferences in 1979 but the participants in the debates soon realized that they had to broaden the party's appeal and scope in discussion with social movement representatives and MDB politicians such as Fernando Henrique Cardoso—although the latter never joined the PT. The party not only emerged from the same socio-political transformations as the new unionism movement, but it also occupied a new space on the left of the political spectrum, attractive to social movement activists and people who had become disillusioned with the existing political parties.[53] In the early years, the party unapologetically viewed itself as a "political project for workers to achieve power, thus creating the conditions for social transformation towards a society without exploitation and on the road to socialism".[54] This agenda clearly appealed to the many new unionists who not only wanted democracy but also social change, particularly as the party identified itself as a channel for the political articulation of social movement demands based on grassroots decision-making.[55] Although many new unionists participated enthusiastically in the PT's foundation, the unions associated with UnS and traditionally connected with the PCB rejected the PT, partly because the PT would compete with the PCB and also because they feared that the PT's radicalism could jeopardize the transition.[56] Other than mirroring the political divisions that had emerged within the union movement, the PT's electoral concerns resonated within organized labour as the democratic transition progressed, eventually turning into a source of political moderation. Apart from founding the PT as an expression of new unionism's political agenda, labour activists also began thinking about uniting the union movement to strengthen its political position at a national level.

The first step towards unifying labour's political agenda and institutionalizing the new unionist movement was the decision to establish a national union organization. In August 1981, after months of regional meetings and discussions, 5000 representatives from over 1000 unions, representing all political groupings in the trade unions, together with international observers, met in the National Congress of the Working Classes (Congresso Nacional das Classes Trabalhadoras—CONCLAT).[57] CONCLAT's ambitious purpose was not only to institutionalize and unify the union movement nationally but also to develop a joint political agenda focused on wages and working conditions, labour reform, and democracy. CONCLAT participants voiced demands related to working conditions, wages, and employment, including reducing the working week and the end of wage adjustment by government decree. They also demanded the reform of the corporatist labour relations system, with special reference to union autonomy, the liberalization of the right to strike, and the right to unionize for public sector workers. Moreover, the CONCLAT resolutions included a series of democratic changes, such as the end of repression, amnesty, and the establishment of a constituent assembly.[58]

However, rather than unifying the union movement, the debates reflected the different political and strategic considerations that had emerged within the various groupings. According to a conference report, despite negotiations that lasted all night—in the hope that "the participants were sufficiently mature to overcome party-political and ideological questions"[59]—the various groupings could not agree on a single list of candidates for the committee that would found a national organization. They formed two competing lists instead,[60] broadly corresponding to Unidade Sindical and the new unionists respectively, the latter led by Lula. As the report described, "[t]he atmosphere before the plenary vote was tense. In a matter of seconds, representatives of both lists had improvised pieces of paper with the numbers 1 and 2",[61] effectively creating an impasse between the two positions until a committee was finally elected with two presidents. The paralysis in CONCLAT reflected union leader Osvaldo Bargas' observation that "in reality, the Brazilian labour movement talks a lot about unity today. But this unity proposed by the majority of Brazilian unionists is a unity of discourse, unity at the top"[62] of the union movement. Despite the rhetoric about unity, the CONCLAT debates therefore reflected profound disagreements about the union movement's strategies and political agenda, ultimately leading to an irreconcilable split between the new unionists and the more moderate Unidade Sindical unions.

The divisions that emerged in the late 1970s and early 1980s did not represent a straightforward split between militant and moderate strategies, illustrating instead the complex factors that shaped labour militancy. These events underline the argument proposed here that labour militancy emerged and escalated in response to adverse political conditions and the unionists' recognition of the connections between wages, labour rights, and democracy. Nevertheless, when considering the purpose and outcomes of militant union strategies, negotiation and particularly wage bargaining with employers and the state remained a key aspect of labour strategies. In 1998, the then president of the ABC Metalworkers' Union, Luiz Marinho, said that "we went on strike in 1978 to open up spaces for negotiation. The dictatorship impeded this negotiation. Our entire struggle in 1978 was about negotiation".[63] While Marinho's quote downplays labour militancy's wider political impact in this period, it illustrates the interdependence between labour conflicts and negotiation. The failure to achieve appropriate wage increases through institutional channels and the unionists' dissatisfaction with the organizational resources at their disposal triggered the strike movement. While the most radical response to the structural constraints was to completely reject corporatist structures as the Union Oppositions proposed, for the vast majority of unionists, working within these structures offered advantages because of the associated financial and organizational resources, even if corporatism restricted the potential for militant, politicized action. These political disagreements illustrate how trade unionists constructed their associational power in a rapidly changing political context while these debates also responded to trade unionists' perceptions of effective union action based on experiences in the 1970s. They also underline that the union activists actively considered how their organizational structures could be maximized to achieve their political aims of labour action, linking associational with political power. In practice, and as the 1979 metalworkers' strike illustrates, the existing union structures operated as a vehicle for strike action while negotiations and militancy were not mutually exclusive, as labour militancy functioned to pressurize employers, complemented during the 1980s by a significant element of compromise and moderation in response to changing economic and political circumstances.

4.3 Economic Crisis and the Consolidation of New Unionism: 1983–1985

After the successful strikes of the late 1970s, labour activists discovered that they had to redefine some of their demands and ideas about militancy, negotiation, and political participation. In contrast with the late 1970s, Brazil experienced a severe economic downturn in the early 1980s, which led to a reduction of private sector strikes as well as an increased emphasis on political strikes and demonstrations at a national level.[64] In the late 1970s, workers' realization that wages did not reflect economic growth and inflation rates had provoked the strike movement, but the economic context worsened significantly as Mexico's default on its external debt in 1982 triggered a region-wide economic crisis. During this period, the political system also gradually became normalized through the introduction of several formal aspects of democracy, namely a new party system and democratic elections at all levels except the presidency.[65] As the opportunities for democratic participation evolved, the opposition's focus became more diffuse and, in some respects, more complicated. The transition's increasingly institutional focus meant that the opposition was split between political parties which positioned themselves at the forefront of political negotiations and the social movement opposition (including the trade unions), the latter generally more sceptical about the benefits of negotiation while wanting to maintain civil society's political influence during and after the transition. When negotiation and political participation became concrete possibilities, even if civil society still faced political restrictions and repression, the opposition's emphasis began to shift from the military regime to questions about the shape of democratic politics as well as the distribution of wealth and income, complemented by the difficult task of redefining the union agenda in an era of economic crisis.[66] The union movement itself experienced growing divisions along party-political lines, with the differences that had emerged within CONCLAT solidifying during this period. The argument here is that labour mobilization became more difficult due to repression and job losses, which meant that the new unionist movement focused on the foundation of the CUT, signifying the consolidation of the uneasy relationship between the different political convictions within the unions rather than national unity. In this sense, the unions' relationship with the PT began to shape labour militancy in this period, also illustrating the nature of internal debates about the political nature of labour action, while leading activists to question the desirability of political alliances as well as the relationship between the party, the union leadership, and grassroots activists.

During the early 1980s, the strike movement lost momentum as a result of the recession, at the same time that it suffered from increased government repression and strategic dismissals. As a result, the total number of strikes dropped from 246 in 1979 to 144 in 1980 and 150 in 1981, with the majority of strikes taking place in higher education and the health sector,[67] where job security initially shielded workers from the recession. As a result, union action became more defensive due to the effects of the economic crisis as labour conflicts focused on protecting rather than increasing employment and wages. If private sector strikes occurred, they focused on establishing workplace representation and preventing dismissals—which often targeted union representatives[68]—instead of the progressive wage demands of the late 1970s. As an example, 9000 Ford workers in São Bernardo do Campo went on strike in 1981 to protest against job losses and for the formal recognition of their factory commission,[69] which had become the main negotiator in this labour conflict. At the same time, although Mercedes-Benz had fired the most militant unionists among its employees, their colleagues began to talk among themselves to identify like-minded activists, planning a strike against unfair wage adjustments in 1981. Rather than the confrontational approach which had worked so well in the late 1970s, the strike leaders had to operate more carefully to avoid being fired and to demonstrate that they could negotiate on behalf of their colleagues. A Mercedes-Benz union activist described how he and his colleagues established the conditions for negotiations by demonstrating that they represented their fellow workers and by rejecting violence: "We had the capacity to lead our people, there was no aggression, we didn't break the machines, we didn't destroy anything belonging to the company, so they [the management] saw that in reality we could be in charge."[70]

In 1983, workers had elected factory commissions in 20 companies in Greater São Paulo, rising to 101 in 1986 and peaking at 211 in 1993.[71] The factory commissions not only represented one of the new unionists' key demands—workplace representation and direct bargaining between workers and employers—but also signalled a shift in the unions' strategies. Although strike action forced the employers to recognize the commissions, they also represented a partial move away from the confrontational strategies of the late 1970s due to their focus on establishing grounds for direct wage bargaining with employers. While employers continued to threaten militant unionists with dismissal and repression, the factory commissions also represented an attempt to consolidate the new unionist model of union organization in the workplace, using strikes to force employers to the negotiating table, thereby legitimizing the commissions.

Despite the continuing economic problems, the year 1983 saw a resurgence of labour militancy as the number of strikes more than doubled compared to the previous year[72] due to growing dissatisfaction with the government's attempts to deal with the debt crisis,[73] and particularly the effect on wages, jobs, and living standards. The government placed part of the blame for the economic crisis on the wage adjustments demanded by workers and imposed wage increases at 80% below the official inflation rate in early July 1983, a measure backed by the IMF.[74] The austerity package also included plans to fire workers in state-owned companies, offering the remaining employees a reduced salary. In response, workers in state-owned oil refineries in the states of São Paulo and Bahia went on strike to protest against these measures. The government hit back by declaring the strikes illegal according to the 1964 strike law, which limited the right to strike in "essential" economic sectors such as oil, followed by intervention in the oil workers' union, repression, and dismissals, which provoked a solidarity strike by 60,000 metalworkers in São Bernardo do Campo.[75] The leaders of this solidarity protest hoped that these events would trigger a general strike as opposition to the austerity measures spread from the public to the private sector.[76] Faced with government repression, the solidarity strike proved hard to maintain and as workers began to return to work, the union decided to suspend the strike.[77] Despite the initial failure to turn this conflict into a general strike, which metalworkers' leader Jair Meneguelli attributed to the lack of willingness in the union movement to mobilize workers, the new unionist leaders were keen to present the protests as proof that they were capable of organizing a political strike.[78] Rather than going on strike as part of the wage-bargaining process, as stipulated by the labour laws, this strike focused directly on supporting colleagues in a different economic sector in protest against government policy, which signified a clear departure from earlier years.

The dynamics of labour conflicts and government intervention in 1983 also show that repression continued to fuel labour militancy, which, together with the increasingly difficult economic conditions, turned strikes into a political instrument to oppose authoritarianism. Although it took several months before the unions finally managed to organize a general strike, the escalation of labour conflict illustrates how strikes became explicitly political in 1983, contesting the military regime from a workers' perspective. In response to the oil workers' strike, the Comissão Nacional Pró-CUT, established at CONCLAT two years previously, elected a strike committee to prepare a general strike, representing both Authentic and UnS unionists. The July 21, 1983, general strike took place primarily in São Paulo, resulting in almost complete adherence in Greater São Paulo with three-quarters out of 400,000 metalworkers on strike in the city of São Paulo.[79] Although the strike never quite turned general or national, further strikes and demonstrations also took place in other parts of the country.[80] Despite the strike's success in new unionism's heartlands, it highlighted that unions struggled to represent and mobilize workers outside of these strongholds. The strike nevertheless managed to unify the union movement's political groupings one last time,[81] while also establishing a precedent for another attempt at a general strike.

A few weeks afterwards the CUT was founded in late August 1983, representing further divisions rather than unity.[82] The founding congress of the CUT in 1983 took place without the participation of the UnS unionists as the divisions between the Authentics and the UnS—particularly about the desirability of another general strike[83]—meant that they could not reach an agreement.[84] The newly established umbrella organization soon began planning another general strike to be held in late 1983. To trigger the strike, the CUT's new leadership planned to present an ultimatum to President Figueiredo, including demands such as abolishing the wage decrees, rejecting the IMF package, and introducing various labour reforms.[85] However, when the general strike failed to materialize, this sparked intense internal debates about the reasons and implications for the newly formed national union organization. An article in the PT magazine *Boletim Nacional* from November 1983 attributed the failure to the union movement's divisions and sabotage from within: "Union leaders who are immobile, conciliatory, *pelegos*, or simply wrong, formed a strange and spurious united front to torpedo and boycott any initiative to unite the Brazilian working class."[86] The article also questioned whether the unions could have tapped into the growing discontent with government policy among the general population, which had mobilized the unemployed and led to occupations, marches, and even occasional looting and vandalism. The CUT's first national congress led to similar soul-searching, which pointed to the political divisions within the organization, while arguing that the CUT's foundation had led to a sense of euphoria which made the organization insufficiently decisive at a crucial time for the opposition. The document identified the general strike as the most important political instrument in the hands of the union movement, taking advantage of the intensification of smaller-scale labour conflicts to generalize labour mobilization, as was the case in 1983. Congress delegates argued that the CUT had hesitated too much with the strike, while the strike organizers failed to connect the struggle to the campaigns for direct presidential elections, which would have helped broaden the protest.[87] These internal responses to the difficulties of maintaining high levels of mobilization while widening labour opposition to mass mobilization beyond trade unions illustrate how questions about political strategies at times paralysed new unionism. At the same time, institutionalizing the national umbrella organization diverted attention away from developing effective militant strategies, explaining the struggle to connect localized strikes with the national opposition movement.

The fact that debates about the general strike resonated not only within the CUT but also in the PT is evidence of the close relationship between the two organizations, translating into insightful debates about their respective political roles. Throughout the early to mid-1980s, these debates proved to be intense and at times highly critical, reflecting both the unionists' awareness of the political nature of the economic pressure they faced and the deliberately politicized nature of labour mobilization. PT publications in this period echoed these debates, providing useful insights not only into how union-party relations shaped labour militancy but also—from the party's perspective—in terms of the debates taking place within the unions themselves. Although the Labour Code prohibited formal and institutionalized relations between unions and political parties, the emergence of the PT and the CUT shows that their strategies and ideas were related. For the unionists who founded the party, "the PT was to be an extension of and at the same time separate from labor organized institutionally in unions, and was—as a party—to respect the autonomy of those unions. At the same time ... [t]he party was not so much to lead workers as to express in the political arena the demands of social movements and workers".[88]

Although the party's nature and history meant that unions as a political constituency and a source of leadership were crucial for its strength as a political organization, functioning merely as a political front for social movements could limit the party's electoral appeal. The PT attempted to resolve the issue by stating that unions could not be used for party-political purposes or organized along party-political lines, while also arguing that labour conflicts were inherently political,[89] recognizing the political impact of the strikes while also differentiating the role of the party and the unions. The CUT also saw its role as different from political parties: "[t]he CUT engages in class struggle through labour conflicts, articulating economic struggles with political objectives ... to aim for the construction of a socialist society, but it should not be confused with a political party and always maintains its autonomy in relation to state power and parties."[90] The reality of their relationship was rather different as the party became inextricably linked with new unionism while the PT and the union movement had many activists in common, resulting in the PT and the CUT experiencing similar political and strategic divisions.

Both the new unionist movement and the PT held heated debates about the position of the internal political groupings that emerged from the strike movement, which also included questions about the PT's role within individual unions and the representation of political and ideological differences within the CUT and the PT. These debates showed that "the party walked a fine discursive line between recognizing its identity as a class party and attempting to transcend its class language and concerns".[91] Despite its central role in new unionism and the PT, the emphasis on grassroots activism and social movements posed problems as the party's grassroots, bottom-up model was not always easy to maintain or to reconcile with electoral strategies. For example, in 1984, in the PT's own evaluation the party had registered 220 PT circles in the state of São Paulo but many of them had already disappeared "because the space reserved for the *núcleos* (grassroots circles) had never been clearly defined within the party's power structure".[92] This debate is exemplified by a 1985 article published in the PT magazine *Boletim Nacional* about a CUT internal debate, reporting that several participants felt that there was a lack of information about the role and presence of the PT within the union movement. The PT's response was to propose the creation of party *núcleos* in trade unions as well as integrating union representation within the party organization. To strengthen the party message within the unions, the party argued that *petista* (PT-supporting) union leaders needed to maintain "their organic link" with the party in their union activism: "the *petista* militant should talk like a worker, constantly reflecting the general demands of workers."[93] This debate echoes the tensions within new unionism between the grassroots union activists who believed that workers' real power was located in workplace mobilization and representation while the dominant groups within new unionism veered towards a more explicitly political agenda.

As a result of these tensions between grassroots mobilization and party discipline, the PT experienced internal divisions similar to the CUT; the political groupings had also become institutionalized within the party as conflicts arose not only about the party's relationship with grassroots activists but also concerning the voters the party would target. In the 1985 debate cited in the previous paragraph, some participants argued that political divisions weakened the unions while others remarked that allowing political and ideological differences within the unions and the party was democratic,[94] reflecting the party's ideals of political pluralism. Regarding the latter point of view, the report cited Raul Pont, then a member of the PT's Diretório Nacional (National Executive), as arguing that the party needed to find a common denominator among the multiplicity of political views, expecting that this heterogeneity would strengthen rather than weaken the party.[95] In other words, representing a wide spectrum of political views would allow the party to cast the widest possible net to attract progressive voters while keeping radical political activists within the party fold, people who would otherwise have joined parties to the left of the PT. However, problems emerged when the political differences created conflicts and undermined the movement's unified message, mirroring the political divisions within the union movement. As in the CUT, within the PT the *direito de tendência* (the right to participate in the party as a distinct political group) was officially recognized at the party's national congress in 1986, but only as long as these groups obeyed the general party line. The party leadership also argued that it did not just tolerate any political views nor did it function "as a front for political organizations", as illustrated when it expelled a number of PT militants who robbed a bank in Salvador to raise money for the Nicaraguan revolution.[96] These examples show how the PT's political debates became closely intertwined with the union movement in the early to mid-1980s, signalling that the party's electoral concerns and political agenda had also begun to shape the labour movement's strategies. Widening the PT's political appeal together with electoral participation gradually led to compromises and a degree of moderation, as evident in the debate about political alliances.

Questions about political alliances came to the forefront of the debate when the PT tried to transform itself from a party based on grassroots activity to a party which was institutionalized and broad enough in its electoral appeal to compete in local and national elections. For the PT, with its roots in the labour movement, successful opposition also raised questions about alliances, which the leadership viewed as necessary to avoid its own isolation and divisions among the progressive opposition. In the party's relationship with the unions, the priority was first to disseminate the PT's ideas among working-class organizations, followed by other groups who did not necessarily support the PT,[97] such as middle-class voters. As reported in articles in PT publications, these strategies sparked internal debates about whether it was desirable to cooperate with parties and organizations that were not *classista* (working-class based).[98] Despite the emphasis on the party's working-class roots, a 1984 PT document expressed doubts about the readiness of the Brazilian working class for political power:

> to change the nature of the state and to contribute to the transformation of society, we want not only the government, but also power. But this opportunity has not yet taken clear and conscious root in the working class. Aside from this, you don't just take power, you also construct it.[99]

In response to this and to broaden the party's electoral appeal, the party started to expand its conception of class, moving beyond its roots in the trade union movement. During the 1980s, although the PT continued to view the working class (*classe operária*) as the most important political constituency in strategic terms, the party started to include rural workers, the marginalized and excluded, the informal sector, and the middle class.[100] These debates demonstrate that mass mobilizations in the campaign for direct presidential elections in 1984–1985 showed both the PT and the CUT saw the potential benefits of a broad-based alliance and began to recognize that alliances could also be of use in future elections.

To conclude this section, the drop in labour militancy in the early 1980s highlights the combined effect of the worsening economic conditions and repression on strikes. However, labour militancy increased again in 1983 in response to growing discontent with the government's austerity measures, underlining that union leaders recognized this as an opportunity to politicize labour's strategies. While militancy increased among individual unions, the failure of the general strike in late 1983 and the internal conflicts this provoked illustrate several key points about the evolution of militant and moderate labour strategies in this period. These developments illustrate the tensions between the mobilization of unions' structural and associational power, and translating these resources into political influence. The latter depended on organizational strengths beyond individual unions as well as coalition building. In addition, rather than unifying the unions, institutionalization at a national level functioned to consolidate political differences. On the one hand, these divisions raised the threshold for successful large-scale mobilization because the CUT needed to convince the unions associated with the moderate Unidade Sindical to participate in strike action. On the other hand, the need to establish the CUT's national organization took up much of the union leaders' time and efforts—often away from their local unions—leading to internal criticism of the CUT's failure to respond quickly and decisively when an opportunity to protest arose. Finally, the debates within the CUT and the PT point to the struggle to connect labour militancy to the wider opposition movement, particularly the extent to which the general strike organizers could have taken advantage of the mass pro-democracy movement that emerged during this period.

4.4 Economic Decline, Direct Presidential Elections, and a New Constitution: 1985–1989

In the second half of the 1980s three interconnected factors shaped labour militancy: mass pro-democracy mobilization, the government's failure to handle the economic crisis, and questions about political participation in the new democratic regime, particularly the Constituent Assembly. Reflecting Brazilians' generalized discontent with repression and economic crisis, the strike movement helped create the conditions for the growing pro-democracy coalition in the early to mid-1980s by mobilizing large protests, largely through the unions' own networks with social movements. The campaign for direct presidential elections in 1983–1985 (Diretas Já!—"Direct Elections Now!") formed the basis for unprecedented unity among the opposition forces, consisting of "mass demonstrations to educate the public about the proposed constitutional amendment for direct elections and rally pressure against recalcitrant members of congress".[101] The Diretas Já campaign inspired a sense of empowerment, building on the successful opposition campaigns held since the late 1970s and signalling the beginning of a broad alliance between opposition groups.[102] While the campaign failed to achieve the desired result—the first civilian president was to be elected by an Electoral College—it provided the opposition movement with a degree of unity, particularly because the campaign focused on the single issue of direct elections. With this focus, opposition groups avoided more fundamental questions about political change, which was less threatening to the moderate forces in the alliance than a call for constructing a socialist society.[103] Another dimension of political change in the latter years of the dictatorship was that the political process became normalized through elections while the rules of the emerging democratic regime became subject to negotiation, shifting the focus of the opposition's political struggle from the streets to state institutions and political parties. While the broadening of the pro-democracy movement was a positive development for the unions in that it led to mass mobilization, it also created strategic dilemmas as to whether the CUT and the PT should enter political alliances and negotiate the terms of the democratic transition.

Apart from the impact of mass mobilizations and the changing political scene, union action post-1985—whether militant or concentrating on political participation—was also strongly conditioned by the government's failure to stabilize the economy. The civilian government under José Sarney (1985–1990) started off with positive economic indicators but had inherited severe financial and inflation problems. Politically, Sarney was not as popular as Tancredo Neves, who was elected president by the Electoral College but died before he could be sworn in. The result was that the Sarney government not only struggled with a severe economic crisis, but it also lacked legitimacy, which made the government appear indecisive and ineffective.[104] The deepening economic crisis and the opportunity to exert political pressure in a democratic context spurred labour militancy, as Fig. 4.1 shows, with the number of strikes approaching 2000 in 1989 and 1990.

In response to the government's failure to control inflation and reverse the economic crisis, and mindful of the successful mobilizations against the IMF-backed austerity plans of 1983, the union movement organized two general strikes, in 1986 and in 1987. The Cruzado Plan, introduced in early 1986, included wage and price freezes as well as ending the indexation of wage increases in line with inflation. The Plan soon failed to stabilize the economy, resulting in shortages, black markets, and parallel

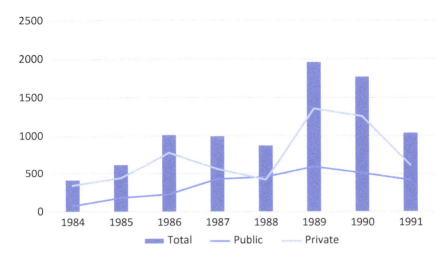

Fig. 4.1 Public and private sector strikes—1984–1991. (Public sector strikes include strikes in state-owned companies in this figure. Source: DIEESE, "Balanço das greves em 2013," *Estudos e Pesquisas* 79 (2015), 42)

exchange rates, while the end of indexation increased uncertainty in the financial markets. Now operating in a democratic context, the government decided it needed to secure popular support for the Plan, which included compensatory measures for workers, inviting unions to negotiate a social pact with the government. In 1985, CUT-affiliated union leaders had already started to speak out against social pacts; such that CUT secretary-general Paulo Paim emphasized that negotiation was conditional upon the government first committing to a range of fundamental labour, agrarian, and social reforms.[105] This position reflected the view prevalent in the new unionist movement at the time that militant strategies could force the government to introduce these reforms without the need for concessions or moderation on the part of the unions. In fact, based on this point of view, moderating workers' demands weakened rather than strengthened the union movement's position. As a report on relations between the CUT and European trade unions stated, due to the difficult political and economic conditions in Brazil negotiation could only work combined with confrontation: "Differentiating strategies of negotiation and confrontation deepens political divisions within the [working] class and dilutes unity."[106] Based on this perspective, the CUT refused to participate in the negotiations and called a general strike in December 1986, mobilizing approximately 3.5 million workers around the country.[107] For the CUT, the general strike's success reinforced the leadership's rejection of negotiating social pacts[108] but maintaining this level of mobilization and militancy proved challenging, signalling the gradual shift towards a greater acceptance of negotiation.

After yet another stabilization plan (the Bresser Plan) failed to produce the desired results, the CUT called a second general strike in 1987. This time the strike plans failed to mobilize similar numbers of strikers due to organizational problems, with a resultant loss of momentum as the leadership postponed the strike several times when union organizers struggled to coordinate the strike with the other union umbrella organizations.[109] Furthermore, a PT analysis of the strike highlighted the lack of a clear set of demands associated with the strike, resulting in the PT believing that the CUT leadership failed to articulate workers' immediate concerns, such as job and wage losses, as connected to opposition to the government. In these conditions, the PT's National Executive argued that attempts to translate a "diffuse sense of dissatisfaction" among workers into an effective strike had become more difficult than before, implying that stronger cooperation between the opposition forces—and particularly between the CUT and the PT—would have made a difference.

The PT's comments on the 1987 general strike also provide insights into the party leadership's view of the division of labour between the party and the CUT, reflecting a degree of frustration with the way union-party relations had evolved. The party leadership diagnosed a lack of coordination between the PT, the CUT, and the unions, in what the PT executive viewed as confusion among trade unionists about the union-party relationship: as it remarked at the time, a large number of *petista* union militants and leaders "consider the party structure as something external to the unions and the CUT, and they don't feel committed to the party's discussions and decisions".[110] These rather critical comments suggest that the PT intended to strengthen its organizational and political relations with the CUT without turning the party into a political front for the union movement,[111] while also expressing concerns about the extent to which the party and the unions could work together. For CUT leaders, even if they were often PT activists themselves, the union movement could not simply function as the PT's union branch, valuing pluralist representation instead. For example, the CUT president Jair Meneguelli commented in 1988 that he hoped a plurality of political parties could be represented within the CUT but until that time, "many comrades confuse the specific role of trade unions ... with that of a political party, as in the PT's case".[112] These internal discussions illustrate the close but sometimes constrained relations between the unions and the party, as the CUT faced the decision whether to participate in the Constituent Assembly and the PT began to prepare for the 1989 presidential elections.

The Constituent Assembly held in 1987 and 1988 was a major opportunity for the union movement and progressive sectors in Brazilian society to introduce some of their demands into the national political arena. The Assembly was set up to facilitate broad-based participation so that civil society organizations could make proposals ("popular initiatives") by collecting a sufficient number of signatures to back a particular proposal. For the majority of the CUT, the Assembly represented an opportunity to open up the democratic decision-making process, moving the political debate away from the formal political arena back to civil society.[113] Left-wing groups within the CUT initially opposed the Constituent Assembly,[114] proposing to delegitimize the decision-making process through mobilizations but eventually decided to participate in an attempt to strengthen workers' rights under the democratic regime.[115] Labour issues formed a prominent part of the constitutional debates and the reason why social and labour rights were included in the first place was the result of social movement and union pressure. To put pressure on the constitutional debate, the CUT distributed hundreds of thousands of pamphlets in support of its proposals, with photos of Assembly members suspected of voting against the CUT's agenda, and also organizing symbolic stoppages and marches in Brasília to underline their demands.[116] The unions' proposals ensured that principles such as union autonomy from the state and the right of unionization within the public sector were now constitutionally enshrined. Furthermore, the Constitution made union participation in collective bargaining obligatory, legalized workplace representation, and removed the military's restrictions on the right to strike.[117]

Despite these positive outcomes, the union movement as a whole had been unable to reach a consensus on labour reform, resulting in a half-hearted attempt at reform of the corporatist system. In fact, although the Constitution established freedom of association and organizational autonomy from the state, it maintained several important pillars of the corporatist system—particularly the monopoly of representation and the compulsory union tax.[118] Trade union participation in the Constituent Assembly illustrates a shift towards the new unionists' gradual acceptance that political participation could be a valuable strategy in a democratic context, inevitably requiring concessions and moderation to avoid paralysis. Regarding the institutional context in which the union movement operated, however, the constitutional provisions formalized a labour relations system in which significant corporatist elements remained, which restricted new unionist ambitions to make unions more representative of the working population and to strengthen workplace representation, effectively continuing the much-criticized moderating effects of corporatism into the new democratic era.

4.5 Conclusion

The late 1970s and 1980s are often considered to be the heyday of labour militancy in Brazil, leaving not only a legacy of successful militant political strategies but also sharp conflicts between militant and moderate groups within the union movement about issues such as the workers' position in the formal political arena, including relations with the PT, appropriate responses to the economic crisis, and labour's political agenda under a democratic regime. Despite the legacy of successful militancy, however, this chapter has argued that confrontation and negotiation often functioned as interdependent approaches, as the union movement's response to the rapidly changing economic and political circumstances changed the balance between the two strategies. The dynamics of labour and political conflict in the late 1970s and 1980s demonstrate that labour conflicts experienced cycles of militancy and moderation, conditioned both by developments in the national economic and political context, mediated by the union movement's own debates about its strategies and political position.

The conditions in the late 1970s illustrate the effect of repression and political exclusion on strike action, giving rise to new unionism's famed militancy and innovative approach to worker mobilization. Building on the rapidly developing grassroots opposition to authoritarianism, the new unionists politicized labour conflicts by organizing strikes and other forms of militant action in the most dynamic sectors of the Brazilian economy. Their confrontational strategies focused not only on pressurizing employers to meet their wage demands but also on establishing the conditions for effective direct negotiation, as the story of the strike movement in Greater São Paulo shows. As the democratic transition evolved and the economic circumstances worsened, union leaders attempted to replicate these achievements with renewed ebbs and flows of militancy and mobilization but they were not always successful, as seen in the case of the general strikes in the

1980s. The imminent transition to civilian rule turned the political representation of workers' interests into a central question for trade unionists, creating internal debates about political strategies and sparking differences between militant and pragmatic groups. These debates focused in particular on whether the union movement should continue to operate outside the formal political arena, pressurizing the government to respond to workers' demands. While this strategy had proven to be effective during the strike movement, the new unionists struggled to link immediate concerns about job losses and wage cuts to mass mobilization against austerity plans. The evolution of the union movement's relationship with the PT in this period shows how party-political and electoral considerations entered the debate, as union leaders valued their autonomy but also recognized the potential of acting through a political party, resulting in a gradual shift towards a greater acceptance of negotiation.

NOTES

1. Herbert de Souza, quoted in "Dignidade para quem faz o país," *De Fato* September (1993), 22.
2. "As multinacionais fabricam a miséria": a media headline shown in the documentary "Greve!" ("Strike!") about the 1979 metalworkers' strike in Greater São Paulo (directed by João Batista de Andrade, 1979).
3. As shown in the documentary "Greve!".
4. Eduardo Noronha, "A explosão das greves na década de 80," in *O sindicalismo brasileiro nos anos 80*, ed. Armando Boito Jr. (Rio de Janeiro: Paz e Terra, 1990), 105.
5. Iram J. Rodrigues, "A trajetória do novo sindicalismo," in *O novo sindicalismo: Vinte anos depois*, ed. Iram J. Rodrigues (São Paulo: Vozes, 1999), 76–7; Leigh A. Payne, "Working Class Strategies in the Transition to Democracy in Brazil," *Comparative Politics* 23(2) (1991): 229.
6. Although the metalworkers' strikes are the best-known aspect of the late 1970s protests, significant strikes also occurred outside the urban centres of Brazil's southeast. Sugarcane workers went on strike in 1979 in the northeastern state of Pernambuco but did not develop the same political agenda as the metalworkers' unions. According to Pereira, their position reflected the historical "reality that democratic rights had been extended differentially in Brazil and that some unions had greater rights to consultation than others", which facilitated the politicization of union action in the southeast, Anthony W. Pereira, *The End of the Peasantry: The Rural Labor Movement in Northeast Brazil, 1961–1988* (Pittsburgh PA: University of Pittsburgh Press, 1997), 70. See also Robert J. Alexander, *A History of Organized Labor in Brazil* (Westport, CN: Praeger, 2003), 175–7.

7. Maria H. Tavares de Almeida, *Crise econômica e interesses organizados: O sindicalismo dos anos 80* (São Paulo: EDUSP, 1996), 37–9; Thomas E. Skidmore, *The Politics of Military Rule in Brazil, 1964–1985* (Oxford: Oxford University Press, 1988), 205.
8. The Instituto Brasileiro de Geografia e Estatística (IBGE) calculated the official interest rate and DIEESE offered an alternative calculation based on actual living costs, see Ademir Figueiredo and Clemente Ganz Lúcio, "O DIEESE no século XXI," *Revista Ciências do Trabalho* 5 (2015), 60–2.
9. Gay W. Seidman, *Manufacturing Militance: Workers' Movements in Brazil and South Africa, 1970–1985* (Berkeley, CA: University of California Press, 1994), 154–9.
10. The fact that the proposal combined wage increases and labour reform—including full freedom of organization, bilateral wage bargaining between unions and employers, and the right to strike—led the conservative *Veja* magazine to identify the issue that would dominate the union agenda for the next decades: "The demand for a wage increase … began to demonstrate the intimate link with the problem of workers' and union rights of workers", Veja, "A questão operária," 14 September 1977, 20.
11. Folha de São Paulo, "Metalúrgicos tentarão repor salários através de acordo," 3 September 1977; O Estado de São Paulo, "São Bernardo não desiste dos 34.1%," 29 November 1977.
12. "Entrevista Gilson Menezes, parte I", *Memórias operárias*, accessed July 11, 2016, http://memoriasoperarias.blogspot.nl/2015/12/entrevista-gilson-menezes-parte-i.html
13. The strike movement not only strengthened the position of existing unions but also motivated the formation of new unions. The number of new unions increased even more rapidly after the approval of the 1988 Constitution, which allowed for the establishment of public sector trade unions, see Adalberto Moreira Cardoso, *Sindicatos, trabalhadores e a coqueluche neoliberal: A era Vargas acabou?* (Rio de Janeiro: Fundação Getúlio Vargas, 1999), 48–50.
14. Beverly J. Silver, *Forces of Labor: Workers' Movements and Globalization Since 1870* (Cambridge: Cambridge University Press, 2003), 55.
15. Seidman, *Manufacturing Militance*, 148.
16. Marco Aurélio Santana, "Ditadura militar e resistência operária: O movimento sindical brasileiro do golpe à transição democrática," *Política e Sociedade* 13 (2008), 297.
17. Diario do Grande ABC, "Operários da Scania entram em greve," 13 May 1978.
18. Maria H. Moreira Alves, *State and Opposition in Military Brazil* (Austin, TX: University of Texas Press, 1985), 194.

19. "Entrevista Gilson Menezes". The company and police reaction to the strike give an indication of how the workers had organized the action in secret. A Delegacia de Ordem Social (DOS) document shows that the company had searched the workers' lockers for evidence of advance organization and found a handwritten note in a coat pocket with the text (in English) "Good nigth goes stoped Monday, day 15 [sic]," which the company denounced to the police. Several workers were detained but they denied any connection with the strike, claiming they did not speak English, after which the case was closed. Delegacia de Ordem Social, Dossiês Movimentos Grevistas/Auto, Vítima: Saab-Scania do Brasil S/A, OS 0378, 1978.
20. "Entrevista Gilson Menezes".
21. A 1983 PT evaluation of the strike movement viewed the motive for the strikes between 1978 and 1980 as primarily economic with implicit political dimensions, PT, "Movimento sindical," *Boletim Nacional*, November 20, 1983, 8–10. See also, Margaret E. Keck, *Workers' Party and Democratization* (New Haven: Yale University Press, 1992), 260; Leôncio Martins Rodrigues, "As tendências políticas na formação das centrais sindicais," in *O sindicalismo brasileiro nos anos 80*, ed. Armando Boito Jr. (Rio de Janeiro: Paz e Terra, 1991), 29, fn 31.
22. According to Osvaldo Bargas, secretary-general of the Sindicato dos Metalúrgicos de São Bernardo do Campo and Diadema in the early 1980s, Ford workers had more freedom to organize while Scania and Volkswagen isolated the union. Interview transcript with Osvaldo Bargas, Transnationals Information Exchange archive, box 38, International Institute of Social History, Amsterdam (1982), 3–4.
23. Barbara C. Samuels, *Managing Risk in Developing Countries: National Demands and Multinational Responses* (Princeton, NJ: Princeton University Press, 1990), 63–5.
24. Mario dos Santos Barbosa, "Sindicalismo em tempos de crise: A experiência na Volkswagen do Brasil" (MA diss., Universidade Estadual de Campinas, 2002), 85–7.
25. Alves, *State and Opposition*, 196.
26. In addition, Sluyter-Beltrão attributes the union leadership's ability to convince the workers to end the strike to Lula's "charismatic authority" and the growing centralization of power in the metalworkers' union, indicating a shift away from the grassroots, see Jeffrey Sluyter-Beltrão, *Rise and Decline of Brazil's New Unionism: The Politics of the Central Única dos Trabalhadores* (Oxford: Peter Lang, 2010), 94–5.
27. Alves, *State and Opposition*, 198.
28. Reconstrução de Lutas Operárias, "Comissões de Fábrica em São Paulo: Dados sobre comissões de fábrica no estado de São Paulo, sua origem, lutas, composição, estatutos e outros itens," Caderno 6 (São Paulo: Reconstrução, 1985), 3.

29. On the intersection between the strike movement and women's movements in the late 1970s, see Sonia E. Alvarez, *Engendering Democracy in Brazil: Women's Movements in Transition Politics* (Princeton, NJ: Princeton University Press, 1990), 105–7. On the role of the Catholic Church, see Scott Mainwaring, *The Catholic Church and Politics in Brazil, 1916–1985* (Stanford CA: Stanford University Press, 1986); Kenneth P. Serbin, "The Catholic Church, Religious Pluralism, and Democracy in Brazil," in *Democratic Brazil: Actors, Institutions, and Processes*, ed. Peter R. Kingstone and Timothy J. Power (Pittsburgh, PA: University of Pittsburgh Press), 144–61.
30. Santana, "Ditadura militar," 293–4.
31. Thomas C. Bruneau, *The Church in Brazil: The Politics of Religion* (Austin TX: University of Texas at Austin, 1982), 101; Daniel Zirker, "The Brazilian Church-State Crisis of 1980: Effective Nonviolent Action in a Military Dictatorship", in *Nonviolent Social Movements: A Geographical Perspective*, ed. by Stephen Zunes, Lester Kurtz, and Sarah B. Asher (Oxford: Blackwell, 1999), 259–78.
32. One such organization is the Centro Pastoral Vergueiro in central São Paulo, established in 1973 and home to a unique archive on social movement struggles in the 1970s and 1980s.
33. James Holston, *Insurgent Citizenship: Disjunctions of Democracy and Modernity in Brazil* (Princeton, NJ: Princeton University Press, 2008), 238.
34. Seidman, *Manufacturing Militance*, 208.
35. Rodrigues, "As tendências políticas", 17.
36. Rodrigues, "As tendências políticas", 28.
37. The communist parties supported the moderate sectors within the labour movement for reasons related to the history of Brazilian communism. Throughout its existence, the PCB had supported a class alliance with the progressive elements of the national bourgeoisie, based on an assumed political convergence with working-class interests against international capital's influence in Brazil. During the dictatorship, the party saw unions as a way to "reactivate" the workers' movement, encouraging party members to become union activists. The party argued that Brazil first required liberal democracy and national capitalist development before a revolution could be contemplated. This position continued during the military regime, when the PCB focused on creating a broad-based anti-authoritarian movement within the opposition party MDB. During the transition, the PCB associated itself with the party it expected to be in power after the return to democracy, the MDB and later the PMDB (Partido do Movimento Democrático do Brasil, Brazilian Democratic Movement Party), even using the MDB as an electoral vehicle for its candidates before the PCB was legalized in 1985. Similarly, union leaders associated

with the PCB focused on strengthening the party's position within the official union structure as their main strategy to promote the interests of the working class, generally rejecting new unionism's focus on political autonomy. See Marco A. Santana, "Política e história em disputa: O 'novo sindicalismo' e a idéia da ruptura com o passado," in *O novo sindicalismo: Vinte anos depois*, ed. Iram J. Rodrigues, (São Paulo: Vozes, 1999), 133–61; Santana, "Ditadura militar," 284–7.
38. Vito Giannotti, *História das lutas dos trabalhadores no Brasil* (Rio de Janeiro: Mauad, 2007), 237–9. Giannotti—himself a former metalworker and author of various histories of the Brazilian labour movement—discusses how in 1980 a PCB representative tried to stop a metalworkers' strike, arguing that the political moment was not right.
39. The "socialist left" within the labour movement aligned with groups such as the Union Oppositions, Alternativa Sindical Socialista (Socialist Union Alternative) and Corrente Sindical Classista (Classist Union Current). The Union Oppositions sometimes accused the Authentics that their strategies for union reform were not radical enough, undermining grassroots mobilizing and allowing corporatism to continue to exist, see Leôncio Martins Rodrigues, *CUT: Os militantes e a ideologia* (São Paulo: Paz e Terra, 1990), 20; Ricardo Antunes, *O continente do labor* (São Paulo: Boitempo, 2011), 102–3. In the eyes of most radical groupings that emerged in the wake of the strike movement, the union movement did not merely function politically to improve of the position of workers but as a revolutionary instrument in the struggle for socialism, Iram J. Rodrigues, *Sindicalismo e política: A trajetória da CUT* (São Paulo: Edições Sociais, 1997), 201.
40. The 1979 documentary "Braços cruzados, máquinas paradas" ("Arms Crossed, Machines Stopped", by Sergio Toledo Segall) depicts the strike movement in Greater São Paulo in 1978 and 1979, including grassroots mobilization outside the factory gates and union elections in which the *oposições sindicais* challenged the official leadership.
41. For further analysis of the emergence of the Oposição Sindical Metalúrgica de São Paulo in the 1960s and 1970s, its political and labour agenda, see Rodrigues, *Sindicalismo e política*, 54–64; Rodrigues, "As tendências políticas", 24–5.
42. Giannotti, *História das lutas*, 238.
43. The military regime introduced a new strike law in 1964 which "virtually eliminated the possibility of conducting a legal strike". The law banned strikes in the public sector, state-owned companies, and essential services while the law stipulated organizational requirements which made a legal decision to go on strike all but impossible. Sanctions for breaking the law were also severe, including interventions in union affairs and other forms

of repression, see Wendy Hunter, *Eroding Military Influence in Brazil: Politicians against Soldiers* (Durham, NC: University of North Carolina Press, 1997), 76.

44. Interview transcript with Waldemar Rossi, Oposição Metalúrgica São Paulo, Transnationals Information Exchange archive, box 38, International Institute of Social History, Amsterdam [c. 1982], 2–3; 'Entrevista Waldemar Rossi—Oposição Metalúrgica de São Paulo', *Memorias Operárias*, accessed July 11, 2016, http://memoriasoperarias.blogspot.nl/2014/05/entrevista-waldemar-rossi.html. Like Rossi, Osvaldo Bargas also emphasized the importance of informing workers and direct conversations, calling news bulletins an instrument "to mobilize, organize, and to create awareness", interview transcript Osvaldo Bargas, 5.

45. The 2004 documentary "Peões" ("Metalworkers", by Eduardo Coutinho) features interviews with participants in the strike movement, many of whom, like Lula, had migrated to São Paulo from the Brazilian northeast.

46. Private sector unions, particularly in the industrial sector in São Paulo, dominated in this group, as represented by the metalworkers' unions' dominant position. For the Greater São Paulo context, see also John Humphrey, "Auto Workers and the Working Class in Brazil," *Latin American Perspectives* 6(4) (1979), 71–89; Francisco Barbosa de Macedo, "Social Networks and the Urban Space: Worker Mobilization in the First Years of 'New Unionism' in Brazil," *International Review of Social History* 60 (2015), 37–71; Mark Anner, *Solidarity Transformed: Labor Responses to Globalization and Crisis in Latin America* (Ithaca, NY: Cornell University Press, 2011), 39–44.

47. Rodrigues, "As tendências políticas", 27. For further analysis of the emergence of the *autênticos* in Greater São Paulo in the 1970s, see Rodrigues, *Sindicalismo e política*, 64–80.

48. See interview transcript Rossi, 10.

49. Reconstrução de Lutas Operárias, *Comissões de fábrica*, 3–4; Kjeld Jakobsen, who would later become a prominent figure in the CUT, reported that in the early 1980s the opposition group within an electricity workers' union suffered from repression and dismissals as well as a lack of experience, resources, and fear, see Kjeld A. Jakobsen, "Oposição sindical dos trabalhadores na indústria de energia eléctrica de Campinas," undated, Transnationals Information Exchange archive, box 33, International Institute of Social History, Amsterdam.

50. Barbosa de Macedo, "Social Networks and Urban Space," 47.

51. Idem, 56.

52. Interview transcript, Waldemar Rossi, 10.

53. Keck, *Workers' Party and Democratization*, 73.

54. PT, "Movimento sindical", 16.
55. Keck, *Workers' Party and Democratization*, 91.
56. Keck, *Workers' Party and Democratization*, 79–81.
57. See Comissão Nacional Pró-CUT, "Tudo sobre a I CONCLAT: À caminho da Central Única" (São Paulo: Centro de Informação, Documentação e Análise Sindical, 1981), 9–10.
58. For a full overview, see Comissão Nacional Pró-CUT, "As resoluções oficiais da I CONCLAT", reproduced in Comissão Nacional Pró-CUT, "Tudo sobre a I CONCLAT: À caminho da Central Única" (São Paulo: Centro de Informação, Documentação e Análise Sindical, 1981). CONCLAT continued to exist after the CUT's foundation in 1983, becoming the moderate trade union federation CGT (Central Geral dos Trabalhadores, General Workers' Central) in 1986, see Rodrigues, "As tendências políticas," 35–9; Alexander, *History of Organized Labor*, 186–90.
59. José Francisco da Silva, President of CONTAG, quoted in Comissão Nacional Pró-CUT, *Tudo sobre a I CONCLAT*, 24.
60. For a detailed discussion about the political divisions and voting arrangements at CONCLAT, see Sluyter-Beltrão, *Rise and Decline of Brazil's New Unionism*, 116–21.
61. Comissão Nacional Pró-CUT, *Tudo sobre a I CONCLAT*, 25.
62. Interview transcript Osvaldo Bargas, 9.
63. Cited in Teones França, *Novo sindicalismo no Brasil: Histórico de uma desconstrução* (São Paulo: Cortez, 2014), loc. 1082. In 2001, an article in the magazine *Isto É Gente* described him as a "relentless negotiator", Isto É Gente, "O negociador implacável," Dec. 17, 2001. Marinho later became labour minister under Lula's first government, overseeing minimum wage negotiations, and then mayor of São Bernardo do Campo.
64. Noronha, "Explosão das greves"; Salvador Sandoval, "The Crisis of the Brazilian Labor Movement and the Emergence of Alternative Forms of Working-Class Contention in the 1990s," *Revista Psicologia Política* 11(1) (2000), 173–95.
65. Bolivar Lamounier and Alexandre H. Marques, "Tendances électorales des années 1980 aux années 1990," *Problèmes d'Amérique Latine*, 9 (1993), 18–9.
66. Seidman, *Manufacturing Militance*, 16.
67. Noronha cited in Ricardo Antunes, "Recent Strikes in Brazil: The Main Tendencies of the Strike Movement of the 1980s," *Latin American Perspectives* 21(1) (1994), 26; Maria Hermínia Tavares de Almeida, "O sindicalismo brasileiro entre a conservação e a mudança," in *Sociedade política no Brasil pós-64*, ed. by Bernardo Sorj and Maria Hermínia Tavares de Almeida (São Paulo: Brasiliense, 1983), 296; Alves, *State and Opposition*, 207.

68. Márcia de Paula Leite, "Reinvindicações sociais dos metalúrgicos," Caderno no. 3 (São Paulo: CEDEC, 1983), 31–2.
69. Dos Santos Barbosa, "Sindicalismo em tempos," 62–4; Alves, *State and Opposition*, 209. On the Ford factory commission in the years after 1981, see María Helena Moreira Alves and Roque Aperecido Silva, "Nas fábricas, a volta dos velhos tempos," *Lua Nova* 3 (1987), 48–50.
70. Interview transcript, Mercedes-Benz employee, São Bernardo do Campo, Transnationals Information Exchange archive, box 38, International Institute of Social History, Amsterdam [c. 1982], 6.
71. According to data collected by the Sindicato dos Metalúrgicos do ABC, cited in dos Santos Barbosa, "Sindicalismo em tempos," 67–8. There is little information available about workplace representation in other parts of Brazil, indicating that factory commissions were limited to companies with strong union representation.
72. Noronha cited in Antunes, "Recent Strikes in Brazil," 26; Almeida, "Sindicalismo brasileiro," 296.
73. Keck, *Workers' Party and Democratization*, 108, 111–2.
74. Almeida, *Crise econômica*, 50–1.
75. Diario do Grande ABC, "Metalúrgicos vão parar hoje," *Diario do Grande ABC*, July 7, 1983; Folha de São Paulo, "Decretada intervenção nos petroleiros de Campinas," *Folha de São Paulo*, July 7, 1983.
76. Gazeta Mercantil, "Petroleiros em greve preventiva," *Gazeta Mercantil*, July 6, 1983.
77. Folha de São Paulo, "Murilo intervém no Sindicato de São Bernardo," *Folha de São Paulo*, July 9, 1983.
78. Folha de São Paulo, "Assembléia de 4 mil suspende greve em São Bernardo," *Folha de São Paulo*, July 11, 1983.
79. Alves, *State and Opposition*, 243.
80. CUT, *Nasce a CUT: Embates na formação de uma central classista, independente e de luta* (São Paulo: CUT, 2007), 75.
81. Keck, *Workers' Party and Democratization*, 243–4.
82. For the CUT's own perspective on the debates surrounding its foundation, see CUT, *Nasce a CUT*. For further analysis of the debates preceding the CUT's foundation, see Sluyter-Beltrão, *Rise and Decline*, 141–52.
83. Rodrigues, *CUT: Os militantes*, 3; Diario do Grande ABC, "CUT: O motivo da divisão," *Diario do Grande ABC*, August 12, 1983.
84. Margaret E. Keck, "The New Unionism in the Brazilian Transition," in *Democratizing Brazil: Problems of Transition and Consolidation*, ed. Alfred Stepan (New York: Oxford University Press, 1989), 273–8; Rodrigues, "As tendências,", 30–3.
85. CUT Diretoria Nacional, correspondence about the Diretoria Nacional meeting on September 10–11, 1983, Archive Sindicato dos Bancários, accessedAugust19,2016,http://www.adb.inf.br/arc02/?p=digitallibrary/digitalcontent&id=57#.V7lDCJN94fE

86. PT, "Movimento sindical," 8–10.
87. CUT, "Uma vitória dos trabalhadores," *Jornal da CUT* 2(1) (1984), 5. As Rodrigues points out, the Congress's resolutions on the general strike were "confused and contradictory", more than likely reflecting the intensity of the debates, see Rodrigues, *CUT: Os militantes*, 5.
88. Keck, *Workers' Party and Democratization*, 180–1.
89. Keck, *Workers' Party and Democratization*, 84–5.
90. Central Única dos Trabalhadores, *Resoluçoes da Segunda Congresso Nacional da CUT*, August 1986, Rio de Janeiro, 8.
91. Diane E. Davis, "New Social Movements, Old Party Structures: Discursive and Organizational Transformations in Mexican and Brazilian Party Politics," in *Politics, Social Change, and Economic Restructuring in Latin America*, ed. William C. Smith and Roberto P. Korzeniewicz (Miami, FL: North-South Center Press, 1997), 163.
92. PT, "Prioridade para os núcleos," *Boletim Nacional*, June 15, 1984, 3.
93. PT, "Libertar os sindicatos e fortalecer a CUT," *Boletim Nacional*, no. 10, June 1985, 4–5.
94. PT, "Libertar os sindicatos," 4–5.
95. PT, "O que é o PT? Um partido ou uma frente de partidos?" *Boletim Nacional*, no. 25, 1987, 8–9.
96. PT, "Encontro Nacional," *Boletim Nacional*, no. 19, June 1986, 8–9.
97. PT, "Movimento sindical," 17–8.
98. PT, "As discussões que agitam o PT," *Boletim Nacional*, February 27, 1984, 3.
99. PT, "Por um PT de massa," *Boletim Nacional, Suplemento Especial*, no. 6, April 1, 1984.
100. Marieke Riethof, "Changing Strategies of the Brazilian Labor Movement: From Opposition to Participation," *Latin American Perspectives*, 31(6) (2004), 36. These changing perspectives on class can be found in the following PT documents: PT, "Plano de ação política e organizativa do Partido dos Trabalhadores para o período 1986/87/88," in *Resoluções de Encontros e Congressos, 1979–1998*, ed. Fundação Perseu Abramo (São Paulo: Editora Fundação Perseu Abramo, 1998), 246–94; PT, "7º Encontro Nacional: O socialismo petista," in *Resoluções de Encontros e Congressos, 1979–1998*, ed. Fundação Perseu Abramo (São Paulo: Editora Fundação Perseu Abramo, 1998), 429–35.
101. Maria H. Moreira Alves, "Interclass Alliances in the Opposition to the Military in Brazil: Consequences for the Transition Period," in *Power and Popular Protest: Latin American Social Movements*, ed. Susan Eckstein (Berkeley, CA: University of California Press, 1989), 295.
102. For further analysis of the groups, parties and individuals involved in organizing the Diretas Já movement, see Edilson Bertoncelo, *A campanha das Diretas e a democratização* (São Paulo: Associação Editorial Humanitas, 2007), 120–34.

103. Alves, "Interclass Alliances," 291–5.
104. Salvador Sandoval, *Os trabalhadores param: Greves e mudança social no Brasil: 1945–1990* (São Paulo: Editora Ática, 1994), 184–7; Almeida, *Crise económica*, 33.
105. IBASE, "Avaliação das políticas sociais do governo federal," Rio de Janeiro: IBASE, October 1985, 16.
106. CUT, "A crise atual e o movimento sindical europeu," undated, Transnationals Information Exchange archive, box 33, International Institute of Social History, Amsterdam.
107. Jornal da Tarde, "CUT: A greve obrigou o governo a propor negociação?", *Jornal da Tarde*, December 13, 1986.
108. See CUT, "Plano geral de ação da CUT/87," *InformaCUT* 1(26) (1987), 4.
109. Almeida, *Crise económica*, 99.
110. PT, "PT avalia a greve: Aprendemos com nossos erros," *Boletim Nacional* 31 (1987), 8. Tirso Marçal (PT trade union secretary) similarly criticized the CUT of acting like a "fluid articulation of unions" rather than a well-coordinated instrument for worker mobilization, Tirso Marçal cited in PT, "As novas tarefas da CUT," *Boletim Nacional* 36 (1988), 6.
111. For a similar point in the run-up to the 1989 presidential elections, rejecting the view of unions as "party appendices", see PT, "Este é o Brasil que a gente quer: Um resumo do texto base do Programa Alternativo de Governo do PT," *Boletim Nacional* 33 (1987–88).
112. Meneguelli quoted in PT, "O teste da unicidade," *Boletim Nacional* 38 (1988), 12.
113. Folha de São Paulo, "CUT e CONCLAT discutem campanha pró-Constituinte," *Folha de São Paulo*, Feb. 27, 1985; Globo, "CUT define tarefas para seus filiados," *Globo*, June 17, 1988.
114. Alvaro A. Comin, "A estrutura sindical corporativa: Um obstáculo à consolidação das centrais sindicais no Brasil" (MA diss., Universidade de São Paulo, 1995), 99; Rodrigues, *CUT: Os militantes*, 22–3.
115. Adalberto Moreira Cardoso, *A trama da modernidade: Pragmatismo sindical e democratização no Brasil* (Rio de Janeiro: Editora Revan/IUPERJ-UCAM, 1999), 194.
116. Jornal do Brasil, "CUT arma defesa dos itens pró-trabalhador," *Jornal do Brasil*, July 23, 1988; Jornal do Brasil, "Contag, CUT e CGT levam milhares," *Jornal do Brasil*, June 12, 1988; Almeida, *Crise económica*, 184–6.
117. Javier Martínez-Lara, *Building Democracy in Brazil: The Politics of Constitutional Change, 1985–95* (London: Macmillan; New York: St. Martin's Press, 1996), 104–6, 121–3.
118. Cardoso, *Sindicatos, trabalhadores*, 38–9.

BIBLIOGRAPHY

Alexander, Robert J. with Eldon M. Parker. 2003. *A History of Organized Labor in Brazil.* Westport: Praeger.

Almeida, Maria H. Tavares de. 1983. O sindicalismo brasileiro entre a conservação e a mudança. In *Sociedade política no Brasil pós-64*, ed. Bernardo Sorj and Maria H. Tavares de Almeida, 279–312. São Paulo: Brasiliense.

———. 1996. *Crise econômica e interesses organizados: O sindicalismo dos anos 80.* São Paulo: EDUSP.

Alvarez, Sonia E. 1990. *Engendering Democracy in Brazil: Women's Movements in Transition Politics.* Princeton: Princeton University Press.

Alves, Maria H. Moreira. 1985. *State and Opposition in Military Brazil.* Austin: University of Texas Press.

———. 1989. Interclass Alliances in the Opposition to the Military in Brazil: Consequences for the Transition Period. In *Power and Popular Protest: Latin American Social Movements*, ed. Susan Eckstein, 278–297. Berkeley: University of California Press.

Alves, María H. Moreira, and Roque Aperecido Silva. 1987. Nas fábricas, a volta dos velhos tempos. *Lua Nova* 3: 48–50.

Anner, Mark. 2011. *Solidarity Transformed: Labor Responses to Globalization and Crisis in Latin America.* Ithaca: Cornell University Press.

Antunes, Ricardo. 1994. Recent Strikes in Brazil: The Main Tendencies of the Strike Movement of the 1980s. *Latin American Perspectives* 21 (1): 24–37.

———. 2011. *O continente do labor.* São Paulo: Boitempo.

Barbosa, Mario dos Santos. 2002. Sindicalismo em tempos de crise: A experiência na Volkswagen do Brasil. MA Diss., Universidade Estadual de Campinas.

Barbosa de Macedo, Francisco. 2015. Social Networks and the Urban Space: Worker Mobilization in the First Years of 'New Unionism' in Brazil. *International Review of Social History* 60: 37–71.

Bertoncelo, Edilson. 2007. *A campanha das Diretas e a democratização.* São Paulo: Associação Editorial Humanitas.

Bruneau, Thomas C. 1982. *The Church in Brazil: The Politics of Religion.* Austin: University of Texas at Austin.

Cardoso, Adalberto Moreira. 1999a. *A trama da modernidade: Pragmatismo sindical e democratização no Brasil.* Rio de Janeiro: Editora Revan/IUPERJ-UCAM.

———. 1999b. *Sindicatos, trabalhadores e a coqueluche neoliberal: A era Vargas acabou?* Rio de Janeiro: Fundação Getúlio Vargas.

Central Única dos Trabalhadores (CUT). 1984. Uma vitória dos trabalhadores. *Jornal da CUT* 2 (1): 5.

———. 1986. *Resoluçoes da Segunda Congresso Nacional da CUT.* Rio de Janeiro: CUT, August.

———. 1987. Plano geral de ação da CUT/87. *InformaCUT* 1 (26): 4.

———. 2007. *Nasce a CUT: Embates na formação de uma central classista, independente e de luta*. São Paulo: CUT.
Comin, Alvaro A. 1995. A estrutura sindical corporativa: Um obstáculo à consolidação das centrais sindicais no Brasil. MA diss., Universidade de São Paulo.
Comissão Nacional Pró-CUT. 1981. *Tudo sobre a I CONCLAT: À caminho da Central Única*. São Paulo: Centro de Informação, Documentação e Análise Sindical.
Davis, Diane E. 1997. New Social Movements, Old Party Structures: Discursive and Organizational Transformations in Mexican and Brazilian Party Politics. In *Politics, Social Change, and Economic Restructuring in Latin America*, ed. William C. Smith and Roberto P. Korzeniewicz, 151–186. Miami: North-South Center Press.
Departamento Intersindical de Estatística e Estudos Socioeconômicos (DIEESE). 2015. Balanço das greves em 2013. *Estudos e Pesquisas* 79, December.
Diario do Grande ABC. 1978. Operários da Scania entram em greve. *Diario do Grande ABC*, May 13.
———. 1983a. CUT: O motivo da divisão. *Diario do Grande ABC*, August 12.
———. 1983b. Metalúrgicos vão parar hoje. *Diario do Grande ABC*, July 7.
Estado de São Paulo. 1977. São Bernardo não desiste dos 34.1%. *O Estado de São Paulo*, November 29.
Figueiredo, Ademir, and Clemente Ganz Lúcio. 2015. O DIEESE no século XXI. *Revista Ciências do Trabalho* 5: 55–90.
Folha de São Paulo. 1977. Metalúrgicos tentarão repor salários através de acordo. *Folha de São Paulo*, September 3.
———. 1983a. Assembléia de 4 mil suspende greve em São Bernardo. *Folha de São Paulo*, July 11.
———. 1983b. Murilo intervém no Sindicato de São Bernardo. *Folha de São Paulo*, July 9.
———. 1983c. Decretada intervenção nos petroleiros de Campinas. *Folha de São Paulo*, July 7.
———. 1985. CUT e CONCLAT discutem campanha pró-Constituinte. *Folha de São Paulo*, February 27.
França, Teones. 2014. *Novo sindicalismo no Brasil: Histórico de uma desconstrução*. São Paulo: Cortez.
Gazeta Mercantil. 1983. Petroleiros em greve preventiva. *Gazeta Mercantil*, July 6.
Giannotti, Vito. 2007. *História das lutas dos trabalhadores no Brasil*. Rio de Janeiro: Mauad.
Globo. 1988. CUT define tarefas para seus filiados. *Globo*, June 17.
Holston, James. 2008. *Insurgent Citizenship: Disjunctions of Democracy and Modernity in Brazil*. Princeton: Princeton University Press.
Humphrey, John. 1979. Auto Workers and the Working Class in Brazil. *Latin American Perspectives* 6 (4): 71–89.

Hunter, Wendy. 1997. *Eroding Military Influence in Brazil: Politicians against Soldiers*. Durham: University of North Carolina Press.
Instituto Brasileira de Análises Sociais e Econômicas (IBASE). October 1985. *Avaliação das políticas sociais do governo federal*. Rio de Janeiro: IBASE.
Isto É Gente. 2001. O negociador implacável. *Isto É Gente*, December 17.
Jornal da Tarde. 1986. CUT: A greve obrigou o governo a propor negociação? *Jornal da Tarde*, December 13.
Jornal do Brasil. 1988a. CUT arma defesa dos itens pró-trabalhador. *Jornal do Brasil*, July 23.
———. 1988b. Contag, CUT e CGT levam milhares. *Jornal do Brasil*, June 12.
Keck, Margaret E. 1989. The New Unionism in the Brazilian Transition. In *Democratizing Brazil: Problems of Transition and Consolidation*, ed. Alfred Stepan, 252–298. New York: Oxford University Press.
———. 1992. *The Workers' Party and Democratization in Brazil*. New Haven: Yale University Press.
Lamounier, Bolivar, and Alexandre H. Marques. 1993. Tendances électorales des années 1980 aux années 1990. *Problèmes d'Amérique Latine* 9: 15–26.
Leite, Márcia de Paula. 1983. Reinvindicações sociais dos metalúrgicos. In *Caderno*, vol. 3. São Paulo: CEDEC.
Mainwaring, Scott. 1986. *The Catholic Church and Politics in Brazil, 1916–1985*. Stanford: Stanford University Press.
Martínez-Lara, Javier. 1996. *Building Democracy in Brazil: The Politics of Constitutional Change, 1985–95*. London/New York: Macmillan/St. Martin's Press.
Memorias Operárias. 2016. Entrevista Gilson Menezes, parte I. *Memórias operárias*. http://memoriasoperarias.blogspot.nl/2015/12/entrevista-gilson-menezes-parte-i.html. Accessed 11 July 2016.
Noronha, Eduardo. 1990. A explosão das greves na década de 80. In *O sindicalismo brasileiro nos anos 80*, ed. Armando Boito Jr., 93–135. Rio de Janeiro: Paz e Terra.
Partido dos Trabalhadores (PT). 1983. Movimento sindical. *Boletim Nacional* (20 November 1983): 8–18.
———. 1984a. Prioridade para os núcleos. *Boletim Nacional* (15 June 1984): 3.
———. 1984b. As discussões que agitam o PT. *Boletim Nacional* (27 February 1984): 3.
———. 1984c. Por um PT de massa. *Boletim Nacional, Suplemento Especial* 6 (1 April 1984).
———. 1985. Libertar os sindicatos e fortalecer a CUT. *Boletim Nacional* 10 (June 1985): 4–5.
———. 1986. Encontro Nacional. *Boletim Nacional* 19 (June 1986): 8–9.
———. 1987a. Este é o Brasil que a gente quer: Um resumo do texto base do Programa Alternativo de Governo do PT. *Boletim Nacional* 33 (1987–88).

———. 1987b. PT avalia a greve: Aprendemos com nossos erros. *Boletim Nacional* 31 (1987): 7–9.
———. 1987c. O que é o PT? Um partido ou uma frente de partidos? *Boletim Nacional* 25 (1987): 5–9.
———. 1988a. O teste da unicidade. *Boletim Nacional* 38 (1988): 12.
———. 1988b. As novas tarefas da CUT. *Boletim Nacional* 36 (1988): 6.
———. 1998a. 7° Encontro Nacional: O socialismo petista. In *Resoluções de Encontros e Congressos, 1979–1998*, ed. Fundação Perseu Abramo, 429–435. São Paulo: Editora Fundação Perseu Abramo.
———. 1998b. Plano de ação política e organizativa do Partido dos Trabalhadores para o período 1986/87/88. In *Resoluções de Encontros e Congressos, 1979–1998*, ed. Fundação Perseu Abramo, 246–294. São Paulo: Editora Fundação Perseu Abramo.
Pereira, Anthony W. 1997. *The End of the Peasantry: The Rural Labor Movement in Northeast Brazil, 1961–1988*. Pittsburgh: University of Pittsburgh Press.
Payne, Leigh A. 1991. Working Class Strategies in the Transition to Democracy in Brazil. *Comparative Politics* 23 (2): 221–238.
Reconstrução de Lutas Operárias. 1985. Comissões de Fábrica em São Paulo: Dados sobre comissões de fábrica no estado de São Paulo, sua origem, lutas, composição, estatutos e outros itens. In *Caderno 6*. São Paulo: Reconstrução.
Riethof, Marieke. 2004. Changing Strategies of the Brazilian Labor Movement: From Opposition to Participation. *Latin American Perspectives* 31 (6): 31–47.
Rodrigues, Leôncio Martins. 1990. *CUT: Os militantes e a ideologia*. São Paulo: Paz e Terra.
———. 1991. As tendências políticas na formação das centrais sindicais. In *O sindicalismo brasileiro nos anos 80*, ed. Armando Boito Jr., 11–42. Rio de Janeiro: Paz e Terra.
Rodrigues, Iram J. 1997. *Sindicalismo e política: A trajetória da CUT*. São Paulo: Edições Sociais.
———. 1999. A trajetória do novo sindicalismo. In *O novo sindicalismo: Vinte anos depois*, ed. Iram J. Rodrigues, 73–94. São Paulo: Vozes.
Samuels, Barbara C. 1990. *Managing Risk in Developing Countries: National Demands and Multinational Responses*. Princeton: Princeton University Press.
Sandoval, Salvador. 1994. *Os trabalhadores param: Greves e mudança social no Brasil: 1945–1990*. São Paulo: Editora Ática.
———. 2000. The Crisis of the Brazilian Labor Movement and the Emergence of Alternative Forms of Working-Class Contention in the 1990s. *Revista Psicologia Política* 11 (1): 173–195.
Santana, Marco A. 1999. Política e história em disputa: O 'novo sindicalismo' e a idéia da ruptura com o passado. In *O Novo Sindicalismo: Vinte Anos Depois*, ed. Iram J. Rodrigues, 133–161. São Paulo: Vozes.
———. 2008. Ditadura militar e resistência operária: O movimento sindical brasileiro do golpe à transição democrática. *Política e Sociedade* 13: 279–309.

Seidman, Gay W. 1994. *Manufacturing Militance: Workers' Movements in Brazil and South Africa, 1970–1985.* Berkeley: University of California Press.
Serbin, Kenneth P. 2000. The Catholic Church, Religious Pluralism, and Democracy in Brazil. In *Democratic Brazil: Actors, Institutions, and Processes*, ed. Peter R. Kingstone and Timothy J. Power, 144–161. Pittsburgh: University of Pittsburgh Press.
Silver, Beverly J. 2003. *Forces of Labor: Workers' Movements and Globalization Since 1870.* Cambridge: Cambridge University Press.
Skidmore, Thomas E. 1988. *The Politics of Military Rule in Brazil, 1964–1985.* Oxford: Oxford University Press.
Sluyter-Beltrão, Jeffrey. 2010. *Rise and Decline of Brazil's New Unionism: The Politics of the Central Única dos Trabalhadores.* Oxford: Peter Lang.
Veja. 1977. A questão operária. *Veja*, September 14.
Zirker, Daniel. 1999. The Brazilian Church-State Crisis of 1980: Effective Nonviolent Action in a Military Dictatorship. In *Nonviolent Social Movements: A Geographical Perspective*, ed. Stephen Zunes, Lester Kurtz, and Sarah Beth Asher, 259–278. Oxford: Blackwell.

CHAPTER 5

Economic Crisis, Reform, and the Pragmatic Left, 1989–2001

The union movement's success in influencing the transition left a legacy for the CUT that emphasized the virtues of militancy and mobilization, one that viewed negotiation with the government, and "defensive" forms of bargaining with employers with suspicion. However, the economic crisis and the neoliberal reform programme of the 1990s limited the opportunities for this type of trade union opposition. The political debate no longer dealt with the deepening of democratic participation as the economic crisis focused government attention on macro-economic stabilization and institutional reform, which precluded the extension of social and labour rights. Widespread fears of joblessness also constrained the successful organization of strikes, while public sector reform and privatization undermined some of the most important constituent groups in the union movement. The consolidation of neoliberal reforms in the aftermath of democratization therefore created a paradoxical situation in which many unions developed a more flexible approach to capital-labour relations, but also tried to maintain their identity built on the political successes of the 1980s. This paradox underlines the argument presented here that past experiences of successful militancy shaped union strategies, while political ideas began to shift from class conflict to a more accommodationist approach based on the new economic and political circumstances. Throughout the 1990s the balance between militant and moderate strategies therefore shifted, derived less from a deliberate choice than a response to an increasingly challenging economic and political context, posing novel challenges to the new unionist agenda.

This changing economic and political context created new strategic dilemmas, which illustrate the complexity of the union movement's trajectory. In response, union political strategies shifted from what the new unionists began to call "pro-active" bargaining (focused on democratization, progressive wage adjustments, and improved workplace representation), which dominated the 1980s, to "defensive" negotiation (protecting rather than improving wages and working conditions). This strategic shift proved controversial and was seen in the inner circles of the unions as an unnecessary departure from the new unionist movement's earlier successes using militant strategies. However, the urgent need to deal with issues such as job and wage losses, privatization, and public-sector cuts translated into a shift from loyalty and identity based on the ideological goals of the CUT to a more pragmatic focus on job security and the protection of existing rights.

Yet the economic and political instability of the late 1980s and early 1990s initially resulted in high levels of mobilization and strikes, culminating in the mass demonstrations against President Collor and the government's failure to deal with the deepening economic crisis, as discussed in the first section of this chapter. This period illustrates how union militancy continued to respond to the political and economic context but the democratic context in which the union movement participated began to make militant action a less obvious choice, illustrating the central connection between union militancy and political developments. However, the union movement's trajectory during the 1990s was far from linear as the internal contestation of its political agenda illustrates, with the struggle to formulate an effective alternative often manifesting itself as a choice between militant and moderate strategies. Whereas the CUT's national publications continued to reflect a radical language, the militant rhetoric began to clash with the actual practices of union action, indicating a shift away from radical solutions to a pragmatic responsiveness to the changing political and economic context. These internal debates culminated in conflicts about privatization. Although the union leadership usually supported union involvement in company restructuring in the private sector, they opposed union participation in the privatization of state-owned companies, leaving local unions at a loss when the wholescale rejection of privatization was unsuccessful and rival groups took over the negotiations. This case illustrates why the CUT could often afford to take a more radical position than local unions, whereas the latter had to deal with the thornier immediate problems facing their members.

5.1 Political Strategies in Times of Economic Crisis: 1989–1992

In the 1989 presidential elections, Lula lost to Fernando Collor de Melo in a surprisingly tight race, indicating that a combination of dissatisfaction with the government and Lula's popularity could bring the PT within reach of the presidency.[1] Many unionists supported Lula's decision to run in the presidential elections, reflecting support for the PT's decision to become active on the centre stage of politics rather than acting in the margins. Collor was not only the first directly elected president since 1960 but his government also began dismantling the state apparatus while liberalizing the economy in response to the economic crises of the 1980s. His government programme was neopopulist, attacking the traditional politics of clientelism, patronage, and corruption. As Schneider has observed, the "economically conservative but socially centrist Collor posed effectively as a potential reformer of the widely discredited practices of Brazilian politics",[2] initiating a series of far-reaching reforms focused on privatization and economic liberalization.

Collor's election and the government's struggle to cope with the crisis initially sparked unprecedented levels of mobilization. But the political situation created new strategic dilemmas which eventually put the union movement on the defensive. The government's reform package and the deepening economic and political crisis sparked protests unprecedented in scope and size but also ended up dividing the trade unions. During the first half of the 1990s, a complex set of factors pulled unionists towards militancy and moderation as the key characteristics of new unionism began to change. Paradoxically, high levels of both mobilization and internal conflict characterized this period as trade unions faced dilemmas about whether to participate in negotiations at a local and national level. Firstly, despite the high number of strikes and demonstrations, the union movement's power to mobilize began to suffer as workers faced unemployment and wage losses, which divided the national labour movement between those who supported negotiations to protect jobs and those who believed that only militant action could secure workers' demands. Secondly, unionists dealt with concrete questions about their relationship with the formal political arena as public-sector wage demands challenged PT-led municipal governments. Thirdly, the CUT experienced organizational changes which shifted political representation from grassroots activists to the leadership and resulted in an uneasy balance of power between militant and moderate groups.

In response to the deepening economic crisis, the number of strikes and mobilizations surged in the late 1980s and early 1990s, particularly in opposition to government economic reform plans, as evident in the general strike against the Plano de Verão in 1989. Due to the economic situation, the protests in this period gained an explicitly political focus as workers not only focused on wage bargaining but also opposed the government's reforms. Indeed, the deliberate politicization of labour protests in this period helped escalate the strikes into mass demonstrations. Only months before Collor's election, the March 1989 strike against President José Sarney's Summer Plan mobilized millions of workers against the wage losses resulting from hyperinflation.[3] Collor's radical reforms also provoked large-scale mobilizations with a total of 1773 strikes across the country in 1990 (see Fig. 5.1).[4] However, the number of strikes began to decline in 1991 and in 1992 dropped to almost a fourth of those recorded in 1989. This period also saw a number of high-profile public-sector strikes in response to government spending cuts, including in cities where the PT had gained power. These strikes were emblematic of the new politi-

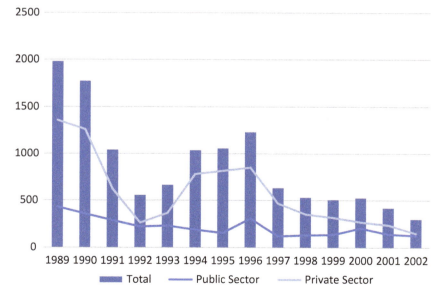

Fig. 5.1 Public- and private-sector strikes—1989–2002. (DIEESE, "Balanço das greves em 2013", 42)

cal context in which electoral considerations and political responsibility had entered the trade union debate. They exemplify how the union movement failed to resolve the thorny question of its position in the formal political arena, a dynamic that would shape the relationship between the trade unions and the PT for decades to come.

The case of the São Paulo public transport strike in the same year illustrates the changing dynamic as mass mobilization and strike action faced increasing challenges. In São Paulo, 60,000 strikers participated in a bus strike lasting nine days and halted 90% of public transport.[5] The strike not only pitched the union against the wage losses resulting from the federal government's economic reforms but also against the PT-led municipal government,[6] as the unions were dissatisfied with the proposed wage increases and with the mismanaged public transport reform plan.[7] At the time of the strike, the city had both a PT-led city council and mayor, meaning that the trade unions expected a sympathetic response to their demands. However, the city government was under budgetary pressure and reluctant to be seen as giving in to the strikers' demands, resulting in the PT mayor Luiza Erundina firing 475 public transport workers.[8] Many members and officials of the CUT-affiliated bus drivers' union were also PT supporters and the union's Edivaldo Santiago Silva believed that the PT administration had expected the union to abandon its demands due to party loyalty. Although the national CUT attempted to mediate in the conflict, it also accused the PT of sending out mixed messages: for instance, the recently elected CUT president Jair Meneguelli said that "the PT didn't have a unified position. There were controversies and different statements".[9] Consequently, the strike put significant political pressure on the PT and its relationship with the unions, leading to internal debates about the extent to which CUT unions should work together with or mobilize against a PT government if it was in their interest, a question that would become amplified after the PT gained power at a national level in 2003.

Another controversial issue regarding the union movement's relationship with the formal political arena was the question whether unions should participate in the federal government's proposal to negotiate economic reforms. Due to the intensifying opposition to his reform programme and recognizing the need to create a political support base, Collor initiated a social pact in June 1990, known as the "Entendimento Nacional", or National Agreement. The intention was to facilitate the implementation of Collor's first stabilization plan in 1990 by negotiating the terms of the reforms with trade unions and employers' organizations. In exchange for union support the government promised to promote wage bargaining without state interference, a long-standing demand of the new unionists. The agreement also included profit-related pay, a public utility rate freeze, and a suspension of plans to dismiss 20% of the country's civil servants. Although the union leadership had initially decided to participate in the social pact negotiations, the radical factions pressurized the leadership into abandoning the talks, arguing that participating in the negotiations meant "giving in" to the government.[10] Fortified by a number of successful national and regional strikes in the transport, oil, and banking sectors in 1990, the CUT decided instead to focus on demanding direct negotiations with employers to guarantee employment stability and compensation for hyperinflation.[11] In 1992 the metalworkers in Greater São Paulo negotiated an agreement with the employers' organization FIESP (Federação das Indústrias do Estado de São Paulo, Federation of Industries of the State of São Paulo) to maintain employment levels. CUT leader Vicente Paulo da Silva ("Vicentinho") viewed this as an example of how "creating a dialogue with other sectors of society" was a better way to represent workers' interests but critics believed that the employers had offered few real concessions.[12] At the same time, these negotiations continued to raise questions about the extent to which the union movement should participate in negotiations with the government without betraying labour's anti-statist principles; arguments which came to a head at the CUT's fourth national congress in 1991.

The CUT's national congress (also known as CONCUT) took place in the context of declining mobilization and Collor's attempts to establish a social pact in support of his reforms. The delegates held many debates on whether activists should provoke a political crisis through strikes and demonstrations to disrupt the regime or whether unionists should participate proactively in the promotion of economic growth and development while promoting workers' participation in the political process. The majority group in the CUT, Articulação, justified its support for negotiations by pointing out that union representatives had contributed to modifications of government policies, arguing that "the CUT's participation in the forum had been a decisive obstacle to the government's … anti-popular project".[13] From the critics' point of view, the experience of privatization in the late 1980s and early 1990s showed that union participation could lead to corruption and inefficiency. "Rather than real democratization," participation functioned as a fig leaf for the government instead of positioning the union movement as a decisive opposition force.[14] Critics argued that labour participation in government bodies equalled acceptance of neoliberalism,[15] stating that a national mass mobilization campaign was essential for a strong position in the negotiations while simultaneously acknowledging the obstacles to successful demonstrations and strikes.[16] The national congress eventually agreed that the Entendimento Nacional's objective was "to isolate and weaken the CUT, developing an official new unionism" in support of the government.[17] When the government decided to proceed with the dismissal of the civil servants, CUT representatives—under pressure from internal criticism—walked out of the negotiations.[18] This debate is indicative of the discussions that took place in the CUT during this period—both in terms of the political agenda and internal conflicts—as questions about political participation versus protest dominated and, in some respects, began to immobilize the union movement by turning the debate inwards.

As the most polarized congress since the foundation of the union organization, the event witnessed heated and often aggressive debates while a physical fight broke out during a meeting about leadership elections.[19] In the meantime, discussions on the value of protests also underlined the conflicts caused by the unionists' dilemma on whether to pursue militant or moderate strategies. Rising unemployment levels, hyperinflation and the privatization programme provoked union mobilizations, strengthening the belief that negotiations did not work and that civil society should provoke a political crisis by stepping up the protests to destabilize the Collor government.[20] However, moderate groups began to question the political value of protests as the number of strikes had begun to decrease in 1991. Citing the lacklustre turnout for a general strike in May of the same year, José Dirceu, then secretary-general of the PT, concluded that "[t]he general strike as a mobilization instrument needs to be re-evaluated. The strike was a half victory. It was successful as a political protest against the government but it did not reach the numbers of a general strike".[21] Dirceu's assessment hints at the growing difficulties trade unions experienced in mobilizing workers, despite efforts to tap into dissatisfaction with the economic situation. These difficulties also illustrate that translating mobilizational power into political influence was not a straightforward process as a faltering of strikes and demonstrations could decrease the unions' leverage. These disagreements about political agendas led to a split between moderate and militant groups,[22] resulting in a turning point for new unionism in strategic and political terms,[23] while the moderate majority candidate Jair Meneguelli narrowly won the CUT presidency.[24] These debates and disagreements about mobilizing strategies constituted a reaction to an increasingly challenging context for labour action, reflected in growing difficulties to exert the level of political influence it enjoyed in the 1980s.

The national congress also marked a crucial shift in the balance of power between different economic sectors in trade unions decision-making structures.[25] Industrial workers remained a key constituency, based on the powerful unions concentrated in urban areas, particularly in Brazil's industrialized south-east. As in the 1980s, the metalworkers in Greater São Paulo continued to have one of the most powerful unions, with considerable influence on the CUT's political strategies. Tellingly, their union began introducing strategic changes during the 1990s that proved crucial for the political reorientation of labour towards a more moderate stance,[26] even though this shift continued to face opposition. The union's dominance in the CUT was also reflected in the fact that, until 2000, the CUT always elected a metalworker as president. During the 1990s, however, the balance of power within the union movement began to turn in favour of the public sector, particularly the banking and education sectors, strengthening the position of unions such as the powerful Bankworkers' Union of São Paulo[27] and education unions such as the Teachers' Union of the State of São Paulo.[28]

The increase of middle-class or white-collar unionism, particularly in services and the public sector, led to a more organized presence of radical and politicized groupings. Despite the increasing importance of these sectors, the official decision-making structures continued to be dominated by the unions that had been strongest since the late 1970s.[29] The changes in the internal balance of power between the late 1980s and early 1990s also marked a shift from rank-and-file delegates to the top-level union leadership, which proved to be more pragmatic in their political choices, as evident in the debate about the Entendimento Nacional. While in 1988 half of the delegates had an executive (*diretoria*) union position, this number increased to 83% of delegates in 1991.[30] Although these changes strengthened the pragmatic groups, the decision to reduce the number of official delegates at the 1991 CONCUT simultaneously sharpened the polarization between militant and moderate approaches. Radical groups achieved the right to participate in the National Congress, including the right to propose policies and position papers at national meetings, while their representatives won several crucial union elections.[31] Despite new unionism's commitment to internal democracy and plural representation, the resulting decision-making structures proved to be "poorly developed"[32] and divisive. The effect of this new balance of power was that while several powerful unions began to move away from militancy towards negotiating strategies, the internal differences between radical and moderate positions became consolidated at a national level, leading to high levels of internal conflict which often froze the organization.

Against the backdrop of the rapidly evolving economic and political crisis of the early 1990s, the CUT experienced a range of organizational and political transformations, reflecting the changing economic and political realities of union activism.[33] Despite the large strikes and demonstrations witnessed in the early 1990s, the unions began to face difficulties mobilizing their members. The reasons for the transformations in labour political strategies in the early 1990s are complex, indicating an uneasy balance between militant and moderate strategies rather than the dominance of one over the other. However, we cannot reduce these changes to the context alone so this section has shown how the implications of these turbulent political and economic times were reflected in union movement's internal debates, which in turn shaped future choices. The contextual changes explain why the unions experienced centrifugal tendencies towards radicalism and pragmatism while the movement's internal political structures and debates mediated the outcomes. As discussed in the next section, these changes not only demonstrate the institutionalization of the new unionism movement and the conflicts that emerged from this process but also underline how organized labour's relationship with other social movements and rival organizations shaped the agenda for the 1990s.

5.2 Competition Within the Labour Movement and Relations with Social Movements

The internal transformations were also reflected in changes in the CUT's traditionally strong relationship with activists from other social movements alongside the emergence of political competition from a rival union organization with an explicitly moderate agenda. As a result, the CUT needed to rethink its position in relation to movements that consciously identified their strategies as either radical or moderate. The CUT also became concerned about losing its political appeal beyond core union members, which was not only part of the organization's political commitment but also an essential precondition for organizing mass demonstrations and establishing effective alliances within civil society. If in the 1980s the alliances between unions and social movements unified the pro-democracy opposition, the political fragmentation of the early 1990s raised questions about the extent to which the new unionist movement might overcome the limitations of traditional trade unionism. With hindsight, according to Rafael Freire Neto, the CUT's secretary of organization between 2000 and 2003, "[t]he third CONCUT [in 1988] ... marked a profound change in the CUT's trajectory. A restrictive vision of the union central prevailed, representing only part of the working class, the unionized, leaving to future generations the task of organizing the unemployed, the informal workers, recovering [the CUT's] mission to represent the entire working class".[34]

Although these concerns translated into the emergence of a broader conception of "class" within both the CUT and the PT—encompassing informal-sector workers, rural workers, white-collar workers, and in some cases, micro-entrepreneurs[35]—the union structures continued to reflect a narrow constituency. For example, while in 1988 the majority of delegates represented rural unions, followed by education and services,[36] by the fourth CONCUT in 1991, rural union delegates had become a marginal presence, making up 12.3% of the delegates while the industrial sector represented 33.4%, with close to half of the delegates from the services sector. From the late 1980s onwards, the number of delegates from the services sector increased from 35.7% in 1988 to 59% in 1997, while the participation of rural workers decreased by one-third between 1991 and 1997.[37] These changes reflected the internal balance of power as well as demographic shifts, and they also opened up space for other organizations to emerge, such as the MST and the moderate union central Força Sindical (Union Force, FS).

Whereas the position of rural workers within the CUT declined between the 1980s and the 1990s, the MST strengthened their political role in Brazil as rural mobilizations and land occupations placed the issue of land reform on the national agenda. The CUT, the PT, and the MST were closely connected during this period, both in organizational and political terms, and "largely shaped by interpersonal linkages among its leaders".[38] As was the case for the CUT, many MST activists were also active party members, campaigning or even running for the PT.[39] The MST also supported protests and mass mobilizations organized by other social movements, such as protests against privatization and mass demonstrations against government reform plans and the occupation of government buildings. The MST's militancy and occasional use of violence was controversial among CUT and PT activists,[40] who sometimes considered this strategy as undermining more moderate forms of protest and negotiations with the government.[41] However, during the second half of the 1990s, the MST became significantly more successful at organizing mass demonstrations and marches than the CUT,[42] underlining the argument that the CUT had started to lose its mobilizational power.

On the other side of the political spectrum, a new central union organization began to challenge the CUT by accepting rather than opposing Collor's reforms, thereby positioning itself as a negotiating partner for the government and championing moderate political strategies.[43] The CUT's emphasis on mobilization and confrontation during the 1990s opened up spaces for the emergence of a more pragmatic unionism, which was based on the view among significant sectors of the union movement that workers had interests in common with the government and employers in overcoming the economic crisis.[44] Founded in 1991, Força Sindical[45] had a pragmatic focus based on *sindicalismo de resultados* or "results unionism". Força Sindical grew quickly in terms of its political importance and the number of unions affiliated to it, although its membership only covered a narrow range of sectors and its connections with individual unions were considered weak.[46] Força Sindical intended to become the principal interlocutor of the government, a space left vacant by the CUT's refusal to participate in the 1991 negotiations. Contrary to the CUT, which continued to promote an ideological perspective on capital-labour relations interpreted as class struggle, Força Sindical emphasized political compromises. For instance, Força Sindical rejected new unionism's focus on general strikes to protest against government policies, working on the basis of an interest convergence between capitalists and labour. According to Força Sindical's political programme, the new unionism model promoted "a climate of permanent conflict between workers' organizations and the government ... threatening its political credibility and ultimately contributing to the destabilization of democratic institutions",[47] reflecting the fear that protests would provoke a return to authoritarianism. Although its non-ideological nature supposedly distanced Força Sindical from political parties, Antonio Rogerio Magri of Força Sindical was appointed Labour Minister in the Collor government.[48] Força Sindical also claimed to be pro-capitalist, based on the idea that trade unions were part of the market and should focus exclusively on wage levels and working conditions rather than political goals.

Faced with competition from Força Sindical and its own internal divisions, the CUT's internal debates reflected on the negative effects of the economic crisis on unions' ability to mobilize workers, as confrontational strategies no longer had the same power they did in the 1980s. The organization's debates during the early and mid-1990s reflected the view that although the struggle against the military regime had unified the opposition forces, this unity soon dissolved when everyday trade union politics began to dominate the labour agenda again. A 1992 CUT publication explained these limitations as caused by the political restrictions the authoritarian regime had imposed on the incoming civilian government alongside the continuing power of the corporatist union structure which limited effective political labour strategies.[49] While this is certainly part of the story, the economic crisis and the union movement's own political divisions also affected the CUT's mobilizational power. Many unionists expressed their disillusionment with Brazilian democracy in union publications, particularly what they saw as the lack of genuine popular participation and social improvement, while also recognizing that the new political conjuncture was affecting the union movement. Reflecting on the early 1990s a CONCUT report from 1997 acknowledged that the political context of labour opposition had changed: "with the end of the dictatorship and re-democratization new social actors emerged and union struggles no longer had the intrinsic democratic character associated with confronting the military dictatorship."[50] Although these comments provide an insight into the connections between political conjuncture and the dynamics of labour conflicts, unionists struggled to translate this into an appropriate political response as internal disagreements continued.

The internal conflicts clearly reflected the struggle to organize effective campaigns as ideological conflicts and leadership elections overtook much-needed debates about political strategies.[51] The inward-looking conflicts continued as competing leadership candidates accused each other of incompetence and of sabotaging campaigns for their own benefit. Gilmar Carneiro, of the powerful São Paulo bankworkers' union and CUT secretary-general, resigned in 1993, citing that the CUT was divided and lacked agility in the face of a growing political crisis.[52] A PT article agreed, arguing that the CUT's divisions had made effective political decision-making all but impossible, while also pointing out that the CUT's problems were not all that different from the much-criticized faults of the official unions and Força Sindical:

> *Gangsterismo* in union elections; unmovable bureaucrats; career leaders; unauthorized use of union vehicles; plenaries, congresses and elections decided before they have even started; abundance of financial resources without having to mobilize the grassroots; none of this is exclusive to Força Sindical.[53]

Durval de Carvalho—a metalworker and Union Oppositions challenger to the CUT leadership—commented that "in light of the [1994] presidential elections[54] and the new adverse scenario created by capitalist changes in production, it should be clear that our disagreements carry much less weight than the [other] conflicts taking place in society".[55]

The most difficult challenge at this point was to develop an effective strategy to represent working Brazilians in the face of a growing economic and political crisis and internal turmoil. The key factors explaining the balance between militant and moderate agendas in this period relate, on the one hand, to the economic and political dynamic at the time and, on the other, to the union movement's response to these transformations. While the transition to civilian rule in the 1980s sparked high levels of protest despite a severe recession, economic conditions had begun to affect the union movement's mobilizing power in the first half of the 1990s. As many individual unions responded to the deteriorating conditions by entering into negotiations about wage and job losses, at a national level the union movement stagnated politically as it struggled to deal with these strategic reorientations while ideological fights came to dominate the debate. Brazil's new democracy also faced significant challenges as the political turbulence of the early 1990s culminated in the movement for Collor's impeachment after accusations of corruption emerged in 1992. As the corruption investigations into Collor's affairs evolved, mass demonstrations and strikes underlined the calls for Collor's resignation. The movement for Collor's impeachment in 1992 led to demonstrations only matched in size by the demonstrations for direct presidential elections in 1983 and 1984. Known as the *caras pintadas* (painted faces), the demonstrators came from a range of different groups, including trade unions, the student movement, and religious groups,[56] providing the strongly divided union movement with a unified focus for political change. After the Senate voted overwhelmingly in favour of prosecuting the corruption charges, Collor resigned in December 1992. Although many unionists considered this outcome a victory for democracy, the future remained uncertain in the context of the deepening economic crisis.

5.3 Mobilization and Strikes in the Aftermath of the Real Plan

After years of failed economic reform plans, the 1994 Plano Real finally achieved what no other stabilization plan had managed to do before, decreasing inflation from four digits to one. Despite the positive effects of the end of hyperinflation on living standards, the Plan's aftermath created new strategic dilemmas for union activists. Besides ending hyperinflation, it produced a simultaneous increase of exports and imports, an improvement of labour productivity, and large inflows of foreign capital, particularly due to the privatization process and stable economic conditions.[57] However, despite the improving economic scenario the trade unions' rank-and-file base was affected by the economic recession of the early 1990s and the budget cuts associated with the Plano Real reforms, which together decreased the number of industrial workers as a proportion of total employment from 25% in 1990 to 16% in 1997.[58] In the city of São Paulo alone, employment in the metalworking sector reduced from 32.6% to 21% between 1993 and 1996, while 476 factories in this sector relocated to other parts of the country.[59] Many of the workers leaving the industrial sector moved to the services sector, often on an informal basis,[60] thereby reducing the number of workers who could be unionized and mobilized. The growing contingent of public-sector unionists suffered from reforms that aimed to streamline the state apparatus by abolishing public sector job security and reforming the pension system, directly affecting some of the most militant trade unionists in the public sector.[61] Combined, these structural changes in the union movement's support base signalled that the challenges to labour's political strategies that emerged in the early 1990s continued into the second half of the decade. Although strike action became less prominent given these difficult circumstances, the union movement together with other civil society organizations began protesting against the government's reform programme.

The neoliberal reforms of the mid-1990s not only affected public-sector trade unions but also challenged trade union strategies in the private sector, as the focus of union action shifted markedly from a political agenda to negotiating protection against job and wage losses. The threat of unemployment led many union agendas to focus on job security, while unions protested against mass job losses and flexible work instead. Traditionally strong unions such as the metalworkers' unions based in multinational corporations in Greater São Paulo began negotiating restructuring agreements to avoid job losses but unions with a weaker bargaining position struggled to do the same.[62] Vicente Paulo da Silva, CUT president between 1994 and 2000, described the period after the introduction of the Plano Real in 1995 as a situation in which unions defended their rights but did not manage to improve their situation, putting the once combative new unionists on the defensive. In his view, the union movement operated in "a situation of constant losses, trying to resist the proposals for flexibilization of labour rights and the deregulation of the labour relations system".[63] Vicentinho's observation not only described the problems that even the strongest unions faced but also marked the general trend that pushed many unions into a defensive stance as the struggles at a local level mirrored the difficulties for trade unions attempting to assume a leading position in mass protests against government policy.

Unsurprisingly, given the implications for the CUT's core supporters, the union organization strongly criticized the Plano Real, arguing that rather than producing development the reforms would lead to Brazil's "subordinate insertion into the globalized economy, with a devastating impact on ... public investment and accelerating the dis-organization of the productive structure".[64] The CUT also disputed the actual positive results of the plan, as seen in its 1997 analysis of the effects of the Real Plan.[65] The pamphlet listed many issues that had not improved during this period: economic growth was not as high as it could be and had not trickled down evenly[66]; the plan had not reduced the use of imported components in industrial products[67]; and finally, the reforms had increased unemployment and informal work.[68] Despite these criticisms, the union organization found it hard to disagree with the immediate effects of the Plano Real on inflation, illustrating the demobilizing effect of the Plan. The benefits to the general population could outweigh the localized losses in sectors such as the automobile industry: "the losses resulting from the economic reforms in specific sectors of the economy ... appear to be a lesser threat to living standards than high inflation so the rapid price reductions produce a large number of beneficiaries in the short term."[69] Lower inflation generally had a positive effect on workers, reducing financial uncertainty, particularly for the many Brazilians without access to a bank account. On this basis, it would be somewhat irrational for the CUT to criticize the effects of the Plano Real on hyperinflation, a dilemma that also affected labour militancy.

The economic stability and rising unemployment levels that the Plano Real brought in its wake combined with the rather uncompromising attitude of the Cardoso government affected the union movement's ability to mobilize workers. Paradoxically, while rising unemployment in the aftermath of the Plano Real challenged unions' mobilizational capacity, the end of hyperinflation also undermined new unionist strategies in the eyes of CUT representative. For the CUT, the end of hyperinflation forced trade unions to focus on issues beyond adjusting wage levels to inflation, which had been a highly effective strategy in the late 1970s and early 1980s. As a CUT document from 1997 observed: the "drastic reduction of inflation had dislocated the union movement's agenda. During the long years of high inflation, we concentrated on the defence of wages and purchasing power but we did not prioritize other themes on the agenda. ... National and union agendas became more complex ... posing new challenges for trade unions".[70] Other figures in the union movement also acknowledged that it had become more difficult to mobilize workers, particularly given the threat of unemployment. Lula stated during a meeting celebrating the twentieth anniversary of CONCLAT (the first and last congress attended by all Brazilian trade unions) in 2001 that while a car equipped with a loudspeaker (*carro de som*) used to be sufficient to call workers to a strike, the current political and economic context no longer worked that way.[71] In an interview, Fernando Lopes of the Confederação Nacional dos Metalúrgicos (National Confederation of Metalworkers—CNM) pointed to the psychological effects of what we could call the "mobilization/inflation paradox". Lopes argued that during hyperinflation, it was easier to demand a high wage increase as this provided a direct incentive to workers: they expected that they could regain the wages that they lost during a strike through the increase achieved if the strike was successful. With low inflation, the percentage of wage demands was lower than in times of hyperinflation, having a negative psychological effect on the willingness to strike, even though the effects on their purchasing power were the same.[72] Thereby, while the Plano Real's implications initially sparked strikes, the paradoxical effect of the end of hyperinflation coinciding with company restructuring strategies such as outsourcing and job cuts pushed unions towards negotiating strategies.

The threat of unemployment associated with outsourcing and the relocation of factories also undermined workers' willingness and ability to engage in militant action. In a prominent illustration of the shift from militant action to a defensive position, unions in the automobile sector focused increasingly on job security in exchange for flexible working hours and wages[73] as employees faced compulsory redundancies and plant closures.[74] For instance, Volkswagen threatened to fire one-third of its workforce in 1997 but introduced a voluntary redundancy programme under union pressure.[75] The CUT's approach towards these initiatives was ambiguous, rejecting them as deregulation and questioning whether such outcomes would create jobs.[76] Accepting the new reality was a difficult step to take for many unionists, leading to internal disagreements as the radical tendencies within the CUT called instead for an openly confrontational approach. In a tour de force, the Sindicato dos Metalúrgicos do ABC, one of the pioneers of negotiated flexibilization, argued in a 1998 union manual on profit-related pay that both the struggle for higher wages and negotiating flexibility were part of the same class struggle: "as one of many contradictory instruments, these [negotiations can be used] to construct class consciousness."[77] The CUT and several of its constituent unions also issued guidelines for negotiators on how to negotiate flexible work and pay, signifying the unions' acceptance of the policy in practice.[78] In a clear example of a pragmatic response to difficult conditions, according to the CUT's department of union affairs the crucial issue for workers and trade unions was not so much whether flexibility was desirable in the first place but whether unions were in a position to negotiate favourable arrangements with employers, effectively a recognition of what local unions were already doing.[79] Mindful of the impact of internal conflicts on union strategies, we can see here that when unions engaged in defensive bargaining they attempted to justify it by using militant and class-based language.

The aftermath of the Plano Real marked the end of a protest cycle which combined core union demands about wages and working conditions with a wider political agenda challenging the government's austerity plans. The initial success can be explained with reference to the legacy of successful mobilization in the 1980s—which the CUT also recognized internally—and a context of political crisis and failed economic reform efforts, which together created the conditions for strikes and mass demonstrations. However, the union movement's capacity to coordinate and mobilize this resistance suffered as a result of the economic crisis and its internal conflicts affected the movement's agility and political appeal. Consequently, the number of strikes at first increased until 1996, primarily due the initial uncertainty about the success of the Plano Real (see Fig. 5.1) but the size of strikes decreased alongside the average number of participants. Meanwhile, the total number of strikes dropped and subsequently stagnated for over ten years. If strikes became less effective and less easy to organize, workers and their unions still had to deal with the consequences of unemployment and wage losses, which led to unions defending their established rights and negotiating the terms of company restructuring. The dynamics of protest during the mid-1990s underline the argument presented here that there was no straightforward correlation between worker mobilization and changing economic conditions. Instead, union responses to economic change were mediated by the political context, internal conflicts, and the dynamics of particular sectors. As we will see in the next section, protests against privatization illustrated a similar dynamic in the public sector as state divestment plans accelerated in the aftermath of the Plano Real, provoking a number of high-profile political strikes in the public sector. Weakened by the economic crisis and riddled with internal conflicts, the union movement was divided between those who fully rejected privatization and those who attempted to negotiate the best possible outcome for employees in the state sector.

5.4 THE STRUGGLE AGAINST PRIVATIZATION AND THE 1995 OIL WORKERS' STRIKE

The protests against privatization illustrate the dilemmas that the unions faced in the 1990s, particularly because the debate about privatizing state-owned companies revealed a central tension within the union movement's political agenda regarding the state's role in national development. Although the new unionist movement rejected corporatist state intervention in industrial relations, the debate about privatization demonstrates that in effect they also expected the state to take a leading role in the development process, resulting in protests against the neoliberal proposal to remove state influence from the economy and society. Although public-sector problems such as corruption and inefficiency were widely known, unions defended state ownership and investment, partly because privatization affected union members—particularly militant constituencies such as unions in the oil, banking, and steel sectors. This position also reflected the belief that the state had an important role to play in national development policy, not least through the social responsibility programmes of major corporations in the state sector. The CUT therefore saw the continued existence of a state-led, industrialized economy, with a diversified range of export products and an active state role in income redistribution, as a condition for economic and social development. In this view, state intervention was not the primary cause of the country's problems, which the government's critics attributed to Brazil's subordinate integration in the global economy.[80] CUT publications from the 1990s identified the causes of the crisis as primarily external: debt and control over domestic policies by organizations such as the IMF resulted in the Brazilian government's decreased policy autonomy.[81] Despite recognizing the external pressures and the state sector's limitations,[82] this diagnosis allowed those who opposed privatization to argue that stabilizing the economy through privatization and budget cuts was a political choice rather than a necessity, thereby politicizing the overly technocratic decision-making surrounding the privatization process. As privatization turned into one of the success stories of the government's reform programme, it also became a traumatic experience for the union movement, illustrating not only their political divisions but also the contradictory dynamics of militant protests and union involvement in negotiations.

While initiated by Fernando Collor de Melo, under Fernando Henrique Cardoso (1995–2002) the privatization programme began to move away from relatively successful enterprises in the industrial sector to controversial cases, such as the mining company Companhia Vale do Rio Doce (CVRD), now Brazil's largest exporter. A 1995 constitutional amendment abolished the state monopoly on public services such as energy, telecommunications, water, and sanitation. These initiatives provoked a great deal of opposition and protest among a wide range of groups,[83] including nationalists, left-wing political parties and movements, as well as sections of the military[84] and many sectors of the trade union movement.[85] Opposition to privatization could also be found in government circles,[86] as public sectors jobs and services often formed part of clientelist networks, serving as an electoral vehicle for some politicians.[87] Additionally, in towns where state-owned enterprises dominated the job market and provided services to local citizens, protestors often found allies in the municipal government.[88] Protests, which sometimes turned violent, were also organized by the people who lived and worked on land owned by state-owned enterprises.[89] An important strategy was to file lawsuits or to challenge the legality and constitutionality of privatization in particular cases.[90] The protesters combined these legal strategies with lobbying efforts at a national level to prevent privatization in particular cases.[91] For example, in the case of the CVRD, the trade union SINDIMINA[92] lobbied Senator José Eduardo Dutra (PT, from the state of Sergipe) and a former CVRD employee, to block privatization through legislative means. This attempt involved the formation of a group of senators from the northeast of Brazil (including former president José Sarney) to reverse the decision to privatize CVRD. Although their legislative proposal was eventually defeated in the Senate, SINDIMINA representatives viewed it as a significant moral victory, as it rallied the opposition to privatization across diverse interest groups. They nevertheless believed that if the act had been accepted, it would probably have been overruled by the executive[93] given the centrality of privatization in Cardoso's reform package. These examples of protests against privatization demonstrate that opposition to state divestment became widespread in several sectors of society, while trade union members faced the direct effects of privatization through job losses which in turn affected union strength.

Privatization in Brazil entailed a reduction of the workforce as part of a restructuring programme in order to make a given company more attractive for potential investors, leading to an immediate negative impact on employees, which also weakened their unions. For instance, the workforce in the steel company Companhia Siderúrgica Nacional (CSN) was reduced by 30% between 1989 and 1993.[94] The number of CVRD employees dropped from around 25,000 to 11,000, most of which was achieved through voluntary redundancies or early retirement. Nevertheless, representatives of one of the CVRD's trade unions (SINDIMINA in Rio de Janeiro) indicated that around 600 job losses occurred without any benefits attached.[95] Unions also accused the CVRD of targeting union activists, while abolishing privileges such as the 1% annual wage increase for seniority and education subsidies for workers and their children.[96] In the case of the privatization of the Brazilian telecommunications system, Telebras reduced its workforce by 6.7% between 1998 and 1999 but in some individual companies job losses exceeded 20% of the total workforce.[97] For many unions in privatized companies, a lower number of employees not only reduced their finances, but it also affected the unions' representative function and organizational power.[98] Although individual trade unions organized many protests against privatization, including strikes, demonstrations, and legal action, they were largely unsuccessful in halting or even influencing the outcome of privatization on favourable terms for employees. These difficulties created tensions between the CUT leadership and individual unions, which had to formulate strategies to deal with the practicalities of privatization, including job losses and the question whether employees should buy shares in privatized enterprises. The conflict about privatization also led to fundamental questions about engaging in confrontational action or negotiation in a situation in which trade unions found themselves defending established rights rather than proactively expanding them as in the 1980s.

The 1995 oil workers' strike signalled the difficulties the union movement faced in mobilizing opposition to privatization, also revealing significant internal political divisions. The national strike of petroleum workers began as a conflict about wage increases, but soon acquired a political dimension as workers turned it into a protest against the privatization of the oil company Petrobras. The stoppage started as a labour dispute with Petrobras in the state of Rio de Janeiro about the company's failure to comply with the Supreme Labour Court's[99] decision to increase wages by 12% instead of 10%, to re-integrate those workers who had lost their jobs during the Collor government, and to maintain the Petrobras retirement programme. The conflict soon spread to other states, provoking protests in other state-owned enterprises in the energy sector, social and health services, and the Federal University of Rio de Janeiro,[100] while inspiring solidarity demonstrations in Greater São Paulo.[101] Because the conflict coincided with the proposed constitutional amendment allowing the flexibilization of the state monopoly in the oil sector, the strike soon began to focus on the proposed constitutional change and privatization.[102] According to Nilson Viana Cesário, of Sindipetro Duque de Caxias, "[w]e understood that the Brazilian state had to be accountable for Petrobras and we would not allow private capital in the company. It was not a strike about wages—wages were an aperitif, a snack. It was a purely political strike."[103] The TST ordered the workers to return to work and allowed those who remained on strike to be fired, leading to 64 dismissals and repression of the strike as the army and the military police occupied several refineries.[104]

The government's decision to repress the oil workers' strike was widely regarded as having outmanoeuvred the unions, as both proponents and opponents of privatization argued that this strike was a lost cause. For example, proponents of privatization saw the strike as a signal that "[t]he tide clearly began to turn against this type of labor tactic".[105] According to representatives of the union movement, linking the original purposes of the strike to privatization had been a tactical mistake, which provoked police repression of the strike while the company refused to meet the workers' demands.[106] Because of the strike's political dimensions, the strikers attempted to defend their position by convincing the general public that they were not just privileged public-sector workers. Various publications disseminated by the oil workers' unions outlined the general arguments against both the liberalization of the state oil monopoly and the often-held view that Petrobras employees were privileged or *marajás* (maharajas), a Brazilian term used to refer to those who benefit from the state. A pamphlet published by the Federação Única dos Petroleiros (Unified Federation of Oil Workers—FUP) stated that it was workers who produced economic development and Petrobras' success in particular. According to the FUP, the repression of the 1995 strike demonstrated that the Brazilian government wanted to destroy Petrobras from within, beginning with its employees.[107] Despite the repression and a public backlash against the strike,[108] a majority of the oil workers' unions decided to maintain the strike until the government resumed negotiations. As the government refused to accept the negotiations and while Petrobras continued to substitute strikers with new workers, the strike ended with none of the workers' demands met,[109] while the oil workers' unions fought to protect their demands from criticisms emanating from government circles, the media, and the union movement itself.

If the oil workers' unions struggled to convince the general public that their demands were worthwhile, they also faced an ambiguous attitude from the CUT and the PT. Following the work stoppages in solidarity with the oil workers in São Paulo, Vicente Paulo da Silva, the then president of the CUT, said in May 1995 that the oil workers needed support from the CUT because the striking workers had been "humiliated, suffocated, their agreement broken".[110] Although the national CUT and the PT initially supported the Petrobras strike, the CUT's involvement in government negotiations on social security and constitutional reforms complicated its unconditional support for the strike. Vicentinho attempted to defuse the conflict by arguing that the strike concerned a labour conflict rather than a political strike that contested the government's neoliberal reforms. The CUT's and the PT's official perspective was that the strike should have ended after the court's decision but this view angered left-wing groups within the CUT and the PT. While the oil unionists saw their strike as "a first step towards a general strike",[111] the CUT postponed a planned general strike to reinforce their official position on the Petrobras strike, leading to further anger about the union central's apparent willingness to sacrifice the oil strike in exchange for a favourable position in government negotiations.[112] As a result of these conflicts, the 1995 Petrobras strike became symptomatic of the internal debates generated by the government's privatization policy, signalling intensifying conflicts about the appropriateness of militant or moderate strategies to deal with the political and economic challenges of the 1990s.

Privatization's political importance turned the process into a traumatic experience for the union movement as both individual trade unions and the CUT found it hard to formulate an effective strategy in response.[113] These problems not only underlined the union movement's political dilemmas but also reflected the internal balance of power between private- and public-sector unions within the movement. Throughout the 1990s, the CUT developed an ambiguous attitude to privatization without defending the state sector at all costs, or, as Jair Meneguelli, the then president of the CUT, commented in relation to the privatization of Usiminas in 1991: "Real existing socialism has already proved that statism is not always the best solution."[114] While the CUT officially supported the individual unions' protests and initiatives, the organization's publications during this period reflected the view held by many private-sector unionists that workers in the public sector and state-owned enterprises enjoyed many privileges: public-sector workers "were certainly not among those who were excluded by the now outdated development model" based on state ownership.[115] Consequently, the CUT argued that public-sector workers had to be accountable for building a more transparent state sector geared towards social development, also recognizing that this sector could form a source of political patronage and corruption. Despite these criticisms CUT publications warned against the temptation of co-optation in the privatization process through participation or the purchase of preferential shares, which would weaken the public-sector unions[116] and the union movement as a whole.[117] The CUT's somewhat ambivalent concerns about the public sector reflected the increasing importance of public-sector workers in the union movement.[118] A large proportion of the National Executive's membership were originally employed in the public sector,[119] so the national leadership could not easily dismiss the concerns of unions in the public and state-owned sector, resulting in the central union leadership vacillating between an ideological rejection of privatization and the pressure from individual unions to support their position.

Apart from the CUT's internal divisions, privatization ended up creating significant differences between those unions which opposed privatization, as found within the CUT, and Força Sindical, which supported privatization. The practical implications of privatization on the ground led to conflicts within local unions affiliated to the CUT and its main competitor, Força Sindical, which supported privatization by arguing that only neoliberal reforms could bring development to Brazil.[120] This view was reflected in the organization's support for the market mechanism, its "anti-statist" attitude, and a critique of the privileged position of public-sector workers.[121] While the new unionists rejected state interference in labour relations, Força Sindical viewed the interventionist state primarily as an obstacle to economic development, with state-owned companies as "epicentres" of the crisis. Força Sindical's 1993 political programme argued that "the state should not concern itself with constructing steel mills".[122] The position of employees or trade unions in the privatization process did not receive much attention in Força Sindical's lengthy mission statement, although the text argued that the government should mitigate its negative effects on workers and society.[123] However, Força Sindical's support for privatization was not unconditional as it promoted employee involvement through the negotiation of preferential shares.[124] Força's generalized support for privatization posed a problem for the CUT, which had to redefine its own position regarding whether to negotiate or mobilize against privatization as the programme unfolded, while local unions were left to deal with the consequences for their members.

The tensions between the CUT's central leadership and the activities of local unions became particularly apparent in the case of the privatization of the CSN (National Steel Company).[125] The moderate groups in the CUT in Volta Redonda aimed to increase workers' influence on the privatization process but the radicals rejected privatization altogether, accusing the moderates of legitimizing the programme. As a result of these divisions, the CUT lost the leadership of the local metalworkers' union to Força Sindical just before CSN's privatization. Conflicts between the CUT and Força Sindical about wage negotiations and whether to co-operate with or actively oppose CSN managers eventually led to a victory of Força Sindical in union elections in 1992.[126] As the Força Sindical president Luis Antonio de Medeiros put it, the conflict presented unionists with a choice between the CUT's defence of "statism" and his union's "opportunity to widen worker participation in the company's destiny while avoiding scrapping the CSN".[127] The new Força Sindical leadership supported privatization, focusing on negotiating a higher percentage of shares reserved for employees. To facilitate the purchase of shares, the Força Sindical leadership established a Clube de Investidores (investors' club), arguing that this would "democratize" the sale of CSN. In response, the CUT opposition in Volta Redonda launched an independent investors' club to allow the opposition's supporters to also profit from CSN's privatization. Ironically, the stalemate between the two groups meant that the government's attempts to "tie" workers into the privatization process by offering shares succeeded, severely weakening the union opposition. Meanwhile, the national CUT opposed any suggestion that employees would buy shares in privatized companies but failed to formulate an effective answer to the dilemmas of local unionists. The CUT expected participation in privatization to lead to marginalization and an absence of influence on the management of privatized companies, but this did not stop local unions and their members from buying shares.[128] The local unions often considered job security for workers post-privatization—which was negotiated in the case of some electricity companies in the state of São Paulo—and preferential shares for employees as positive gains in the privatization process. Nevertheless, the national CUT continued to interpret these types of negotiations as conceding to the government's privatization efforts in its political statements.

The federal government also recognized that the participation of workers as shareholders in the process could be a valuable instrument when dealing with opposition forces. In the case of the steel company Usiminas, 10% of the shares were offered to Usiminas employees at a reduced price. As a result, unions and employees became involved in setting up investment clubs (which were promoted by the Banco Nacional de Desenvolvimento Econômico e Social [BNDES], National Economic and Social Development Bank), negotiating their participation in the privatization process directly with the BNDES and the company's management. In addition, these shares guaranteed employees a seat on the administrative council of the privatized enterprise.[129] The CVRD unions proposed a social agreement (*Acordo Social*), the result of a visit to privatized companies in several European countries.[130] The document stressed the importance of the agreement for an increase in productivity with participation and consultation of all employees ("a partnership between labour and capital").[131] The document supported the acquisition of shares by CVRD employees, also noting that new management techniques could facilitate employee participation in the administrative council of the company, as in the European experience the unionists had encountered.[132] This strategy was only successful in achieving a 10% offer of preferred shares to the employees but proved impossible to negotiate in terms of the other aspects of the proposal. The experiences of the CVRD unions with participation through shareholding were therefore not wholly positive, as the investor's club that was established in order to take full advantage of the employee offer did not want to be associated with the union, representing the position of workers as shareholders instead.[133] A similar initiative took place in CSN in 1990: a document published by the Sindicato dos Engenheiros stressed that the CSN as a state-owned enterprise should be democratized, which would include core union demands, such as the right to information for trade unions, union representation in the workplace, participation of unions in the formulation of new company policies, and fair hiring procedures for new workers.[134] However, the reality was that these ambitions did not resonate in the privatization debate, leaving individual unions weakened and the national union movement divided.

The failure to reverse privatization therefore contributed to a sense of disillusionment among unions about the effectiveness of labour opposition strategies more generally, compounding the shift towards negotiation-based strategies happening in the private sector. The privatization protests illustrate two central conflicts concerning the union movement's agenda in the 1990s, namely its attitude to the state and the CUT's relationship with individual unions. One refers to the tension between new unionism's anti-statist approach to labour relations, reflected in the movement's strong belief in grassroots union organizing; the other was the equally strong, if more implicit belief in the state as a key driving force of development. In the case of privatization, this tension allowed the CUT's opponents—as in the case of Força Sindical and the media—to argue that the unions defended an inefficient state sector at all costs, in contrast to their opposition to the government's economic reforms. Internally, this debate also affected the fragile balance of power between radical and pragmatic groups while also positioning private- and public-sector unions against each other, as many in the CUT shared the critique of state-owned enterprises while simultaneously considering militant opposition to privatization a logical part of the new unionist agenda. This ambiguity manifested itself in the second conflict between the national union leadership and unions in state-owned enterprises, raising questions about the extent to which these unions should engage in militant, confrontational strategies to oppose privatization or whether they should take the opportunity to participate in negotiations whenever they occurred. This second conflict reveals that while the CUT viewed the defence of its membership in the public sector as a core issue on the labour agenda, there was no consensus on how best to represent these members as the privatization process evolved.

5.5 Conclusion

To deal with the challenge of effective labour strategies in an increasingly adverse political and economic situation during the second half of the 1990s, the CUT proposed in 1997 to widen its political strategies to "resist attacks against workers' rights, elaborate alternative proposals and construct alliances to resist neo-liberalism", signalling a desire to return to the union movement's past militancy.[135] The wish to widen popular resistance against government policies beyond unions through alliances with other social movements[136] partly reflected the union movement's own dilemmas between militant and moderate action, and partly the impressive mobilizing capacity of movements such as the MST in this period. Just as the unions began to struggle, other social movements—with a central position for the MST and the agrarian question—came to the forefront by organizing large marches and demonstrations against the government, leading Sandoval to conclude that the landless workers' struggle had turned into the most important form of working-class contention in the late 1990s.[137] While the CUT experienced crippling internal divisions, the MST's popularity and support increased,[138] particularly after the 1997 march to Brasília to protest against the killing by the military police of 19 landless activists during a land occupation in the previous year—known as the Eldorado dos Carajás massacre.[139] Although the CUT also participated in and supported these demonstrations, they no longer played the central role that they had in the 1980s.

While this shift appears to underline the argument found in some of the literature on the new Latin American left and social movements that trade unions are no longer at the forefront of political contestation, the central argument proposed here is that these struggles—including those of the union movement—are contingent on the political and economic context as well as being mediated by the political dynamics within a movement. Rather than viewing the 1990s as a long road towards political moderation, this chapter has explained how labour militancy increased in the early 1990s, marking a shift in union debates towards a more explicitly political agenda, while mobilization increased again in the late 1990s but this time with a less prominent role for organized labour. During the 1990s protests against matters which the CUT opposed in principle were often unsuccessful, which in turn led to conflicts within the union movement itself, dilemmas which usually manifested themselves as a choice between militant and moderate political strategies. The dilemmas about political participation that emerged in the debate about negotiating the terms of economic reforms with the government and employers' organizations sparked internal conflicts between those who believed that the government could only be opposed through militant action and those who saw political participation as the lesser of two evils.

At the level of individual trade unions, negotiation and participation also became more prevalent as their strategies became more defensive, reflected in a declining number of strikes and the increasing focus on maintaining wage and employment levels as many unions, particularly in multinational corporations, negotiated worker involvement in enterprise restructuring and the flexibilization of labour contracts. As the protests against privatization illustrate, the internal divisions reflected a central union organization torn between pragmatism and ideology, while local unions were often more concerned with survival and real issues on the ground. As evident in the case of anti-privatization protests and the oil workers' strike in 1995, it was often difficult to reconcile ideological positions at a national level with the need to formulate a practical union strategy dealing with changes in ownership structures and labour relations, particularly when the opposition was unable to reverse the privatization programme. Unsurprisingly, these dilemmas often resulted in pragmatic decision-making at a local level, decisions which were sometimes difficult to accept by both the CUT's leadership as well as the various political groupings within the unions.

As the CUT struggled to reconcile the new unionist ideals with the political realities of the 1990s, opposition to the Cardoso administration increased while the PT prepared for another run in the 2002 presidential elections. Similar to other cases in Latin America, both dissatisfaction with neoliberal reforms and widespread popular opposition to the government contributed to Lula's election victory. In his campaign, Lula walked a fine line "between opposition and adaptation",[140] and between relying on social movement support and developing a wider public appeal, mindful of accusations that the PT government would be incapable of managing the economy and that Lula would give in to social movement demands. As discussed in the next chapter, after his election victory many of Lula's supporters were dissatisfied and surprised by the PT-led government's pragmatism, although studies about the PT now usually trace this shift back to the 1990s.[141] While the union movement's trajectory in the 1990s also signals a shift from militancy to moderation, this change was neither universal nor uncontested as demonstrated in this chapter, leading to further conflicts about militancy and moderation in the 2000s.

NOTES

1. Wendy Hunter, *The Transformation of the Workers' Party in Brazil, 1989–2009* Cambridge: (Cambridge University Press, 2010), 109–116.
2. Ronald M. Schneider, *Brazil: Culture and Politics in a New Industrial Powerhouse* (Boulder, CO: Westview Press, 1996), 111.
3. CUT, "Resolução da reunião extraordinária da executiva da Direção Nacional da CUT realizada no dia 16/3, em São Paulo", *InformaCUT*, 55, 20–27 March (1989), 1–2; Vito Giannotti, *História das lutas dos trabalhadores no Brasil* (Rio de Janeiro: Mauad, 2007), 262.

4. In 1990, the media accused the CUT of organizing political strikes to support the PT, referring to "setembro negro" ("black September") but CUT representatives such as José Mirande de Oliveira—the CUT's union secretary at the time—insisted that the strikes purely focused on wages in light of government economic policies. See PT, "Setembro é mês de primavera e não de terror," *Boletim Nacional*, 52 (1990), 12.
5. PT, "O momento político em debate," *Boletim Nacional* 54 (May 1991): 5.
6. For an overview of conflicts within PT-led municipalities and between the party and municipal workers' unions in the early 1990s, see Kathleen Bruhn, *Urban Protest in Mexico and Brazil* (Cambridge: Cambridge University Press, 2008), 72–4.
7. The union demanded a 89% wage increase compared to the 77% offer, see "Todos nos perdemos," *Brasil Agora* 15 (May–June 1992), 4. On the challenges facing the PT administration in São Paulo in the political context of the early 1990s, see Lúcio Kowarick and André Singer, "A experiência do Partido dos Trabalhadores na prefeitura de São Paulo," *Novos Estudos CEBRAP* 35 (1993), 195–216; Bruhn, *Urban Protest*, 86–8; Hunter, *Transformation of the Workers' Party*, 89–92. For an analysis of the 1989 PT election victory in São Paulo and the public transport reform plans, see Fiona Macaulay, "'Governing for Everyone': The Workers' Party Administration in São Paulo, 1989–1992," *Bulletin of Latin American Research* 15 (2) (1996), 213–9.
8. Folha de São Paulo, "Há 20 anos termina greve de motoristas e cobradores de ônibus em São Paulo," *Folha de São Paulo*, May 20, 2012.
9. For a frank and critical inside account of the strike and its aftermath, see PT, "A greve em que todos perdemos," *Boletim Nacional* 64 (July 1992), 14–15.
10. CUT, *Resoluções do 4o CONCUT*, São Paulo: CUT, September 4–8, 1991, 4–5.
11. PT, "CUT não negocia emprego e salário," *Boletim Nacional*, May (1990), 3.
12. "A aposta do ABCD," *Brasil Agora* 12 (April 1992), 6–7 and Carlos Eduardo Carvalho, "Não devemos exagerar: Triunfo histórico ou acordo defensivo e questionável," *Brasil Agora* 12 (April 1992), 7; França goes as far as arguing that the metalworkers had abandoned class struggle in favour of negotiation by 1992, thereby effectively supporting neoliberal reforms, see Teones França, *Novo sindicalismo no Brasil: Histórico de uma desconstrução* (São Paulo: Cortez, 2014), loc. 273–322.
13. The resolution also criticized those against negotiation, arguing that these critics limited the range of possibilities for union action by precluding negotiation. It also stated that the opponents' criticisms masked their own ineffectiveness and "lack of capacity of these sectors to mobilize their unions' constituencies", see CUT, *Resoluções do 4o CONCUT*, 5.

14. "A CUT mostra a cara," *Brasil Agora* 10 (March 1992), 4; CUT São Paulo/Escola Sindical São Paulo, "Sindicalismo CUT—20 anos," *Cadernos de Formação*, no. 1 (2001–2002), 76–7. Another negotiation attempt happened when the CUT unsuccessfully tried to convince the Itamar Franco government to introduce a full monthly adjustment of wages to inflation in 1993. See "A CUT mostra: é falsa a desculpa do dinheiro" and "A negociação vista no raio X," *De Fato* 1 (1) (1993), 4–11.
15. Giannotti, *História das lutas*, 279.
16. For example, an article in the magazine *Causa Operária* (published by a left-wing group within the CUT of the same name) argued that the absence of the ABC Metalworkers' union from the 1991 general strike signalled that the CUT's moderate majority had distanced itself from militant action, "Greve geral: Primeiro balanço," *Causa Operária* 131 (May 30, 1991), reproduced in CPV, *Quinzena* 118 (June 1991), 10–11.
17. CUT, *Resoluções do 4o CONCUT*.
18. Although no further national negotiations on wage and price levels occurred, the government increased the representation of trade unions and employers' organizations in social security institutions, signalling the integration of union representatives in parts of the state apparatus. Organized labour also gained a representative on the Administrative Council of the BNDES. See Maurício Rands Barros, *Labour Relations and the New Unionism in Contemporary Brazil* (New York: St. Martin's Press; London: Macmillan, 1999), 47 and Marcio Pochmann et al., "Ação sindical no Brasil: Transformações e perspectivas," *São Paulo em Perspectiva* 12 (1) (1998), 10–23.
19. PT, "O fundo do poço," *Boletim Nacional* 59, October 1991, 8. Jornal do Brasil, "CUT briga na quarta eleição de Meneguelli," September 9, 1991; Jornal da Tarde, "Guerra entre tendências tumultua o congresso da CUT," September 7, 1991.
20. PT, "O PT e o momento político: resolução do Diretório Nacional reunido em 16/03/91," *Boletim Nacional*, April (1990), 5.
21. Gazeta Mercantil, "Greve inexpressiva poderá levar sindicatos ao Congresso," May 24, 1991; Folha de São Paulo, "Meneguelli atribui fracasso à 'falta de empenho'," May 24, 1991.
22. Another major conflict focused on whether the CUT should affiliate with the International Confederation of Free Trade Unions (ICFTU), which critics associated with a moderate political agenda and Cold-War labour politics. Interview Kjeld A. Jakobsen, August 20, 2001; CUT, *A política internacional da CUT: História e perspectivas* (São Paulo: CUT, 2003), 47–9; Hermes A. Costa, "A política internacional da CGTP e da CUT: Etapas, temas e desafios," *Revista Crítica de Ciências Sociais* 71 (2005): 152–3. Gazeta Mercantil, "Divergências políticas dificultam os debates em congresso da CUT," September 6, 1991.

ECONOMIC CRISIS, REFORM, AND THE PRAGMATIC LEFT, 1989-2001   159

23. Echoing the debates in the new unionist movement, Ann Mische argues that the Brazilian student movement experienced "a period of internal evaluation and restructuring" during the same period, reflecting "growing dissatisfaction with the factional entrenchment of the movement", which stifled the movement's creativity and effectiveness in the late 1980s. See Ann Mische, *Partisan Publics: Communication and Contention across Brazilian Youth Activist Networks* (Princeton, NJ: Princeton University Press, 2008), 141–3.
24. Diário Popular, "CUT deve reeleger hoje Jair Meneguelli," *Diário Popular*, September 8, 1991.
25. To strengthen the ties between the CUT and the unions, from 1991 onwards unions had to be formally affiliated to the CUT to participate in national decision-making and the number of delegates each union could send would be based on the number of unionized workers affiliated with the CUT, effectively favouring the larger unions. See CUT, *Resoluções do 4o CONCUT*, 2; Sílvio Costa, *Tendências e centrais sindicais: O movimento sindical brasileiro, 1978–1994* (São Paulo: Editora Anita Garibaldi, 1995), 156–7; Alvaro A. Comin, "A estrutura sindical corporativa: Um obstáculo à consolidação das centrais sindicais no Brasil," (MA diss., Universidade de São Paulo, 1995), 84.
26. Just as the metalworkers' union pioneered factory commissions during the 1980s, its representatives also began negotiating with employers at a company and regional level through sectoral chambers (*câmaras setoriais*). Their remit was to define policies to compensate for the negative effects of economic liberalization on the export sector, particularly in the automobile industry in São Paulo. The unions and employers agreed to reduce car prices by 22% and to involve workers in the restructuring process, which ended up maintaining employment levels and wage adjustments fully linked to monthly inflation. The chambers disappeared in 1994, when sector-specific policies became increasingly discredited within the government. See Departamento de Estudos Sócio-Econômicos e Políticos (DESEP/CUT), "Câmaras setoriais e intervenção sindical," Texto para Discussão 5 (São Paulo: DESEP/CUT, 1992); DESEP/CUT, "Câmaras setoriais: Para além do complexo automotivo," Texto para Discussão 6 (São Paulo: DESEP/CUT, 1993); França, *Novo sindicalismo*, loc. 595–853; Scott B. Martin, (1997) "Beyond Corporatism: New Patterns of Representation in the Brazilian Auto Industry," in *The New Politics of Inequality in Latin America: Rethinking Participation and Representation*, ed. Douglas A. Chalmers et al. (Oxford: Oxford University Press, 1997), 45–71.
27. Sindicato dos Bancários de São Paulo, SBSP.
28. Associação de Professores de Ensino Oficial do Estado de São Paulo, or APEOESP.

29. Despite their relative marginalization in the CUT, rural workers became an increasingly visible and active group in the Brazilian union movement in the 1980s and 1990s. For example, in 1998 the percentage of rural unionization was 24.4%, higher than in any other sector. Although the rural workers' movement was relatively strong, their participation in the CUT congresses decreased from the early 1990s. Rural unionists enjoyed representation proportional to their organizational strength in 1988 but their participation declined during subsequent CONCUTs. In the early 1990s, the rural union confederation Confederação Nacional dos Trabalhadores na Agricultura (CONTAG) began discussing affiliation to the CUT, which many in the CUT saw as an effort to strengthen its roots in the countryside, although some also found CONTAG conservative, see PT, "CUT e Contag no mesmo barco," *Boletim Nacional* 5 (December 1991), 3; PT, "CUT discute Contag," *Boletim Nacional* 42 (July 1993), 11. On the representation of rural unionists within the CONCUT, see Leôncio Martins Rodrigues et al., *Retrato da CUT: Delegados do 3o CONCUT, representação nas categorias* (São Paulo: CUT, undated), 22, 27; CUT, *Resoluções e Registros*, 6o Congresso Nacional da CUT, August 1997, 128.
30. Rodrigues, *Sindicalismo e política*, 185.
31. For example, between the early and mid-1990s the powerful bankers' unions of São Paulo and Rio de Janeiro were almost equally divided between the majority coalition led by Articulação Sindical and opposition groups which favoured confrontation over negotiation. See Folha de São Paulo, "CUT vai dividida à eleição dos bancários," *Folha de São Paulo*, January 17, 1994; CUT São Paulo, "Sindicalismo CUT," 78–9; Estado de São Paulo, "A CUT sofre com luta interna,", *O Estado de São Paulo*, June 2, 1991.
32. Sluyter-Beltrão, *Rise and Decline*, 280.
33. See also Heloísa de Souza Martins and Iram J. Rodrigues, "O sindicalismo brasileiro na segunda metade dos anos 90," *Tempo Social* 11 (2) (1999): 156; Rodrigues, *Sindicalismo e política*, 215.
34. Cited in CUT São Paulo, "Sindicalismo CUT," 9–10.
35. Riethof, "Changing Strategies," 33–5.
36. Rodrigues et al., *Retrato da CUT*, 22, 27.
37. Further information about CONCUT delegates in 1988, 1991 and 1997 can be found in Rodrigues et al., *Retrato da CUT*; Rodrigues, *Sindicalismo e política*, 213; Costa, *Tendências e centrais*, 160; and CUT, *Resoluções e registros*, 128.
38. Hernan B. Gómez, *Lula, the Workers' Party and the Governability Dilemma in Brazil* (New York: Routledge, 2013), 36.
39. Paradoxically given the MST's emphasis on autonomy, it received financial resources from the state to administer several rural social programmes

during the 1990s, as Gómez argues. Although the MST also organized major anti-governments protests, its organizational survival began to depend on state funding, presaging the increasingly close relations between the PT government and the MST from 2003 onwards, see Gómez, *Lula, the Workers' Party*, 46.
40. See footnote 89 on MST involvement in violent protests against the privatization of the Companhia Vale do Rio Doce.
41. Gómez, *Lula, the Workers' Party*, 49–50; Gabriel Ondetti, *Land, Protest, and Politics: The Landless Movement and the Struggle for Agrarian Reform in Brazil* (University Park, PA: Pennsylvania State University Press, 2008), 126–7, 162–3.
42. Salvador Sandoval, "Working-Class Contention," in *Reforming Brazil*, ed. Mauricio Font and Anthony P. Spanakos (Lanham, MD: Lexington Books, 2008), 208–10.
43. On Força Sindical's roots in São Paulo's moderate metalworkers' union, see Mark Anner. *Solidarity Transformed: Labor Responses to Globalization and Crisis in Latin America* (Ithaca: Cornell University Press, 2011), 141–3.
44. Cardoso, *Trama da modernidade*, 68.
45. The central union organization Força Sindical and "pragmatic" unionism have not been studied as widely as the CUT and new unionism. The principal studies on Força Sindical's political role in the 1990s are Leôncio Martins Rodrigues and Adalberto Moreira Cardoso, *Força Sindical: Uma análise socio-política* (São Paulo: Paz e Terra, 1993) and Cardoso, *Trama da modernidade*; see also Costa, *Tendências e centrais* and Barros, *Labour Relations*.
46. Barros, *Labour Relations*, 42.
47. Força Sindical, *Um projeto para o Brasil: A proposta da Força Sindical* (São Paulo: Geração Editora, 1993): 106.
48. Barros, *Labour Relations*, 36–9; Cardoso, *Trama da modernidade*, 36, 47–50. In 2002 Força Sindical's president Paulo Pereira da Silva ("Paulinho da Força) ran as a vice-presidential candidate of Lula's main competitor Ciro Gomes and in 2015 became involved as federal deputy in protecting Congress speaker Eduardo Cunha from prosecution for corruption as part of "Cunha's shock troops". See Globo, "'Tropa de choque' de Cunha reúne deputados de cinco partidos," *Globo*, Dec. 6, 2015.
49. DESEP/CUT, *Câmaras setoriais*, 7.
50. CUT, *Resoluções e Registros*, 19.
51. For example, see PT, "CUT: Balança mas não cai," *Boletim Nacional* 70 (June 1993), 12.
52. Carneiro cited in PT, "Chacoalhada na roseira," *Boletim Nacional* 39 (May 1993), 11.

53. PT, "Uma crise a resolver," *Boletim Nacional* 40 (June 1993), 12.
54. Another heated debate focused on whether the CUT should formally support and finance Lula's 1994 presidential election campaign, vehemently opposed by the minority groups, which often belonged to other political parties. Although these groups lost the vote on other radical proposals, they did manage to block this proposal during the fifth CONCUT in 1994, see Folha de São Paulo, "CUT decide não dar apoio formal a Lula," *Folha de São Paulo*, May 23, 1994.
55. Durval de Carvalho quoted in Gustavo Codas, "Pancadaria nunca mais," *Boletim Nacional* 57 (April 1994), 10.
56. Mische, *Partisan Publics*, 134–5.
57. Renato Baumann, "O Brasil nos anos 1990: Uma economia em transição," In *Brasil: Uma Década em Transição*, ed. Renato Baumann (Rio de Janeiro: Editora Campus/CEPAL, 2000), 21–3.
58. See Sandoval's detailed discussion on how the reforms affected employment prospects for metalworkers as well as workers in the public and banking sectors and the privatized steel industry, where unions were traditionally strong: Sandoval, "Working-Class Contention", 200–7.
59. Sandoval, "Working-Class Contention," 200.
60. Baumann, "Brasil nos anos 1990", 34–5; International Labour Organization, *Panorama Laboral 1999* (Lima: ILO, 1999).
61. Moreover, privatization affected not only workers and individual trade unions in state-owned companies but also divided the union movement as a whole, as analysed in the next section. Gazeta Mercantil, "Mais peso do funcionalismo dentro da CUT," *Gazeta Mercantil*, May 20, 1994; Rubens Penha Cysne, "Aspectos macro e microeconômicos das reformas," in *Brasil: Uma década em transição*, ed. Renato Baumann (Rio de Janeiro: Editora Campus/CEPAL, 2000), 57, 72–3.
62. DIEESE, "A reestruturação negociada na indústria automobilística brasileira," *Boletim DIEESE* 168 (1995), 18–19.
63. Martins and Rodrigues, "Sindicalismo brasileiro," 159–60.
64. CUT, *Resoluções e Registros*, 16–7.
65. Vicente Paulo da Silva, 1° de Julho ou 1° de Abril? (n.d.), http://www.cut.org.br/a20104.htm. 'July 1' in the title refers to the date of the introduction of the Plano Real in 1994, while 'April 1' refers to April Fool's day.
66. During a time before the "Asian model" was discredited, Vicente Paulo da Silva criticized attempts of the Brazilian government to replicate this model by comparing the "Brazilian cat" with the "Asian tigers".
67. Folha da Tarde, "Metalúrgicos do ABC protestam contra importação de autopeças," *Folha da Tarde*, August 3, 1995.
68. DESEP/CUT, "Os gastos sociais no governo FHC" (São Paulo: DESEP/CUT, 1997).

69. Pamela K. Starr and Philip Oxhorn, "Introduction: The Ambiguous Link Between Economic and Political Reform," in *Markets and Democracy in Latin America: Conflict or Convergence?*, ed. Pamela K. Starr and Philip Oxhorn, 1–9. Boulder, CO: Lynne Rienner) 1999), fn 1.
70. CUT, *Resoluções e Registros*, 19.
71. Author's notes, speech Luís Ínacio Lula da Silva, at "Vinte Anos da primeira CONCLAT", São Paulo, August 23, 2001; Interview with Julio Turra, Secretaria de Relações Internacionais (CUT), São Paulo, August 21, 2001.
72. Interview Fernando Lopes, Executive director, Confederação Nacional dos Metalúrgicos (CNM-CUT), São Paulo, August 22, 2001.
73. The Banco de Horas allowed employers to vary the number of hours worked according to production requirements rather than cutting jobs to respond to changing demand. Participação nos Lucros e Resultados (PLR) allowed unions and employers to negotiate profit- and performance-related pay. Carlos E. Freitas, "Alterações na regulamentação das relações de trabalho no governo Fernando Henrique," in *Precarização e leis do trabalho nos anos FHC* (São Paulo: CUT/ Secretaria da Política Sindical, 2001): 11–2.
74. These negotiations represented a typical example of the transformation of labour relations in Brazil: originating in local practices where these negotiations were already common place and resulting in federal legislation in 1998.
75. In November 2001, Volkswagen workers in São Bernardo do Campo accepted a 15% wage cut and reduction in working hours in return for employment protection and proper redundancy schemes. Martins and Rodrigues, "Sindicalismo brasileiro", 176; Raymond Colitt, "Brazil unions adapt to changing times," *Financial Times*, November 22, 2001; Raymond Colitt, "Brazilian workers approve VW pay-cut agreement," *Financial Times* November 21, 2001.
76. CUT/Secretaria de Política Sindical, *A estratégia da CUT em relação ao Banco de Horas* (São Paulo: Secretaria de Política Sindical/CUT, 1998), 2–3.
77. Sindicato dos Metalúrgicos do ABC, *Participação nos lucros e resultados: A visão dos metalúrgicos do ABC* (São Bernardo do Campo: Sindicato dos Metalúrgicos do ABC, 1998), 12.
78. Direct negotiations between employers and employees on issues such as shorter working weeks, temporary dismissal, and a-typical labour contracts (e.g., temporary and part-time contracts) became common in the 1990s, see Maria S. Portella de Castro, "Mercosul e Relaçoes Trabalhistas," Informe OIT, February 1999, mimeo, 39; Maria S. Portella de Castro, *Estratégias sindicales frente a los procesos de globalización e integración regional: Un análisis comparado TLCAN-Mercosur*, 1999, mimeo, 39; Martins and Rodrigues, "Sindicalismo brasileiro", 167–70. The federal

government also reduced the costs of firing employees, a measure facilitated by Congress' approval of withdrawing its ratification of ILO Convention 158 (protection against unjustified dismissals), see Maria L. Cook, "Labor Reform and Dual Transitions in Brazil and the Southern Cone," *Latin American Politics and Society* 44(1) (2002): 18–23.
79. CUT/Secretaria de Política Sindical, *Estratégia da CUT*, 2–3.
80. For the CUT's views on globalization and neoliberalism during the mid-1990s, see CUT, "Modelo de desenvolvimento, política industrial, e reestruturação produtiva: As propostas da CUT," Propostas para Debate (São Paulo: CUT, 1994), 7; CUT, *Resoluções do 5o Congresso Nacional da CUT* (São Paulo: CUT, 1994), 3–10.
81. See, for example, CUT, "Modelo de desenvolvimento," 7.
82. In a 1991 article for the PT magazine *Boletim Nacional*, Jorge Bittar—then a unionist in the state-owned telecommunications sector, later elected as PT councillor and federal deputy—argued that state subsidies had often enriched the elites, causing many of the country's economic problems, while workers were "interested in the distribution of income and wealth as well as the state as instigator of development". Wladimir Palmeira—student activist during the dictatorship and PT co-founder—argued that defending state ownership at all costs was in fact conservative, arguing in favour of active state intervention as a redistribution mechanism instead, quoted in PT, "Privatizações: Duas visões," *Boletim Nacional* 57/58 (September 1991), 6–7.
83. Civil society participation in the privatization process was limited to political lobbying in Congress and the Senate as civil society's only point of access to the decision-making process. These efforts contributed to a parliamentary inquiry into the implementation of the privatization programme in 1993. See Congresso Nacional, *Relatório final da Comissão Parlamentar Mista de Inquérito (Destinada a investigar fatos decorrentes da execução do Programa Nacional de Desestatização*, Relatório n. 3, 1994-CN, published as a supplement to Diário do Congresso Nacional, no. 32, 21 July 1994; Alexandre Ferraz, "Sindicatos e política de privatização no Brasil," MA diss., University of São Paulo, 2002, 79; interview with Argemiro Pertence Neto, Secretário de Comunicação, Associação de Engenheiros da Petrobras (Association of Engineers of Petrobras, or AEPET), Rio de Janeiro, September 6, 2001. The judiciary was another important focal point for the opposition, allowing protestors to challenge the legality of privatization.
84. Thomas J. Trebat. *Brazil's State-Owned Enterprises: A Case Study of the State as Entrepreneur* (Cambridge: Cambridge University Press, 1983), 69.
85. Author's interview with Mozart Schmitt Queiroz, general secretary of the Sindicato dos Trabalhadores na Indústria Petróleo no Estado de Rio de Janeiro (Petroleum Workers' Unions of Rio de Janeiro, SINDIPETRO-RJ), Rio de Janeiro, September 17, 2001. See also Licinio

Velasco Jr., *A economia política das políticas públicas: Fatores que favoreceram as privatizações no período 1985/94*, Texto para Discussão 54 (Rio de Janeiro: BNDES, 1997): 20.

86. Within the public sector opposition to privatization could be found among staff of state-owned enterprises, politicians connected to the public sector, in contrast with governmental institutions committed to privatization, such as the BNDES, see Velasco, *Economia política*, 20; Werner Baer, *The Brazilian Economy: Growth and Development* (Westport, CN: Praeger, 1995), 261–2; Luigi Manzetti, *Privatization South American Style* (Oxford: Oxford University Press, 1999), 54–5.

87. A participant from the Brazilian northeast at the trade union-organized Third Regional Energy Conference (Rio de Janeiro, September 2001) commented to me that privatization was slow to develop in the northeast due to clientelism and corruption as local politicians often had a stake in state-owned enterprises and distributed jobs in exchange for votes and political favours. See also, Globo, "Trevisan denuncia pressões contra a desestatização," *Globo*, April 13, 1986; Gazeta Mercantil, "Congresso ameaça privatização," *Gazeta Mercantil*, March 14, 1990.

88. For example, in the case of the steel company Cosipa in the state of São Paulo, the municipal government supported union protests against mass dismissals in the run-up to privatization, see PT, "Cosipa: Demissões suspensas," *Boletim Nacional* 79 (December 1993), 3. On the similar case of CSN, see Edilson J. Graciolli, "Um laboratorio chamada CSN: Greves, privatização e sindicalismo (A trajetoria do Sindicato dos Metalúrgicos de Volta Redonda - 1989/1993)," (PhD thesis, Universidade Estadual de Campinas, 1999), 224. A related argument was that state-owned companies funded social and cultural projects. For example, CVRD had to place 8% of its annual turnover in a social fund, which financed schools, environmental projects, and trade union services. Post-privatization, the new owners only have to pay for projects that had already been approved. Interview with Marcelo Sereno, December 17, 1999; Centro de Pesquisa Vergueiro (CPV), "Muito além da Vale," in *CVRD: Privatização da Vale do Rio Doce* (São Paulo: CPV 1997).

89. The CVRD owned significant amounts of land in the Amazon region, provoking protests among rubber tappers and the MST against the company's privatization and the potential sale of these lands. An example of violent protests against the privatization of CVRD was the destruction of a CVRD-owned port in the state of Espírito Santo in December 1998. Other examples of protest included road blocks, occupations, demonstrations at privatization auctions, and hunger strikes, see Folha de São Paulo, "Bloqueio causa prejuízo de R$ 5 mil à Vale," *Folha de São Paulo*, July 10, 1996; Folha de São Paulo, "Exército pode retirar garimpeiros no PA," *Folha de São Paulo*, Oct. 21, 1996; Folha de São Paulo, "Termina greve de fome na Vale," *Folha de São Paulo*, Dec. 2, 1997; Folha de São Paulo,

"Protesto destrói porto no Espírito Santo," *Folha de São Paulo*, Dec. 3, 1998; Folha de São Paulo, "Meneguelli defende ocupação da Usiminas," *Folha de São Paulo*, Sept. 20, 1991.

90. See Gazeta Mercantil, "Urucum não impede venda da Vale," *Gazeta Mercantil*, April 16, 1997; Folha de São Paulo, "Leia a principal ação contra a venda da Vale," *Folha de São Paulo*, May 2, 1997.
91. Folha de São Paulo, "Projeto de PT sofre investida," *Folha de São Paulo*, November 26, 1996.
92. Sindicato dos Trabalhadores nas Indústrias de Prospecção, Pesquisa e Extração de Mineríos (Union for Workers' in the Mineral Prospecting, Research and Extraction Industries).
93. Interview with Luiz Vieira and Celso Vianna de Fonseca, respectively president and communications officer of SINDIMINA. Rio de Janeiro, September 15, 2001.
94. The average job losses in state-owned enterprises between 1991 and 1994 were 49% of the workforce, and 75% of this reduction happened in the process of preparing companies for privatization. Excluding dismissals in the process of pre-privatization restructuring, 39,631 workers were fired from 22 former state-owned enterprises between the early and mid-1990s. Armando Castelar Pinheiro, *No que deu afinal a privatização?* Texto para Discussão 40 (Rio de Janeiro: Banco Nacional de Desenvolvimento Econômico e Social, 1996); Chico Santos, "'Privatizados' cortam 39,6 mil empregos," Folha de São Paulo, March 3, 1997; Francisco Galrão Carneiro, "Privatizações na América Latina: Seus efeitos e impactos sobre o mercado de trabalho," *Estudos Empresariais* (3)2 (1998): 8; Graciolli, "Laboratorio chamado CSN," 221–2.
95. Interview with two representatives of the Human Resources Department of CVRD, Rio de Janeiro, November 9, 2001; Interview with Luiz Vieira and Celso Vianna de Fonseca, September 15, 2001.
96. Interview with two representatives of the Human Resources Department of CVRD, Rio de Janeiro, September 11, 2001; Interview with Luiz Vieira and Celso Vianna de Fonseca, September 15, 2001; Interview with Marcelo Sereno, December 17, 1999; PT, "Nota 10, bilhete azul," *Brasil Agora* 7 (January 1992), 5.
97. An increase in jobs at EMBRATEL (a long-distance telecom company), call centres, and tele-sales obscured the total job losses in TELEBRAS. Furthermore, telecom companies began outsourcing some of their activities, leading to a loss of job security and occasionally to more precarious working conditions. See DIEESE/Subseção FITTEL, *Evolução do Emprego no Setor de Telecomunicações*, DIEESE/Subseção FITTEL, May 2000; International Monetary Fund. *Brazil: Recent Economic Developments*. IMF Staff Country Reports no. 98/24 (Washington D.C.: IMF, April 1998): 14.

98. Interview with Luiz Vieira and Celso Vianna de Fonseca, September 15, 2001; author's notes during visit to Cosipa trade union office and interview with trade union official, Cubatão, April 20, 1999.
99. Tribunal Superior de Trabalho, or TST.
100. Martins and Rodrigues, "Sindicalismo brasileiro," 157–8.
101. Diário do Grande ABC, "Metalúrgicos da região param em solidariedade a petroleiros," *Diário do Grande ABC*, May 20, 1995.
102. Many public-sector strikes in 1995 focused on privatization and employment after the job losses of the early 1990s, including in the electricity sector, education, and telecommunications, see DIEESE, "As greves de maio de 1995," *Boletim DIEESE* 171, June (1995), 53.
103. Cited in Petrobras, *União e força: Memória das organizações dos trabalhadores da Petrobras, 1954–2009* (Rio de Janeiro: Petrobras, 2009), 19.
104. Folha de São Paulo, "Operação foi determinada por FHC na 2a," *Folha de São Paulo*, May 25, 1995.
105. Manzetti, *Privatization South American Style*, 199.
106. Interview with Argemiro Pertence Neto, Secretario de Comunicação, Associação de Engenheiros da Petrobrás (AEPET), Rio de Janeiro, September 6, 2001; Interview with Julio Turra, Diretor Executivo (Secretaria de Relações Internacionais), CUT, São Paulo, August 21, 2001.
107. See Federação Única dos Petroleiros (FUP), "Carta Aberta á População Brasileira," Rio de Janeiro: FUP, September 1995; Assessorias de Imprensa dos Sindicatos de Petroleiros do Estado de São Paulo, "Defender o monopólio do petróleo: Um desafio para a imprensa sindical," São Paulo: Sindicatos de Petroleiros do Estado de São Paulo, 1995.
108. The reaction of the press and the Brazilian government to the Petrobras strike illustrates the image of public-sector workers as benefiting from state protection, see Estado de São Paulo, "Os perigos da greve," *O Estado de São Paulo*, Oct. 3, 1995. In clear support of the government, the newspaper O Estado de São Paulo argued in an article entitled "FHC knocks out the left in one year" that "this type of unionism, which lives off the monopolies inherited from an obsolete state and which confuses its corporatist interests with the defence of the national interest, is ... one of the pillars of our backwardness", see Estado de São Paulo, "FHC nocauteia esquerdas em um ano," *O Estado de São Paulo*, Nov., 6, 1995. An article in Veja suggested a convergence of interests between the CUT, public-sector management and public-sector unions, with the latter benefiting from Brazil's economic and political crisis: "As defenders of a strong state, the leaders of these [public-sector unions] only managed to enlarge their union basis among public workers in the last ten years because they faced a state in crisis," see Veja, "A nova cara do ABC," *Veja*, May 25, 1994, 44.

109. DIEESE, "Greves de maio," 53–4; Diário do Grande ABC, "Petroleiros acabam com a greve de 31 dias sem conseguir nada," *Diário do Grande ABC*, June 3, 1995.
110. Diário do Grande ABC, "Metalúrgicos da região"; Diário do Grande ABC, "Sindicatos da região preparam apoio à greve dos petroleiros," *Diário do Grande ABC*, May 20, 1995.
111. Estado de São Paulo, "Lula e Vicentinho recorrem ao ABC," *O Estado de São Paulo*, May 28, 1995.
112. Gazeta Mercantil, "Acordos terão novo tom," *Gazeta Mercantil*, June 5, 1995; Estado de São Paulo, "Movimento abriu crise no PT," *O Estado de São Paulo*, June, 3, 1995; PT, "Carta Aberta de Lula," *Linha Direta*, June 5, 1995.
113. See also Salvador Sandoval, "The Crisis of the Brazilian Labor Movement and the Emergence of Alternative Forms of Working-Class Contention in the 1990s," *Revista Psicologia Política* 11(1) (2000), 181.
114. Folha de São Paulo, "Meneguelli defende."
115. CUT, "Análise da Lei de Concessões," preparatory document for seminar "A Empresa Pública e seu controle social", São Paulo: CUT, 1995, mimeo, 6.
116. DESEP/CUT, *A crise brasileira e os trabalhadores*. São Paulo: DESEP/CUT, August 1993, 14; Paulo R. Schilling, "Privatização: Lucros concentrados e prejuízos socializados," *Contexto Pastoral* 20, May–June 1994, 15.
117. CUT, *Resoluções e registros*, 18.
118. At the sixth National Congress of the CUT in 1997, 35.7% of the delegates were civil servants and 19.3% of the delegates were employed by state-owned enterprises, CUT, *Resoluções e registros*, 128.
119. Sidney Jard da Silva, "'Companheiros Servidores': Poder político e interesses econômicos do sindicalismo do setor publico na CUT," MA diss., Universidade de São Paulo, 1999, 65–6, 70–2.
120. Ferraz, "Sindicatos e política de privatização", 82–4.
121. Força Sindical, *Um projeto*, 106–7, 272; Patricia Vieira Trópia, "O neoliberalismo no movimento sindical: Uma análise das bases sociais da Força Sindical," Paper presented at the 23rd Encontro Anual da Associação Nacional de Pós-Graduação em Ciências Sociais, Caxambu, 1999, 6.
122. Força Sindical, *Um projeto*, 48.
123. Força Sindical, *Um projeto*, 229–31.
124. Even though the national directorate of Força Sindical supported privatization and the "flexibilization" of state monopolies, several of its affiliates disagreed and opposed privatization. For further analysis, see Trópia "Neoliberalismo no movimento sindical," 7, 10–2.
125. A similar conflict happened in the case of Usiminas in 1991, see PT, "As duas maracutaias da Usiminas," *Brasil Agora* 2 (October 1991), 8–9;

Folha de São Paulo, "Presidente do sindicato defende privatização: Sindicalistas divergem sobre destino da Usiminas," *Folha de São Paulo* October 3, 1991; Veja, "A praça da bagunça: O leilão da Usiminas é derrubado em meio a um festival de selvageria," *Veja*, Oct. 2, 1991.
126. Ferraz, "Sindicatos e política de privatização", 85–110.
127. Quoted in PT, "Os demônios da impotência," *Brasil Agora* 21 (August 1992), 4.
128. CUT, *O papel das empresas*, 10.
129. Velasco, *Economia Política*, 24–33; Enrique Saravia, "Proceso de privatización en Argentina y Brasil: Consecuencias en materia de mercado de trabajo y desempeño empresarial, practicas utilizadas para el ajuste de personal." Working Paper 97 (Geneva, International Labour Organization, 1996): 12–3; Ferraz, "Sindicatos e política de privatização", 52–4.
130. SINDIMINA, "Proposta: 'Os trabalhadores da CVRD diante da privatização'" (Aracaju: Sindimina, 1996); interview with Luiz Vieira and Celso Vianna de Fonseca, September 15, 2001.
131. SINDIMINA, "Proposta: 'Os trabalhadores'".
132. SINDIMINA, "Proposta: "Os trabalhadores'".
133. Interview with Luiz Vieira and Celso Vianna de Fonseca; Interview with Maria Lucia Garcia, InvestVale (Investors' Club CVRD), Rio de Janeiro, September 11, 2001.
134. Sindicato dos Engenheiros de Volta Redonda (SENGE/VR), *Privatização? Não Obrigado!* May, (Volta Redonda: SENGE/VR, 1990): 35–6.
135. CUT, *Resoluções e Registros*, 15.
136. Ferrero also notes this shift, calling attention to increased networking among social movements and arguing that it was easier to mobilize popular support by organizing political campaigns rather than strike action, see Juan Pablo Ferrero, *Democracy against Neoliberalism in Argentina and Brazil: A Move to the Left* (Basingstoke: Palgrave Macmillan, 2014), 95–6, 108.
137. Sandoval, "Working-Class Contention," 209–10.
138. There were parallels between the MST's experience and the widening of new unionism's political agenda and conception of class in the late 1980s and early 1990s. As Wolford argues, the MST underwent a shift from identifying as a workers' movement focused on agrarian reform to a broadly conceived anti-neoliberal agenda which appealed to a wide range of people, see Wendy Wolford, *This Land is Ours Now: Social Mobilization and the Meanings of Land in Brazil* (Durham, NC: Duke University Press, 2010), 95–101.
139. Lúcio F. de Almeida and Félix Ruiz Sánchez, "The Landless Workers' Movement and Social Struggles against Neoliberalism," *Latin American Perspectives* 27(5) (2000), 20–3.
140. Hunter, *Transformation of the Workers' Party*, 137.

141. For example, see Hunter's argument about the relationship between the PT's experience in local government and political pragmatism, Hunter, *Transformation of the Workers' Party*, Ch. 4. See also Gómez, *Lula, the Workers' Party*, Ch. 5 about the changing relationship between the PT and civil society in the 1990s; and Samuels, "Socialism to Social Democracy," about internal changes.

Bibliography

Almeida, Lúcio F. de, and Félix Ruiz Sánchez. 2000. The Landless Workers' Movement and Social Struggles Against Neoliberalism. *Latin American Perspectives* 27 (5): 11–32.
Anner, Mark. 2011. *Solidarity Transformed: Labor Responses to Globalization and Crisis in Latin America*. Ithaca: Cornell University Press.
Assessorias de Imprensa dos Sindicatos de Petroleiros do Estado de São Paulo (SPESP). 1995. *Defender o monopólio do petróleo: Um desafio para a imprensa Sindical*. São Paulo: Sindicatos de Petroleiros do Estado de São Paulo.
Baer, Werner. 1995. *The Brazilian Economy: Growth and Development*. Westport: Praeger.
Barros, Maurício Rands. 1999. *Labour Relations and the New Unionism in Contemporary Brazil*. New York/London: St. Martin's Press/ Macmillan.
Baumann, Renato. 2000. O Brasil nos anos 1990: Uma economia em transição. In *Brasil: Uma Década em Transição*, ed. Renato Baumann, 11–53. Rio de Janeiro: Editora Campus/CEPAL.
Brasil Agora. 1992a. Todos nos perdemos. *Brasil Agora* 15, May–June: 4.
———. 1992b. A aposta do ABCD. *Brasil Agora*, April 12: 6–7.
———. 1992c. A CUT mostra a cara. *Brasil Agora*, March 10: 4.
Bruhn, Kathleen. 2008. *Urban Protest in Mexico and Brazil*. Cambridge: Cambridge University Press.
Carneiro, Francisco Galrão. 1998. Privatizações na América Latina: Seus efeitos e impactos sobre o mercado de trabalho. *Estudos Empresariais* 3 (2): 3–13.
Carvalho, Carlos Eduardo. Não devemos exagerar: Triunfo histórico ou acordo defensivo e questionável. *Brasil Agora* 12 (April 1992): 7.
Castelar Pinheiro, Armando. 1996. *No que deu afinal a privatização?* Texto para Discussão 40. Rio de Janeiro: Banco Nacional de Desenvolvimento Econômico e Social.
Castro, Maria S. Portella de. 1999a. *Estratégias sindicales frente a los procesos de globalización e integración regional: Un análisis comparado TLCAN-Mercosur*. São Paulo: mimeo.
———. 1999b. *Mercosul e Relaçoes Trabalhistas*. Informe OIT, mimeo, Febraury.
Causa Operária. 1991. Greve geral: Primeiro balanço. *Causa Operária* 131. Reproduced in Centro Pastoral Vergueira, Quinzena 118: 10–11.

Central Única dos Trabalhadores (CUT). 1989. Resolução da reunião extraordinária da executiva da Direção Nacional da CUT realizada no dia 16/3, em São Paulo. *Informa CUT* 55: 1–2.

———. 1991. *Resoluções do 4o CONCUT*. São Paulo, CUT.

———. 1993a. A CUT mostra: é falsa a desculpa do dinheiro. *De Fato* 1 (1): 4–5.

———. 1993b. A negociação vista no raio X. *De Fato* 1 (1): 10–11.

———. 1994a. *Resoluções do 5o Congresso Nacional da CUT*. São Paulo: CUT.

———. 1994b. Modelo de desenvolvimento, política industrial, e reestruturação produtiva: As propostas da CUT. Propostas para Debate, São Paulo: CUT.

———. 1995a. *Relatório do Seminário 'A Empresa Pública e seu controle social'*. Brasília: CUT.

———. 1995c. O papel das empresas públicas e seu controle social. Discussion document and preparatory document for seminar "A Empresa Pública e seu controle social". São Paulo: CUT/mimeo.

———. 1997. *Resoluções e Registros*. 6o Congresso Nacional da CUT, August.

———. 1998. *Política industrial e de geração de empregos: As propostas da CUT*. São Paulo: CUT.

———. 2003. *A política internacional da CUT: História e perspectivas*. São Paulo: CUT.

Codas, Gustavo. 1994. Pancadaria nunca mais. *Boletim Nacional* 57: 10.

Colitt, Raymond. 2001a. Brazil Unions Adapt to Changing Times. *Financial Times*, November 22.

———. 2001b. Brazilian Workers Approve VW Pay-Cut Agreement. *Financial Times*, November 21.

Comin, Alvaro A. 1995. A estrutura sindical corporativa: Um obstáculo à consolidação das centrais sindicais no Brasil. MA dissertation, Universidade de São Paulo.

Congresso Nacional. 1994. *Relatório Final da Comissão Parlamentar Mista de Inquérito (Destinada a investigar fatos decorrentes da execução do Programa Nacional de Desestatização*. Relatório n. 3, 1994-CN, published as a supplement to *Diário do Congresso Nacional*, no. 32, July 21.

Cook, María L. 2002. Labor Reform and Dual Transitions in Brazil and the Southern Cone. *Latin American Politics and Society* 44 (1): 1–34.

Costa, Sílvio. 1995. *Tendências e centrais sindicais: O Movimento Sindical Brasileiro, 1978–1994*. São Paulo: Editora Anita Garibaldi.

Costa, Hermes A. 2005. A política internacional da CGTP e da CUT: Etapas, temas e desafios. *Revista Crítica de Ciências Sociais* 71: 141–161.

Coutinho Jorge. 1997. Muito além da Vale. In *CVRD: Privatização da Vale do Rio Doce*. São Paulo: CPV.

CUT São Paulo/Escola Sindical São Paulo. 2001–2002. Sindicalismo CUT – 20 anos. *Cadernos de Formação*, 1.

CUT/Secretaria de Política Sindical. 1998. *A estratégia da CUT em relação ao Banco de Horas*. São Paulo: Secretaria de Política Sindical/CUT.

Cysne, Rubens Penha. 2000. Aspectos macro e microeconômicos das reformas. In *Brasil: Uma década em transição*, ed. Renato Baumann, 56–99. Rio de Janeiro: Editora Campus/CEPAL.

De Fato. 1993a. A CUT mostra: é falsa a desculpa do dinheiro. *De Fato* 1 (1): 4–5.

———. 1993b. A negociação vista no raio X. *De Fato* 1 (1): 7–11.

Departamento de Estudos Sócio-Econômicos e Políticos (DESEP)/CUT. 1992. Câmaras setoriais e intervenção sindical. Texto Para Discussão no. 5. São Paulo: DESEP/CUT.

———. 1993a. *A crise brasileira e os trabalhadores*. São Paulo: DESEP/CUT.

———. 1993b. Câmaras setoriais: Para além do complexo automotivo. Texto Para Discussão 6. São Paulo: DESEP/CUT.

———. 1997. *Os gastos sociais no governo FHC*. São Paulo: DESEP/CUT.

Departamento Intersindical de Estatística e Estudos Socioeconômicos (DIEESE). 1995a. As greves de maio de 1995. *Boletim DIEESE* 171, June: 12.

———. 1995b. A reestruturação negociada na indústria automobilística brasileira. *Boletim DIEESE* 168: 18–20.

———. 2015. Balanço das greves em 2013. *Estudos e Pesquisas* 79, December: 1–43.

Diário do Grande ABC. 1995a. Petroleiros acabam com a greve de 31 dias sem conseguir nada. *Diário do Grande ABC*, June 3.

———. 1995b. Sindicatos da região preparam apoio à greve dos petroleiros, *Diário do Grande ABC*, May 20.

———. 1995c. Metalúrgicos da região param em solidariedade petroleiros. *Diário do Grande ABC*, May 20.

Diário Popular, 1991. CUT deve reeleger hoje Jair Meneguelli, *Diário Popular*, September 8.

DIEESE/Subseção FITTEL. 2000. *Evolução do emprego no setor de telecomunicações*. Brasília: DIEESE/Subseção FITTEL, May.

Estado de São Paulo. 1991. A CUT sofre com luta interna. *O Estado de São Paulo*, June 2.

———. 1995a. Movimento abriu crise no PT. *O Estado de São Paulo*, June 3.

———. 1995b. FHC nocauteia esquerdas em um ano. *O Estado de São Paulo*, November 6.

———. 1995c. Os perigos da greve. *O Estado de São Paulo*, October 3.

———. 1995d. Lula e Vicentinho recorrem ao ABC. O Estado de São Paulo, May 28.

Federação Única dos Petroleiros (FUP). 1995. *Carta aberta á população brasileira*. Rio de Janeiro: FUP.

Ferraz, Alexandre. 2002. Sindicatos e política de privatização no Brasil. MA dissertation, Department of Political Science, University of São Paulo.

Ferrero, Juan Pablo. 2014. *Democracy Against Neoliberalism in Argentina and Brazil: A Move to the Left*. Basingstoke: Palgrave Macmillan.
Folha da Tarde. 1995. Metalúrgicos do ABC protestam contra importação de autopeças. *Folha da Tarde*, August 3.
Folha de São Paulo. 1991a. Presidente do sindicato defende privatização: Sindicalistas divergem sobre destino da Usiminas. *Folha de São Paulo*, October 3.
———. 1991b. Meneguelli defende ocupação da Usiminas. *Folha de São Paulo*, September 20.
———. 1991c. Meneguelli atribui fracasso à 'falta de empenho'. *Folha de São Paulo*, May 24.
———. 1994a. CUT decide não dar apoio formal a Lula. *Folha de São Paulo*, May 23.
———. 1994b. CUT vai dividida à eleição dos bancários. *Folha de São Paulo*, January 17.
———. 1995. Operação foi determinada por FHC na 2a. *Folha de São Paulo*, May 25.
———. 1996a. Projeto de PT sofre investida. *Folha de São Paulo*, November 26.
———. 1996b. Exército pode retirar garimpeiros no PA. *Folha de São Paulo*, October 21.
———. 1996c. Bloqueio causa prejuízo de R$ 5 mil à Vale. *Folha de São Paulo*, July 10.
———. 1997a. Termina greve de fome na Vale." *Folha de São Paulo*, December 2.
———. 1997b. Leia a principal ação contra a venda da Vale. *Folha de São Paulo*, May 2.
———. 1998. Protesto destrói porto no Espírito Santo. *Folha de São Paulo*, December 3.
———. 2012. Há 20 anos termina greve de motoristas e cobradores de ônibus em São Paulo. *Folha de São Paulo*, May 20.
Força Sindical. 1993. *Um projeto para o Brasil: A proposta da Força Sindical*. Geração Editora: São Paulo.
França, Teones. 2014. *Novo sindicalismo no Brasil: Histórico de uma desconstrução*. São Paulo: Cortez.
Freitas, Carlos E. 2001. Alterações na regulamentação das relações de trabalho no governo Fernando Henrique. In *Precarização e leis do trabalho nos anos FHC*, ed. CUT/Secretaria da Política Sindical. São Paulo: CUT/Secretaria da Política Sindical.
Gazeta Mercantil. 1990. Congresso ameaça privatização. *Gazeta Mercantil*, March 14.
———. 1991a. Divergências políticas dificultam os debates em congresso da CUT. *Gazeta Mercantil*, September 6.
———. 1991b. Greve inexpressiva poderá levar sindicatos ao Congresso. *Gazeta Mercantil*, May 24.
———. 1994. Mais peso do funcionalismo dentro da CUT. *Gazeta Mercantil*, May 20.
———. 1995. Acordos terão novo tom. *Gazeta Mercantil*, June 5.

———. 1997. Urucum não impede venda da Vale. *Gazeta Mercantil*, April 16.
Giannotti, Vito. 2007. *História das lutas dos trabalhadores no Brasil*. Rio de Janeiro: Mauad.
Globo. 1986. Trevisan denuncia pressões contra a desestatização. *Globo*, April 13.
———. 2015. 'Tropa de choque' de Cunha reúne deputados de cinco partidos. *Globo*, December 6.
Gómez, Hernan B. 2013. *Lula, the Workers' Party and the Governability Dilemma in Brazil*. New York: Routledge.
Graciolli, Edilson J. 1999. Um laboratorio chamada CSN: Greves, privatização e sindicalismo (A trajetoria do Sindicato dos Metalúrgicos de Volta Redonda – 1989/1993). PhD Thesis, Universidade Estadual de Campinas.
Hunter, Wendy. 2010. *The Transformation of the Workers' Party in Brazil, 1989–2009*. Cambridge: Cambridge University Press.
International Monetary Fund. 1998 *Brazil: Recent Economic Developments*. IMF Staff Country Reports no. 98/24, Washington, DC: IMF.
Jard da Silva, Sidney. 1999. 'Companheiros Servidores': Poder político e interesses econômicos do sindicalismo do setor publico na CUT. MA dissertation, Universidade de São Paulo.
Jornal da Tarde. 1991. Guerra entre tendências tumultua o congresso da CUT, September 7.
Jornal do Brasil. 1991. CUT briga na quarta eleição de Meneguelli, September 9.
Kowarick, Lúcio, and André Singer. 1993. A experiência do Partido dos Trabalhadores na prefeitura de São Paulo. *Novos Estudos CEBRAP* 35: 195–216.
Macaulay, Fiona. 1996. 'Governing for Everyone': The Workers' Party Administration in São Paulo, 1989-1992. *Bulletin of Latin American Research* 15 (2): 211–229.
Manzetti, Luigi. 1999. *Privatization South American Style*. Oxford: Oxford University Press.
Martin, Scott B. 1997. Beyond Corporatism: New Patterns of Representation in the Brazilian Auto Industry. In *The New Politics of Inequality in Latin America: Rethinking Participation and Representation*, ed. Douglas A. Chalmers et al., 45–71. Oxford: Oxford University Press.
Martins, Heloísa de Souza and Iram J. Rodrigues. 1999. O sindicalismo brasileiro na segunda metade dos anos 90. *Tempo Social* 11 (2): 155–182.
Mische, Anne. 2008. *Partisan Publics: Communication and Contention Across Brazilian Youth Activist Networks*. Princeton: Princeton University Press.
Ondetti, Gabriel. 2008. *Land, Protest, and Politics: The Landless Movement and the Struggle for Agrarian Reform in Brazil*. University Park: Pennsylvania State University Press.
Partido dos Trabalhadores (PT). 1990a. Setembro é mês de primavera e não de terror. *Boletim Nacional* 52: 12.
———. 1990b. CUT não negocia emprego e salário. *Boletim Nacional* 53, May: 3.

———. 1991a. CUT e Contag no mesmo barco. *Boletim Nacional* 61, December: 3.
———. 1991b. O fundo do poço. *Boletim Nacional* 59, October: 8.
———. 1991c. As duas maracutaias da Usiminas. *Brasil Agora* 2, October: 8–9.
———. 1991d. Privatizações: Duas visões. *Boletim Nacional* 57/58, September: 6–7.
———. 1991e. O momento político em debate. *Boletim Nacional* 54, May: 5.
———. 1991f. O PT e o momento político: Resolução do Diretório Nacional reunido em 16/03/91. *Boletim Nacional* 5, April: 5.
———. 1992a. Os demônios da impotência. *Brasil Agora* 21, August: 4.
———. 1992b. A greve em que todos perdemos. Boletim Nacional 64, July: 14–15.
———. 1992c. Nota 10, bilhete azul. *Brasil Agora* 7, January: 5.
———. 1993a. Cosipa: Demissões suspensas. *Boletim Nacional* 79, December: 3
———. 1993b. CUT discute Contag. *Boletim Nacional* 42, July: 11.
———. 1993c. CUT: Balança mas não cai. *Boletim Nacional* 40, June: 12.
———. 1993d. Uma crise a resolver. *Boletim Nacional* 40, June: 12.
———. 1993e. Chacoalhada na roseira. *Boletim Nacional* 39, May: 11.
———. 1995. Carta aberta de Lula, *Linha Direta*, June 5.
Petrobras. 2009. *União e força: Memória das organizações dos trabalhadores da Petrobras, 1954–2009*. Rio de Janeiro: Petrobras.
Pochmann, Marcio, Reginaldo Muniz Barreto, and Sérgio E.A. Mendonça. 1998. Ação sindical no Brasil: Transformações e perspectivas. *São Paulo em Perspectiva* 12 (1): 10–23.
Rodrigues, Leôncio Martins, and Adalberto Moreira Cardoso. 1993. *Força Sindical: Uma análise socio-política*. São Paulo: Paz e Terra.
Rodrigues, Leôncio Martins, Maria S. Portella de Castro, Suzanna Sochaczewski, and Iram J. Rodrigues. *Retrato da CUT: Delegados do 3o CONCUT, representação nas categorias*. São Paulo: CUT/mimeo.
Sandoval, Salvador. 2000. The Crisis of the Brazilian Labor Movement and the Emergence of Alternative Forms of Working-Class Contention in the 1990s. *Revista Psicologia Política* 11 (1): 173–195.
———. 2008. Working-Class Contention. In *Reforming Brazil*, ed. Mauricio Font and Anthony P. Spanakos, 195–215. Lanham: Lexington Books.
Santos, Chico. 1997. 'Privatizados' cortam 39,6 mil empregos. *Folha de São Paulo*, March 3.
Saravia, Enrique. 1996. Proceso de privatización en Argentina y Brasil: Consecuencias en materia de mercado de trabajo y desempeño empresarial, practicas utilizadas para el ajuste de personal. Working Paper 97, Geneva: International Labour Organization.
Schilling, Paulo R. 1994. Privatização: Lucros concentrados e prejuízos socializados. *Contexto Pastoral* 20, May–June: 3–20.
Schneider, Ronald M. 1996. *Brazil: Culture and Politics in a New Industrial Powerhouse*. Boulder: Westview Press.

Silva, Vicente Paulo da. 1999. 1 de Julho ou 1 de Abril? http://www.cut.org.br/a20104.htm. Accessed 22 June 1999.

Silva, Vicente Paulo da, and Sereno, Marcelo. 1999. A quem interessa a privatização da Vale do Rio Doce?! undated. http://www.cut.org.br/a2012.htm. Accessed 24 June 1999.

Sindicato dos Engenheiros de Volta Redonda (SENGE/VR). 1990. *Privatização? Não Obrigado!* Volta Redonda: SENGE/VR.

Sindicato dos Metalúrgicos do ABC (SMABC). 1998. *Participação nos lucros e resultados: A visão dos metalúrgicos do ABC*. São Bernardo do Campo: Sindicato dos Metalúrgicos do ABC.

SINDIMINA. 1996. *Proposta: "Os trabalhadores da CVRD diante da privatização"*. Sindimina: Aracaju.

Sluyter-Beltrão, Jeffrey. 2010. *Rise and Decline of Brazil's New Unionism: The Politics of the Central Única dos Trabalhadores*. Oxford: Peter Lang.

Starr, Pamela K., and Philip Oxhorn. 1999. Introduction: The Ambiguous Link Between Economic and Political Reform. In *Markets and Democracy in Latin America: Conflict or Convergence?* ed. Pamela K. Starr and Philip Oxhorn, 1–9. Boulder: Lynne Rienner.

Trebat, Thomas J. 1983. *Brazil's State-Owned Enterprises: A Case Study of the State as Entrepreneur*. Cambridge: Cambridge University Press.

Trópia, Patricia Vieira. 1999. O neoliberalismo no movimento sindical: Uma análise das bases sociais da Força Sindical. Paper presented at the 23rd Encontro Anual of the Associação Nacional de Pós-Graduação em Ciências Sociais, Caxambu.

Veja. 1991. A praça da bagunça: O leilão da Usiminas é derrubado em meio a um festival de selvageria." *Veja*, 2 October 1991.

———. 1994. A nova cara do ABC. *Veja*, 44, 25 May 1994.

Velasco, Licinio, Jr. 1997. *A economia política das políticas públicas: Fatores que favoreceram as privatizações no período 1985/94*, Texto para Discussão 54. Rio de Janeiro: BNDES.

Wolford, Wendy. 2010. *This Land Is Ours Now: Social Mobilization and the Meanings of Land in Brazil*. Durham: Duke University Press.

CHAPTER 6

Labour Strategies and the Left in Power: Moderation, Division, and Renewed Militancy from Lula to Dilma

While Brazilian unions had struggled with the effect of economic crisis and ever-tightening macroeconomic reforms during the 1990s, the presidential election campaigns in 2002 provided unionists with new prospects for political change. However, after Lula's breakthrough election victory, the PT's emphasis on radical social transformation during the 1980s made way for a more pragmatic agenda, including the maintenance of the previous government's economic policies, supported by a new programme of social policies aimed at poverty reduction. In this new political environment, significant sections of the union movement benefitted from increased access to political influence as unions moved closer to the government agenda and several senior trade unionists took up ministerial posts, thereby absorbing the party's electoral and governmental logic. Yet the new union-party relations with the PT in power proved controversial as new unionism's close ties with the party sparked significant conflicts in terms of pursuing either radical or gradualist strategies. By examining these conflicts during the PT-led governments (2003–2016), this chapter moves away from the emphasis on political moderation evident in much of the literature.[1] Instead, the argument proposed here is that while the drive towards moderation was strong during this period, disagreements about political agendas and strategies as well as changing economic conjunctures sparked not only divisions but also a new wave of labour militancy from 2009 onwards.

© The Author(s) 2019
M. Riethof, *Labour Mobilization, Politics and Globalization in Brazil*,
Studies of the Americas,
https://doi.org/10.1007/978-3-319-60309-4_6

The relationship between the union movement and the PT governments between 2003 and 2016 illustrates organized labour's struggle to identify and redefine its position in a new political landscape. This period marked the gradual adoption of political strategies in the institutional sphere, particularly through participation in policy forums and integration into the government, which led to a moderate approach focused on negotiation with politicians and government actors. As a result, many union leaders echoed the government's policy rationale and hesitated to challenge the PT administration for fear of destabilizing it. This approach reflected the national union leadership's focus on political influence using party and government channels, rather than pressurizing the government through protests. Labour mobilization's stagnation during the Lula administrations reflected a certain continuity with the unions' difficulties during the 1990s, when the latter focused on defensive struggles to protect jobs and labour rights, thereby dampening labour militancy. However, echoes of the union movement's more militant past re-emerged when contesting policy issues such as social security and labour reforms and, from the late 2000s onwards, which further underlined internal conflicts when the number of strikes increased as economic growth began to decelerate.

Because the union-party relationship was such a powerful driving force behind labour political agendas during this period, the chapter begins by discussing the impact of the PT's balancing act between maintaining economic growth, improving social indicators, and managing congressional majorities. The first years after Lula's election showed the limitations of the union movement's political influence under the new configuration. The successful minimum wage campaign and organized labour's failure to halt controversial pension reforms illustrates how union leaders had absorbed the PT's governmental logic, while the government had also become less receptive to the labour agenda. During the second half of Lula's first administration, the government's proposals to address the corporatist system became an even more divisive debate. Even if the proposed reforms opened up the opportunity to introduce changes that had been at the heart of the new unionist agenda since the late 1970s, the discussions ended up dividing the unions, underlining the difficulty of maintaining an autonomous stance in the new political environment. Combined, these events resulted in the political fragmentation and weakening of the union movement, which increased internal conflicts and competition. Finally, as the economy began to falter in 2009, a new wave of strikes signalled a return to militant labour strategies as well as a growing social and political polarization, which would culminate in mass demonstrations from 2013 onwards and Dilma Rousseff's impeachment in 2016. The largely unrecognized role of labour militancy in the years preceding the 2013 protests show that while the new political context pulled trade union leaders towards political moderation, internal conflicts and dissatisfaction with politics-as-usual and the outcomes of Brazil's development model pushed others towards renewed militancy and mobilization.

6.1 Trade Unions, Lula's Election Victories, and the PT's Trajectory in Government

The political dynamics of the early years after Lula became president in 2003 illustrate how trade union debates about militant and moderate political strategies evolved in a new political context. Labour's political dilemmas mirrored what happened in the PT in this period, which meant that unions were reluctant to force the government to introduce far-reaching progressive reforms. The unions' close relationship with the PT played a major role in moderating the labour agenda, particularly given the unions' hesitance to challenge the government's policy choices from 2003 onwards. As several key union figures entered the government as ministers and politicians under Lula, the CUT's leadership became closer politically to the PT's agenda in power. In addition, union leaders were involved in running Brazil's powerful state-owned enterprises, pension, and investment funds. The integration of the new unionists in the PT-led governments has led authors such as Francisco de Oliveira, Alvaro Bianchi, and Ruy Braga to conclude that the *cutista* unionists formed a new political class under the working-class president, which in their view meant that the transformation of new unionism into a moderate force was irreversible.[2] The relationship between the PT and its social movement supporters changed as the party offered channels of political influence but the party also became less responsive to more radical social movement demands, lessening the effectiveness of civil society participation. Similarly, opportunities for union participation in major policy debates, such as labour reforms, contributed to a more gradualist approach, as union leaders struggled to reconcile access to political influence and effective opposition. Nevertheless, even if the government consulted civil society representatives regarding major policy reforms, the proposals proved highly controversial, bringing up debates and disagreements which had divided the unions since the late 1970s. As discussed in this section, the internal debate became increasingly fractious, resulting in disagreements about the extent to which unionists should absorb the PT's logic about the realities of government and electoral concerns.

Shortly before his election victory, Lula made what seemed to be a political volte-face by maintaining many of the macroeconomic policies introduced by Cardoso, his predecessor. When US Treasury Secretary Paul O'Neill visited Brazil as part of a Latin American trip in August 2002, Brazil's economy was in a severe crisis and US support for renewed IMF loans and debt renegotiation meant that there was little room for manoeuvre for any of the presidential candidates, including Lula. In his *Carta ao Povo Brasileiro*, Lula called for a leap of faith, arguing that the only way his ambitious social agenda could be achieved was by maintaining the economic framework of the previous government. This argument dominated the political agenda of the first Lula administration and union leaders also echoed this rationale in their campaigns. Although the Brazilian economy improved significantly after Lula was elected, many critics were not prepared to step over what they viewed as Lula's "selling out" to global capital, the international financial institutions, and the USA. This episode set the scene not only for the PT's electoral successes, reflecting the argument in favour of combining economic prosperity, political moderation, and social improvements, but it also accounted for the heated debates held within the union movement.

After a slow start, the government's macroeconomic policies began to result in economic growth in 2004, with Brazil maintaining primary budget surpluses and reducing inflation to single digits. High global prices for Brazilian products such as iron ore, soy, and manufactured goods also fuelled the country's economy, leading to trade surpluses and the successful diversification of exports.[3] As a result of this turnaround, the urban unemployment rates that had steadily increased since the mid-1990s decreased consistently after 2004.[4] Sustained economic growth, relatively low inflation, and growing employment all contributed to improvements in social indicators after 2004,[5] as Brazil experienced a significant decline in income inequality, reducing the Gini coefficient by 5.4% points between 1998 and 2009.[6] Increased domestic spending fuelled by increasingly accessible consumer credit, social policies, and higher minimum wage levels not only improved social indicators but also contributed to economic recovery,[7] which lasted until the economy began to slow down in 2009. Underlining the significant role of government policy in these changes,

Lustig et al. attribute the decline in income inequality primarily to the expansion of education, the reduction of geographical and sectoral wage differences, and social policies.[8] As a result of the high levels of economic growth, reduced inflation, minimum wage increases, and social policies, Brazilian society experienced significant improvement from the early 2000s. However, the PT's critics also argued that the party's programme lacked ambition for more fundamental reforms to the country's highly unequal socio-economic and political structures.

Particularly controversial was the PT leadership's belief in the need to maintain a relatively conventional economic agenda built on the unpopular policies of the previous government. At the same time, the party curtailed its supporters' more radical demands by arguing that these policies were necessary to guarantee the PT's ambitious social agenda. Observers of Brazilian politics have focused on the contradiction between maintaining the macroeconomic framework, the expansion of social policies, the lack of fundamental political reforms needed to transform Brazil's highly unequal society, as well as the party's internal conflicts. Despite the high expectations, according to Kingstone and Power, "the PT, by all accounts, has made only the smallest of dents in Brazil's elitist political culture, and 'politics as usual' prevails".[9] For Flynn, the problems in Lula's first term resulted from the contrast between his conservative economic policies, the initial lack of social progress, and the PT's past commitments to social change: "Throughout the left a widespread sense of betrayal focused on policies which Lula had strongly criticised in the past."[10] Nevertheless, French and Fortes reject the commonplace view that the PT betrayed its principles, emphasizing the social transformations that occurred in the 2000s and adding that mass political participation of the poor should be considered a major achievement in a country dominated by elitist politics.[11] Moreover, in her study of the transformation of the PT between 1989 and 2009, Hunter argues that the severe economic crisis in the early 2000s and the characteristics of Brazil's political institutions—particularly the difficult task of managing unstable government coalitions—limited the possibilities for radical reform.[12] In the early years of the Lula government, debates within the union movement also vacillated between these different assessments, manifesting at times in strong disappointment with the lack of progress and at other times in an acute awareness of the electoral and political limitations facing the PT in government.

In light of the contrast between the party's roots in the unions, its progressive past, and the realities of government, research on the PT has ascribed its turn towards political moderation to a variety of factors, including the party's electoral concerns in the 1980s and 1990s, the difficult economic context of the early 2000s, and the quirks of the Brazilian political system. Samuels focuses his explanation of these discrepancies on the party's experience in local government in the 1990s, which resulted in the PT adapting its political agenda to deal with local realities in an act of what he calls "strategic moderation".[13] As argued in Chap. 5, the union movement also absorbed many of these considerations as mass labour mobilization and strikes became less effective as an instrument of political pressure in the 1990s. Hunter emphasizes external factors such as the global economic context leading to Lula's decision to continue Cardoso's macroeconomic framework, which Lula justified by citing the need for economic development as the basis for effective social programmes.[14] Both Gómez and Hunter cite the nature of Brazil's political system in that it is difficult for a president to achieve a parliamentary majority, forcing "Lula to gather support from a majority of voters … in a context of an extremely fragmented electorate and party system".[15] Moreover, Gómez points to the difficulties caused by progressive parties in government having to compromise to gain majority support for their proposals, in what he calls the "governability dilemma" that also resulted in a greater distance between the party and its social movement supporters.[16] The picture that emerges is one of a left-wing party whose potential for a transformative agenda became constrained by electoral concerns, coalition politics, and attempts to balance economic growth with social reforms, all of which became highly divisive dilemmas for the party's supporters.

Another strand of the debate has focused on the PT's relationship with its core supporters and the electorate after Lula's election to the presidency, signalling changing movement-party relations and reflecting growing internal conflicts evident in the union movement. The PT leadership attempted to balance the party's supporters' demands while also managing the government coalition and building majorities in Congress for legislative proposals. The centre of gravity began to move away from the party's core union and social movement supporters, signalling that the relationship between Lula, the PT, and social movements was in flux. Indeed, Morais and Saad-Filho argue that Lula's supporters criticized the lack of progress but also had conflicting agendas, while elites expected moderation and left-wing supporters demanded revolutionary political and social changes.[17] These conflicting agendas were not only evident in party circles but also characterized trade union debates on how to position labour's political agenda in a new context. Diniz Amaral, Kingstone and Krieckhaus believe the contradictions between Lula's economic and social agendas to be the reason why Lula began "to divorce his electoral strategy from the PT's traditional base",[18] including the party's roots in trade unions.

Indeed, in the run-up to the 2005 presidential elections, Lula began to distance himself from the PT, focusing on the beneficiaries of the Bolsa Família social programmes instead.[19] He became more popular than the party, with commentators beginning to refer to *lulismo*, which involved Lula mobilizing the poor to vote for the PT by offering state-sponsored income redistribution, but without challenging existing power structures.[20] *Lulismo* reflected the personalization of the PT leadership, as "most Brazilians are far more interested in Lula's personal story and the concrete benefits he has provided as president than they are in the PT's partisan story and the ideological cues it offers to voters".[21] The PT's growing electoral support base in the northeast of the country and among the poor was another effect of this trend. The shift away from Lula's traditional support base in the southeast of Brazil did not so much indicate an ideological change among the electorate but a pragmatic response to the impact of social programmes on a significant proportion of the electorate.[22] Critics on the left argued that government social policies promoted redistribution through the market[23] rather than radically changing the country's socio-economic structure. This argument echoed the view that the flagship social policies and minimum wage increases did not resolve structural inequalities but merely compensated for the PT's market-based solutions.[24] Nevertheless, Lula's moderate government programme made him and the party acceptable to larger numbers of voters, who would not have voted for a left-wing working-class candidate in the past, even if his traditional supporters felt that the party's principles had been betrayed in the process. Lula's popularity, sustained levels of economic growth, and the social benefits his government offered also explain why election victories occurred despite major corruption scandals and early setbacks in the implementation of social policies.

These debates indicate that even though trade unionists gained political access and absorbed the rationale of the government agenda to a large extent, the shifts in the PT's electoral and political agendas meant that trade union and workers' demands had become peripheral to the PT's government agenda and electoral success. With a government in power that many trade unionists considered relatively sympathetic to labour and social movement demands, the central political dilemma of the 1990s—how to best to oppose government policy that negatively affected workers' rights in a deteriorating economic context—became a balancing act between political participation and opposition. In this context, labour's political power increased significantly in terms of access to political influence while the union movement's power to mobilize people to exert political pressure was effectively diminished. Many in the CUT were reluctant to challenge the government agenda to avoid destabilizing a left-wing party in power and to maintain access to political decision-making, which the government could curtail if faced with radical demands. The debates about militant and moderate political strategies were also realigned according to these new dilemmas, as can be seen in the following examples from the early years of the first Lula government.

6.2 Reluctance to Protest or Co-Optation? The Early Years of the Lula Government, 2003–2004

The political shifts in the trade unions' position mirrored those of the PT, leading to an initial reluctance among many trade unionists to pressure the government through radical demands while also generating considerable debate, fragmentation, and protests. The examples of union political engagement outlined in this section show that the initial union response to the Lula government's agenda was cautious and that several union leaders had absorbed the PT's focus on macroeconomic stability. Based on the expectation that a PT government would introduce positive changes for workers, the party's union supporters focused on negotiating their political participation in policy reform proposals. The union movement's reluctance to press for radical change in the immediate aftermath of Lula's election should not have come as a surprise based on certain trends evident in labour mobilization in the 1990s. As discussed in Chap. 5, under pressure from the economic crisis and a hostile political environment, trade union action became more defensive during this period, and concentrated on protecting wages and jobs rather than the proactive demands of the late 1970s and 1980s.[25] In addition, instead of using the new political context as an opportunity to push a radical agenda, the CUT reached back to the argument that active government intervention could redress the negative social effects of government economic policy. This theme signalled the union movement's focus on the state as the central agent of development as well as a change in trade unionist debates, moving from fundamental socio-economic transformation to a reformist perspective, a development which had already become evident in the 1990s. Reflecting the PT's historical roots in social movements and experiments with participatory democracy in the 1980s and 1990s, the government initiated participatory forums at the federal level to discuss socio-economic reform proposals, including highly controversial topics such as social security and labour reforms. Union influence on these decision-making processes proved to be mixed, which was not only due to the controversial nature of the reforms but also to a lack of civil society mobilization pressurizing the government, indicating a shift in focus from mobilizing associational power to participation in the formal political arena.

Although these examples suggest that the union movement experienced a turn towards political moderation, the relationship between the PT and the unions proved to be more turbulent than is often assumed. As argued here, as soon as proposals such as the controversial social security and pension reforms began to threaten a core labour constituency—namely the public sector—internal conflicts re-emerged, even leading to active opposition to the government as well as significant splits within the CUT and the PT. Thus, the union movement's response to these reforms indicates that the CUT's majority agenda absorbed the PT's governmental and electoral logic to a large extent, also reflected in the incorporation of new unionists in key government posts. Although the controversial reforms were ultimately passed in 2003, they also signalled the articulation of a vocal left-wing section of the union movement, resulting in splits and fragmentation. Another trend seen in the mid-2000s was the distancing of grassroots union activists from the CUT leadership, with the former's demands often more radical than mainstream union leaders were prepared to support. Although labour conflicts stagnated until the late 2000s, trends in strike action during this period illustrate a growing willingness among public-sector unions to go on strike as well as illustrating significant conflicts between grassroots unions and the union leadership about whether to prioritize militant or moderate strategies.

The ongoing economic crisis inherited from the previous government characterized the early years of Lula's first administration, limiting both the unions' ability to mobilize under threat of unemployment and the government's room for manoeuvre. As economic growth dropped to 1.1% in 2003 and urban unemployment continued to grow,[26] civil society organizations began to criticize the lack of social progress as well as the discrepancy between the PT government's project and their own. Initially, protests during Lula's first term can be characterized as "supportive mobilization", used by social movements such as the MST to push the government to pursue the promised progressive policies.[27] Union strategies first focused on criticizing what they saw as the government's conservative macroeconomic agenda. They did not necessarily view the government's economic policy agenda as Lula's political decision but rather saw it as derived from the PT having to accommodate conservative interests in the government coalition. The various national union organizations shared this view and the joint unions proposed a "Pauta do Crescimento" (Platform for Growth) document to the government in September 2003, focused on an anti-cyclical development policy supported by government spending and job creation.[28]

In July 2004, between 80 and 100 unionists demonstrated outside the Ministério da Fazenda against the government's economic policies. While tiny in number, the protest's focus and demands exemplified the early years after Lula's election, appearing to accept the fundamental constraints but demanding active state involvement. According to João Osório da Silva, president of the CUT in the Distrito Federal, "we understand that the government has achieved some positive points in terms of economic recovery but we want this to accelerate," calling for more government investment in job creation. Reflecting Brazil's successful derailment of the Free Trade Area of the Americas (FTAA) negotiations in 2005, the protestors underlined their demands by burning a US flag.[29] The initial response to the reality of the PT in power was therefore cautious, showing again that many trade unionists had absorbed the logic of preserving macroeconomic stability to avoid political destabilization, concentrating instead on promoting policies focused on an active government role[30] in reversing the economic crisis, which included active civil society participation in government decisions.

Trade union participation in national decision-making forums illustrates that this form of political participation was limited in scope and impact.[31] The topics discussed in these forums heightened internal disagreements, which made it harder to organize concerted mobilization to pressurize the government to support a joint labour agenda. Consequently, rather than leading to renewed labour mobilization, the combination of potential influence and the spectre of what would happen if protests destabilized a PT government contributed to political moderation. The PT's approach to policy reform focused on organizing discussions in national forums and consultations with key stakeholders to develop policy proposals and strengthen the support base for controversial changes. At a national level, the first Lula government encouraged civil society participation in national policy-making, increasing the number of participatory opportunities at a federal level.[32] Querying the participatory nature of these forums, however, a 2005 report by the Brazilian NGO IBASE[33] pointed out that potential discussion topics were often restricted and that only selected groups could take part, "favouring entrepreneurs, bankers and trade unionists".[34] As a result, the report called the new dynamics of government-civil society relations the "entrapment of citizenship", presenting a semblance of deepened participation without having substantive influence. More generally, this phrase also pointed towards the declining prominence of citizen initiatives under the PT, including the famous municipal-level participatory budgeting processes. The report's damning conclusion was that active civil society involvement had effectively been brought to a standstill while social movements faced the dilemma of dealing with "a government with a strong popular base, elected with a mandate to reinvent politics",[35] which nevertheless continued to prioritize macroeconomic stability.[36] Although Brazil's participatory initiatives offered opportunities "for the poor in Brazil to claim public goods"[37] and contributed to the redistribution of political authority,[38] the outcomes and the degree to which citizens gained a meaningful say in policy-making at a local and federal level remained limited.

The participatory structures initiated by the Lula government largely aligned with the CUT's agenda concerning active state intervention in socio-economic development with civil society participation in the decision-making process. The tripartite set-up also mirrored the *cutistas*' growing interest since the mid-1990s in conducting negotiations with the government and business actors about wider policy themes, such as social, labour, and economic policy. Nevertheless, while the PT government's participatory initiatives provided access to political influence, their agenda and structure limited the possibility for those fundamental changes desired by civil society. To signal its commitment to civil society participation in government policy, one of the government's first initiatives was the Conselho de Desenvolvimento Econômico e Social (Socio-Economic Development Council, CDES) in May 2003. The CDES was set up as a "broadly corporatist"[39] organization with government, labour, and business representatives as well as some civil society members. Business representatives were over-represented, reflecting the PT's focus on economic development as the government's priority.[40] The council's purpose was to advise the government on social policy reform, such as developing proposals for the highly controversial social security and pension reforms,[41] both discussed below. Critics viewed the initiative not as a forum for political participation but as "devoid of any real participatory features", leading to the co-optation of labour and social movements without a transformation of the much-criticized corporatist framework.[42]

Participants in the policy forums also recognized the shortcomings of these participatory structures as they were constrained not only by the difficult economic context but also by the government's limited commitment to meaningful civil society participation. Based on her experiences as a CDES member between 2003 and 2006, Sonia Fleury commented that the economic context and the government's macroeconomic policies restricted the possibilities for ambitious policy change, a situation reinforced by the over-representation of business in the council, which contributed to a lack of recognition of civil society demands. Furthermore, she argued that the council answered to the executive, which meant that the CDES agenda was dominated by the government while bypassing Congressional oversight.[43] Social movement participants were also unhappy with the consensus approach taken in the council, which in their view watered down the social agenda.[44] Together with social movements such as the MST, the CUT set up the Coordenação dos Movimentos Sociais (Social Movement Coordination, CMS) to develop proposals from a social movement perspective in August 2003.[45] This early experience with participatory policy-making indicates that although the government committed itself to widening political participation, the actual process was more controlled and restricted than the civil society representatives had hoped, including the trade unions. Despite this dissatisfaction, protests against the perceived lack of progress continued to be limited as trade union perspectives at the time continued to chime with the government's macroeconomic priorities.

One of the areas where the tensions between widening political participation and socio-economic reforms manifested themselves was in the government's proposal to reform social security and pensions, which affected a significant proportion of the CUT membership. The growing dissatisfaction with the lack of progressive change under the Lula government revealed severe splits within the union movement at three different levels: between groups who fundamentally disagreed about the desirability of the proposed social reforms; between public- and private-sector unions[46]; and between those groups within the union movement who wanted to push the government towards radical reforms and those who did not want to rock the boat in exchange for political influence. The single most controversial reform during this period was the plan to adjust Brazil's social security and pension systems, which affected public sector workers in particular while illustrating the different political approaches that emerged in the union movement at this moment in time. Following on from Cardoso's reforms, the Lula government proposed to cap retirement benefits while increasing the minimum age and years of service requirements to draw a pension and taxing public sector pension benefits by 11%.[47] In a debate that echoed the conflicts about privatization in the 1990s discussed in Chap. 5, these reforms resulted in significant splits between private- and public-sector unions, with the latter expressing their opposition in a politically radical manner.

The public-sector unions were vehemently opposed to the reforms, viewing it as the government's deliberate decision to erode their rights and entitlements,[48] while they attempted to escalate demonstrations and strike action to force the government to withdraw the proposals.[49] Yet the CUT's national leadership opposed the strikes and declared that they would be negotiating aspects of the proposal instead of rejecting it.[50] When the public-sector unions threatened to set up an alternative central union organization to represent their interests, the CUT's president, Luiz Marinho, argued that if the unions simply opposed the reforms, their demands would fall on deaf ears, so negotiation was essential in his view.[51] Although the proposal passed in Congress, the PT's congressional representation also experienced divisions as the party expelled three deputies and one senator for voting against the proposal; they subsequently set up a party with a political agenda explicitly to the left of the PT, the Partido Socialismo e Liberdade (PSOL). This debate reveals an unresolved conflict about the extent to which unions should actively oppose government policy if it hurt workers' interests. Despite the apparent alignment between trade unions and the PT, this example illustrates that in cases where unions perceived government policy as directly hurting workers' interests—the CUT's large and powerful public-sector constituency in this case—the close union-party relationship was far from representative of the union movement as a whole.

In contrast, the campaign to increase the minimum wage was an area in which union demands and the government agenda coincided more explicitly. The government's minimum wage policy not only represented a key labour demand for wage improvements but also a cornerstone of the government's macroeconomic policy, which was to expand domestic consumption as a source of economic growth. As a result of this policy, the real minimum wage increased significantly in 2005 and 2006 at levels well above inflation. Even when economic growth declined from 2009, the real minimum wage continued to increase, in line with inflation as well as economic growth, while the government's social programmes magnified its social impact.[52] We can in fact consider the minimum wage campaign as one of the most successful labour campaigns waged after 2003 because the government agreed to regular minimum wage increases which had a real effect on people's incomes. Union campaigners demanded that the minimum wage should be adjusted to inflation and economic growth, a proposal which the unions had wanted to include in the 1988 Constitution but which never materialized.[53] The Lula government initially did not meet its promise of a new minimum wage policy "despite considerable pressure" from the unions[54] but proceeded to establish a quadripartite commission, including government, business, union, and pensioner representatives, to discuss the minimum wage.[55] In 2007 the campaign resulted in a policy guaranteeing the annual adjustment until 2023 of the minimum wage according to the previous year's inflation and economic growth.[56] The significance of the minimum wage campaign reflected the new unionism's long-lasting legacy of successful wage claims since the late 1970s, as well as their long-standing moral argument that economic growth should be translated into wage increases and compensate for inflation. The minimum wage campaign also exemplified new forms of labour mobilization to achieve policy changes in a context in which the government opened up channels for political participation.

The minimum wage increases did not just result from coinciding interests between the government and the union movement, they also involved labour mobilization to put pressure on the government to keep to its commitments. In 2004, the national union organizations launched a joint minimum wage campaign, organizing three marches in Brasília in 2004, 2005, and 2006. The marches were symbolic in that the unions aimed to get the government to commit to a policy change that was already likely to happen, rather than using mass mobilization as leverage for policy change.[57] Furthermore, union arguments consciously replicated the government's macroeconomic argument that a higher minimum wage would produce economic growth by increasing purchasing power,[58] underlining the extent to which leading unionists had absorbed the PT's governmental logic. For example, Luiz Cláudio Marcolino, president of the powerful Bankworkers' Union in São Paulo argued that the new minimum wage policy was attractive because it did not require more government spending and simultaneously increased income tax revenues, which would help create more jobs and stimulate economic growth.[59] João Felício, then recently re-elected as CUT president, echoed this sentiment in 2005 with his rather technocratic point that a minimum wage policy would support "the immediate reduction of interest rates and reaching a primary budget surplus", which was necessary for economic growth, employment, social and infrastructural investments.[60] He also pointed out that the new minimum wage policy "was only possible under the Lula government, as before workers were not even heard [by the government]".[61] The CUT's arguments in favour of the minimum wage policy reflected the generally cautious approach of other civil society organizations to the PT, showing that many union leaders came to share or had absorbed the government's argument about the need for macroeconomic stability, viewing compromises as a trade-off for access to decision-making, such as the minimum wage council. However, these examples of union participation in socio-economic policy-making illustrate that the union movement's ability to influence the government was mixed and restricted by macroeconomic considerations while the level of labour militancy continued to be low.

While on the surface it looked as if labour militancy stagnated after Lula's election, the second half of 2003 and early 2004 witnessed increased levels of dissatisfaction with the PT government and with the limitations of the new participatory channels as expressed in public-sector strikes (see Fig. 6.1) and protests against pension reforms. In light of the disillusionment with the discrepancy between the PT's radical past and the realities of governments, these trends indicate that the relationship between the PT, the unions, and social movements was more turbulent in the early years than often suggested in the literature. Although the stagnating levels of labour conflict evident in the 1990s continued under Lula, public-sector strikes began to intensify in this period, reflecting the growing public sector[62] and resulting in protests against the reforms and budget cuts as well as the expectation that the government would be more receptive to public-sector union demands. Private-sector strikes had dominated the landscape of labour conflict in Brazil since the late 1970s but in 2003 the public and state-owned sectors overtook the number of those in the private sector, with 51% of strikes taking place in the public sector in 2003 and 61% in 2004 combined.[63] Even if the total number of strikes remained low at

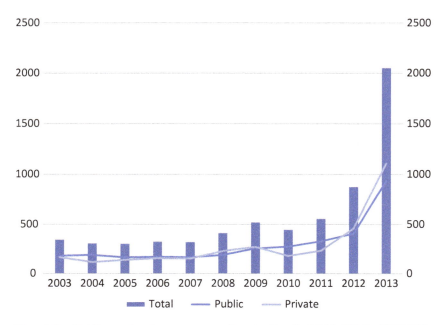

Fig. 6.1 Public- and private-sector strikes in Brazil, 2004–2013. (DIEESE, "Balanço das greves em 2013," *Estudos e Pesquisas* 79 (December 2015), 42)

340 in 2003 and 2004, public-sector strikes became larger and longer as the number of workdays lost to strikes in both the public and the private sector increased after 2003.[64] These trends meant that even if the total number of strikes stagnated, labour conflicts became harder to resolve and more politicized, particularly in the public sector.[65] These trends also indicate the growing space for public-sector unions and left-wing voices to assert their dissatisfaction with the CUT's stance towards government policy.

These internal conflicts also affected the relationship between the CUT and its affiliated unions, signalling the distancing of the national leadership from grassroots unionists given the latter's willingness to contest the focus on political stability. For example, in September 2004 bankworkers went on strike for 30 days, after which the CUT-affiliated National Bankworkers' Confederation (Confederação Nacional dos Bancários, CNB) negotiated a national wage agreement. Nevertheless, grassroots union meetings ended up rejecting the agreement, accusing the CNB of betraying them and pandering to the government's macroeconomic goals while neutralizing union militancy. The CNB in turn accused the opposition groups of protesting without an alternative proposal and ignoring the government's dialogue with social movements.[66] This conflict illustrates growing disagreements within the union movement about the extent to which it should support the Lula government as well as the willingness of grassroots opposition groups to challenge their leadership.

In sum, the first two years of the Lula administration saw the union movement adopt a cautious approach, informed by a reluctance to destabilize a government led by their political allies and a desire to make use of new channels of political influence. Several factors led to political moderation among trade unions in this period, including leading CUT unionists mirroring the government's argument about macroeconomic stability as a precondition for socio-economic reforms, as evidenced by the minimum wage campaign. Maintaining access to decision-making processes through participation in policy forums was another consideration. Set up to build a broad consensus among key stakeholders regarding controversial policy reforms such as social security and pensions, the close union-party relations, the consensus approach, and the prospect of being able to influence major policy areas all had a moderating influence. The union movement's political power and union-PT relations became a key factor in labour political mobilization strategies and militant action. Nevertheless, the assumption that the union movement followed a trajectory of political moderation does not tell the full story as disagreements about the virtues of political participation based on government terms and union-party links emerged. The tendency not to want to upset the political apple cart and the arguments about macroeconomic stability did not resonate with all trade unionists, particularly as it became clear that participation yielded mixed and limited results. The internal conflicts that emerged in this period pointed both to historical priorities, such as labour reforms and wage demands, and to the new challenge of waging effective opposition under a government that was ostensibly sympathetic to the labour agenda.

6.3 Growing Discontent: Conflicts About Labour and Social Reform, 2005–2008

In the second half of Lula's first administration, the debate about labour reform further sharpened disagreements concerning political strategies. Between 2005 and 2008 the combination of economic recovery, proposals for labour reforms, and the worsening corruption crisis all affected the union movement's political strategies. Bearing this in mind, this section illustrates three trends in labour politics under the Lula government that contributed to weakening the union movement's political bargaining position despite a more positive economic context: the growing dilemma of opposition or collaboration with the government; the fragmentation created by political divisions within the union movement; and the increasing distance between union leaders and grassroots activists. Although the tendency towards political moderation evident in the early years of the first PT-led government continued, these dilemmas led to dissatisfaction with the lack of progress. Internal conflicts also became more visible, particularly in the case of social security and labour reforms, leading to mobilization against government proposals. These divisions resulted in strategic immobilization, magnifying the dilemma of the union movement's political power, which translated into access to political decision-making on the one hand, and a lack of progress regarding key labour demands on the other.

As economic growth returned on the basis of the diversification of Brazil's export portfolio and unemployment declined, militant labour action also continued to stagnate. Similar to 2003 and 2004, in the following two years, public-sector strikes continued to dominate the labour scene, while the most significant change was that the more positive economic outlook allowed unions to make progressive wage demands in 69% of strikes, moving away from a defensive position.[67] The question of new unionism's loyalty to the Lula government re-emerged after the *mensalão* corruption scandals surfaced in 2005. The scandal involved vote-buying—on a monthly basis, which explains the term *mensalão* ("big monthly payment")—to ensure majorities for the government's legislative proposals. Although Lula was never directly accused in the *mensalão* investigations, several figures close to the party leadership and senior trade unionists had to resign. The corruption scandals not only affected the PT's reputation as a party with "clean" politics[68] but also illustrated that the party's problems spilled over to its union allies when it became clear that several union leaders were also involved in corruption. The lack of mass protests against the government was a major factor in explaining why the corruption scandals never seemed to touch Lula[69]; however, civil society organizations were also reluctant to mobilize in support of Lula given the scale of the corruption.[70] Both the PT-supporting unions and social movements were torn between their rejection of corruption, the knowledge that several key union figures had been involved, and the realization that the alternative could be much worse if Lula lost the elections. In this challenging political context, the government initiated a debate about reforming the country's corporatist labour and trade union legislation.

The debate about union reform became highly divisive, revealing irreconcilable differences between various groups within the union movement regarding the extent to which corporatism should be reformed, while highlighting strains in the relationship between trade unionists and the PT. As discussed in Chap. 4, labour reform had been a key agenda point for the new unionist movement since the late 1970s. In particular, the new unionists challenged state intervention in trade unions and restrictions on collective bargaining, proposing workplace representation and voluntary union membership instead. Under the PT-led government, the expectations of substantive reforms were high, particularly due to Lula's own radical rejection of corporatism in the late 1970s and 1980s. Up until the mid-2000s, little progress had been made in terms of abolishing corporatism, while previous reforms had focused primarily on liberalizing the labour market.[71] The new unionists initially opposed these reforms but in the adverse context of the 1990s, many unions had already started to negotiate flexible working hours, contracts and performance-related pay in order to avoid job and wage losses.[72] Because a wholesale reform of corporatism seemed out of reach given the disagreements within the union movement itself, the CUT proposed improving individual unions' representative function by making union membership voluntary as well as breaking up the union monopoly in order to replace the existing corporatist fragmentation along occupational lines.[73] These proposals continued to inform the CUT's majority position in the labour reform debate under Lula, reflecting the acceptance in practice of flexible labour relations and collective bargaining, while proposing the abolition of corporatist regulation of trade unions.

Targeting corporatist union legislation and the state-labour relationship, the reform agenda under the Lula government tackled issues such as collective bargaining, the legal position of unions, and the legalization of central union organizations. In fact, the proposals focused primarily on the regulation of unions rather than labour rights, which Lula justified by arguing that unions had to be strengthened first before engaging in negotiations about workers' rights.[74] The government's plan was to strengthen the support for the proposed reforms by including core actors in the consultation process and in the development of the legislative proposals. Similar to the social security reforms, the government first tasked the key stakeholders with debating and developing the proposals in the tripartite Fórum Nacional de Trabalho (National Labour Forum, FNT), created in 2003. The debates not only took place at a federal level but also in state-level consultations and debates, involving around 30,000 participants[75] in the hope that this would increase the legitimacy of what would prove to be a highly controversial process. Although the FNT's purpose was to reform corporatism, the forum's set-up echoed corporatist structures, while union representatives were also divided in their views regarding the desirability of radical reforms. The national-level forum counted 600 government, business, and union representatives; the latter represented eight different central union organizations, including the CUT and Força Sindical. Because union representatives were appointed by the central union organizations, several important groups were marginalized in the debate, particularly teachers, rural workers, and the public sector, with 70% of the FNT union members working in the industrial sector and services.[76] Another concern among the non-*cutistas* was that many CUT representatives had close relations with the PT while several government representatives had been associated with the CUT in the past—including the former CUT presidents Luiz Marinho, Jair Meneguelli, and Vicentinho—contributing to suspicions among other union representatives that the FNT privileged the government agenda.[77] Despite the efforts to widen the discussions about labour reform, the unions ended up largely divided, reflecting both widespread support for state corporatism as well as attempts to increase union autonomy and pluralism.

Apart from questions about how representative the FNT was in terms of Brazil's highly diverse labour market, the debates revealed more divisions than agreements about the nature and extent of the reforms. During the discussions, the dividing lines among the union representatives soon began to materialize, resulting in divergences between the central union organizations as well as within the CUT. The latter's leadership was close to the government, as evident in statements by prominent new unionists repeating the government's proposals. Their suggestions focused on union autonomy and the freedom to organize: particularly the abolition of the compulsory union tax, which was to be replaced by a worker's contribution to the union that represented him or her in collective bargaining; the right to workplace representation; as well as abolishing the rule that only one union could represent a particular category of workers per region (the end of *unicidade sindical*).[78] According to these proposals, the reforms would involve removing geographical and sectoral restrictions on collective bargaining, while forcing unions to represent their membership because their financial resources would become linked to the collective bargaining process.

With reference to the new unionist argument from the 1970s and 1980s that democracy started in the workplace, the CUT leadership presented these demands as the final step in the democratization process, a view echoed by the FNT's president, the PT's Ricardo Berzoini.[79] However, a significant segment of the union representatives vehemently disagreed with these proposals, particularly the abolition of the *unicidade sindical* principle and the union tax, a position that was already evident in the labour reform debates in the 1980s. A major proportion of Brazilian trade unionists continued to support corporatist control because it guaranteed a union's existence and provided financial resources through the union tax, whether they actively represented their members or not. Dissatisfied with the FNT, a coalition of confederations which supported maintaining corporatist unionism set up an alternative discussion forum, the Fórum Sindical dos Trabalhadores (Union Labour Forum, FST) to organize protests against the government's proposals and push for an alternative proposal in Congress.[80] The employers represented in the FNT shared many of the FST's concerns, thereby effectively supporting the continuation of corporatist labour relations, and rejecting the right to workplace union representation.[81] Finally, the government position also faced opposition in Congress from deputies sympathetic to official unionism and business interests respectively. Despite the disagreements, the FNT managed to send a joint proposal for discussion to Congress in March 2005, just weeks before the *mensalão* scandal broke out.

The proposal presented to Congress had incorporated several core new unionist demands, including the abolition of the union tax over three years, replaced by a collective bargaining fee. The proposed reforms also opened up the possibility of multiple unions representing a particular category of workers, with each union required to have a membership of at least 20% of the workforce in a given occupational category. Furthermore, a new Conselho Nacional de Relações de Trabalho (National Labour Relations Council, CNRT) would redefine the 1940s corporatist professional categories still used to organize unions and oversee their representativeness.[82] In the midst of the corruption scandals and Lula's re-election campaign, the union reforms fell by the wayside, with several of the proposal's elements introduced in a piecemeal fashion over the next few years. For example, the CNRT was set up by presidential decree in 2006 but never got off the ground, while central union organizations, whose position was already recognized in practice through their participation in several national forums, were finally legalized in 2010. In fact, the labour reforms primarily benefitted the central union organizations, whose existence was finally legalized, but did not necessarily reduce state control or lead to more union autonomy *vis-à-vis* the state.

The dilemma between autonomy and participation in a climate marred by political instability played out both within the CUT and in the union movement as a whole. Reflecting sharp disagreements about union reforms, critics inside and outside the CUT argued that the organization had lost its autonomy in relation to the PT government. In 2005 and 2006, the internal disagreements about labour reforms and the CUT's relationship with the government exploded. At the CUT's 11th national plenary in May 2005, left-wing groups, such as the Corrente Sindical Classista (Class-based Union Movement, CSC), rejected the FNT proposal as "confused and contradictory" and as a reversal in the struggle for workers' rights.[83] Others argued that negotiating progress in workers' rights without pressurizing the government through protests was a fallacy, rejecting the FNT's compromises and arguing CUT should step up mobilizations to achieve its real agenda.[84] In the end, the plenary voted in favour of a set of minimum principles regarding union reforms[85] but the CUT's left-wing groups, who felt defeated and marginalized in the debate, began to reconsider their position.[86]

These divisions continued the following year at the CUT's national congress, leading to conflicts among left-wing and moderate groups as well as disagreements within the majority Articulação group regarding unions' autonomy in light of Lula's re-election campaign and the fractious outcome of the labour reform debate. Referring directly to the uneasy relationship between political influence and the power to mobilize, left-wing groups such as CSC argued that the CUT had not found a way to "preserve its autonomy when defending workers' concerns. In the new political reality, the CUT has not always applied the principle of union autonomy correctly, often limiting itself to dialogue with the government and underestimating the power of mobilization".[87] Within Articulação, two candidates competed for the CUT presidency: the incumbent João Felício, a representative of the powerful teachers' unions who favoured more autonomy, and Arthur Henrique, a unionist from the electricity sector, and considered to be closer to the government.[88] In the end, Arthur Henrique was elected as president and the CUT voted to support Lula in his re-election campaign. This episode was not only marked by severe disagreements and the eventual victory of the government-supporting camp within the CUT, but it also signalled the distance between the national union leadership and grassroots activists, and the increasing fragmentation of the unions given the rise of competing organizations.

The labour reform process left many unionists dissatisfied with the CUT and the limitations of the government's participatory decision-making process, underlining the divisions the close union-party-union relations created and the dilemmas of opposition under the PT. As a result, alternative central union organizations began to emerge when the Ministry of Labour renegotiated the recognition criteria for national union organizations in 2007.[89] Three organizations were founded by former CUT supporters to occupy a space to the left of the CUT leadership and were associated with left-wing parties that struggled to position themselves within the PT-dominated CUT.[90] The Corrente Sindical Classista left the CUT and set up the Central dos Trabalhadores e Trabalhadoras do Brasil (Brazilian Workers' Central, CTB, affiliated with the PCdoB); disgruntled public-sector unionists set up CONLUTAS (Coordenação Nacional de Lutas, National Struggle Coordination—affiliated with the Trotskyist PSTU); and those who opposed the 2003 social security reforms set up Intersindical (affiliated with the PSOL).[91] Although these alternative union organizations never reached either the size or political profile of the CUT and Força Sindical, they began to position themselves as a left-wing alternative that would represent groups such as public-sector workers while less reluctant to mobilize against the government.[92]

Paradoxically, the long-awaited legal recognition of central union organizations confirmed the distancing between the national leadership and the affiliated unions, as the labour reform proposals "strengthened the top union leaderships, transferring negotiations to the union centrals and therefore restricting the activities of unions and workplace assemblies".[93] Another indication of the growing divisions was the willingness of public-sector workers to go on strike in this period, with large and lengthy strikes in the oil sector, banking, the civil service, teachers and federal universities between 2005 and 2008. This period saw an increase in labour protests with a political agenda, for example, protests against privatization in Petrobras and against corruption in the postal service.[94] As these labour conflicts spread to strategic economic sectors—such as energy, construction, and infrastructure—they created a new surge in labour militancy from 2009 onwards, a less well-recognized aspect of the mass discontent that emerged in 2013.

In sum, although access to political influence had become a real opportunity through the participatory forums with prominent unionists taking up government posts, the CUT leadership faced a trade-off between capitalizing on this close relationship and voicing opposition to the PT; the latter could involve workers losing political influence by destabilizing the government during politically turbulent episodes. However, despite their unprecedented political access, union campaigns had relatively little impact on policy outcomes under the PT-led governments. Nevertheless, these sharp disagreements also created spaces for critical voices, which questioned the PT's socio-economic agenda and, in the case of the CUT, the organization's close relations with the government. Combined with politically motivated splits within the unions, the trends discussed in this section indicate a growing distance between the national leadership and rank-and-file unionists, particularly in the public sector, with the latter increasingly prepared to link strike action to mobilizations against government policy. The developments in this period therefore indicate that the assumptions that the union movement had absorbed the logic of political power and moderated its strategies should be revised by paying attention to internal conflicts, the latter having helped revitalize labour militancy in the 2010s. These trends also signalled increased dissatisfaction, polarization, and a heightening of grievances associated with the government's development agenda and spending priorities, as evidenced by the resurgence of labour militancy from 2009 onwards, several years ahead of the 2013 protests.

6.4 Resurgence of Protest, Revival of the Labour Movement, 2009–2016

In June and July 2013, hundreds of thousands of Brazilians took to the streets, initially to protest against a planned increase of public transport prices but the protests soon morphed into a critique of government spending priorities, the quality of public services, and corruption levels. To start with, the major newspapers did not cover the demonstrations but when the protestors experienced severe police repression, demonstrators began to share information, photos, and videos on social media. Because the protests coincided with the Copa das Confederações football tournament, the demonstrations soon became international news as people carried banners against government spending on the World Cup, while simultaneously decrying stadium construction working conditions. The 2013 protests united people who were not necessarily affiliated with traditional political parties or civil society organizations,[95] particularly exemplified by the leading role of the Movimento Passe Livre (Free Fare Movement, or MPL). Strong sentiments against traditional political institutions such as political parties were also evident: protestors carried banners with slogans such as "O povo unido não precisa de Partido" (The people united do not need parties) and "Nem direita nem esquerda, somos Brasil!" (Neither right nor left, we are Brazil!). In 2015, the protests turned against the government with a particular focus on corruption, coinciding with the "Lava Jato" ("car wash") corruption investigation which implicated many top politicians.[96] Eventually, increasing social and political pressure on the government culminated in Dilma Rousseff's impeachment in August 2016. The demonstrations created new dilemmas for trade unions, including how to respond to and participate in the protest movements as well as how to rethink their relationship with the PT as the government slid into an accelerating crisis.

The country had not seen this scale of protests since the 1980s (the Diretas Já campaign) and 1992 (the mass protests for Collor's impeachment), so they came as a surprise to many observers. However, the roots of the widespread dissatisfaction that provoked these demonstrations can be found in the socio-economic and political developments of the 1990s and 2000s. The unprecedented social mobility Brazilians experienced in the 2000s as a result of economic expansion and government social policies, together with raised expectations of what the government could achieve in a deteriorating economic context, goes some way towards explaining the intensity of the protesters' disillusionment.[97] Mattos views the June 2013 protests as a culmination of the agendas that social movements and unions had promoted for years but which had become weakened and fragmented under the PT-led governments, which in his view, helps account for why the established social movements did not play a major role in the demonstrations.[98] Anger about corruption was another factor which mobilized hundreds of thousands of people against the government in 2015 and 2016. The combination of corruption scandals that reached ever closer to the PT leadership, anger about government spending priorities given the context of decelerating economic growth, and the upcoming presidential elections in 2014 proved to be an explosive mix, leading to massive protests with participants drawn from across the political spectrum.

One of the key characteristics of the mass demonstrations was their diverse demands, strategies, and political views, while trade unions, social movements, and PT supporters initially remained at the margins. Indeed, Tatagiba argues that during the mass demonstrations between 2013 and 2016, protesters' demands ranged from increasing education and health spending, to the implementation of specific social policies, political reforms, tackling police violence and corruption, and finally calls for Dilma

Rousseff's impeachment.[99] The protests were also heterogeneous in terms of the organizations involved and their strategies, ranging from the MPL's horizontal structures to confrontational tactics employed by anarchist-inspired "black bloc" groups. Many protestors criticized political parties and politicians in general while their political views spanned the entire political spectrum, from demands for socially progressive policies to rallying cries for political conservatism. In 2014, the protests became more explicitly conservative and turned against the PT-led government, with protestors calling for Dilma's impeachment and the imprisonment of leading PT figures for corruption, including Lula. New organizations with a right-wing libertarian orientation, such as the Movimento Brasil Livre (Free Brazil Movement, MBL) and Movimento Vem Pra Rua (Come to the Streets Movement, MVR) began to mobilize demonstrators against the government. While most demonstrators did not identify themselves as party political, the protests in 2015 and 2016 split more directly along electoral lines, with pro-impeachment demonstrations dominated by PSDB supporters and counter-demonstrations by PT voters.[100] In the post-2013 context of escalating protests and despite its long history of being at the forefront of political change, the trade union movement was not a major protagonist. Indeed, reports emerged of hostile reactions to protestors with a visible partisan or CUT affiliation,[101] underlining the challenge for groups associated with the PT to tap into the mass discontent. Meanwhile in 2015 and 2016, anti-government forces began to dominate the debate, organizing demonstrations with hundreds of thousands of participants across the country, leaving the CUT and other government supporters with the much harder task of mobilizing in favour of the status quo.

Several trends with roots in recent labour history contributed to the union movement's struggle to respond adequately to the growing political polarization and the widespread dissatisfaction evident in the demonstrations. The union movement's mobilizational power had weakened considerably during the 1990s and 2000s, with union campaigns focusing primarily on negotiating with the government and "defensive struggle[s] against the withdrawal of rights and the politics of austerity".[102] The CUT's close relationship with the PT, based on the idea that a PT-led government was the least-worst option, was a major factor limiting union participation in the protests. Meanwhile, Dilma Rousseff's relationship with the unions and social movements was not as close as Lula's,[103] diminishing the CUT's political access to the government and heightening internal frustrations with the political process. The protests thereby underlined the political differences among various groups within the union movement, focusing once again on the extent to which union action should support or challenge the government.

The key political paradox for the unions in this context was to maintain the union-party relationship as a source of power in the face of widespread popular scepticism about the country's political culture while also mobilizing the public when the demonstrations turned against the unions' political ally. A general strike organized jointly by Brazil's central union organizations in July 2013 happened somewhat late in the day, the first such event since 1996. The general strikes of the 1980s and 1990s were iconic protests against government austerity policies, underlining the union movement's ability to mobilize large numbers across Brazil. In turn, the lack of general strikes from the mid-1990s onwards symbolized the unions' political crisis, meaning that a return to large-scale strikes marked a turning point in the union movement's involvement in the protest waves. In March 2015, however, as the mass protests became explicitly anti-government and anti-PT in character in the context of the deepening Petrobras corruption scandals, the CUT organized somewhat lacklustre demonstrations to support the elected government and the petroleum company, despite the growing public outrage. According to left-wing critics, these protests, which were a lot smaller than the anti-government protests, highlighted the CUT's "governmental" and conciliatory character. A declaration of the Corrente Sindical Classista presented during a meeting of the CUT's national executive urged the organization to use the recent wave of strikes and the economic downturn as an opportunity to protest against the government, as it was "impossible to derail an austerity policy by negotiating it"[104] with the government. As opposition forces began to push for Dilma's impeachment, the central union organizations and social movements—with the MST and MTST (Movimento dos Trabalhadores Sem Teto, Homeless Workers' Movement) at the forefront—began organizing demonstrations against what they saw as a threat to democracy, mobilizations that grew as impeachment became more likely. These examples suggest that the June demonstrations not only highlighted the political dilemmas of the union movement but eventually re-invigorated its ability to mobilize people, despite the many factors that had restricted organized labour's political impact since the mid-1990s.

The struggle between militant and moderate strategies also manifested itself in a new wave of labour militancy, amplifying the internal conflicts and emerging trends in labour mobilization discussed in the previous sections. Less well-known than the mass demonstrations between 2013 and 2016, the sharp increases in labour mobilization that took place after 2009 preceded the more visible political polarization evident in the mass protests. Grassroots unionists and (often non-unionized) workers showed an unprecedented willingness to go on strike, even if the union leadership did not agree with their actions. Labour conflicts, strikes, and protests had already started to increase several years before the mass demonstrations, indicating workers' dissatisfaction with the impact of government policies, as evident in protests focused on large development projects, and the lack of redistribution in what was a growing economy up to 2009. Between 2003 and 2007, public sector workers had been more willing to engage in militant union action compared to the private sector; however, this dynamic began to change in 2011, when the number of private-sector strikes increased. Whereas private-sector strikes were previously concentrated in the southeast, particularly in the São Paulo industrial sector, major strikes emerged in other parts of the country, spreading to sectors not traditionally known for labour militancy,[105] particularly in the construction sector.

Paradoxically, these labour conflicts arose in a context of economic growth and government investment in strategic economic sectors, reflecting workers' ability to mobilize their structural power. When economic growth began to slow down in 2009, this growing dissatisfaction among workers became evident in the steadily increasing number of strikes (see Fig. 6.1) which focused on flagship government projects in strategic sectors such as infrastructure, construction, and energy. Many of the labour conflicts between 2011 and 2016 were directly associated with Brazil's major development projects as part of the Planos de Aceleração do Crescimento (Growth Acceleration Plans, or PAC), focusing not only on the wage increases that dominated the union agenda in the 2000s, but also on working conditions, food, and medical assistance.[106] Protests and strikes associated with resource extraction, hydro-electricity, and large infrastructural projects had already risen in 2009 and spiked in 2013, when the number of strikes quintupled compared to the mid-2000s.[107] Major strikes and protests took place at four hydro-electric dam construction sites in Amazonian states as well as oil refineries and port construction projects in the northeast of the country. For example, between January 2011 and April 2012, DIEESE counted 20 mobilizations and strikes directly focused on football stadiums, with workers' demands concentrated on wages and working conditions. In 2011, a total of 310,000 workers went on strike in the northeastern cities of Salvador, Fortaleza, and São Luis to protest against working conditions in the construction industry, as 59,000 workers held a 29-day strike in Fortaleza in 2012 focusing on working conditions in the World Cup stadiums.[108] The same year, workers went on strike at the Abreu e Lima oil refinery in Pernambuco, the Jirau hydro-electric complex in Rondônia, the Teles Pires hydro-electric dam in Mato Grosso, and at various construction works in Bahia.[109] These episodes highlight that well before the 2013 mass demonstrations workers were willing to contest the negative consequences of the country's economic success,[110] as the protestors contested the government's use of mega-events such as the 2014 World Cup and the 2016 Olympics to promote Brazil's image as a modern economy and society.[111] Another distinctive feature of these labour conflicts was that they took place in sectors and regions where unions were often weak or co-opted, such as construction and infrastructure, or the public sector, where unions were well-organized and left-wing. These trends illustrate that Brazil's labour politics has continued to be more politically diverse than suggested by arguments about the inevitable decline of labour.

To summarize, the upsurge in the number of strikes signalled a new wave of labour militancy after years of relative stagnation and marked a response to the discrepancy between economic growth and working conditions. Although the number and intensity of these labour protests increased in sectors where workers were traditionally well-organized—such as in the industrial southeast—they also mobilized workers who were not necessarily unionized or who felt that their union did not represent their interests and demands. Because these strikes took place in key economic sectors and symbolically important sites, the striking workers managed to mobilize their structural power, often without relying on, or while actively rejecting, existing union structures. In several significant cases, workers' concerns aligned with the protests against public transport fare increases in highly unionized and politicized sectors, such as public transport and education, showing that at a grassroots level trade unionists' interests and strategies were connected to the mass protests. However, the developments in labour militancy in the 2010s also underlined that central union organizations such as the CUT had not managed to position themselves at the forefront of these mobilizations. Indeed, party and union activists had become the political establishment under the PT-led government, which many demonstrators considered a central feature of Brazil's political problems, rather than the union movement's symbolically powerful legacy of political opposition to the dictatorship.

6.5 Conclusion

Faced with the prospect that Dilma would be impeached and replaced by a president who was much less sympathetic to their demands, left-wing parties, movements, and protestors began protesting against impeachment, coalescing around the principle that the president's electoral mandate had to be respected.[112] Although these protests gave the left a new focus, the demonstrations in favour of the president and her democratic mandate proved insufficient to prevent her Senate impeachment in August 2016. Rousseff's fall from power marked a decade of increasing political polarization, leading to a political crisis at the heart of Brazilian political culture, which in turn was reflected in a similar political crisis for the union movement. This chapter has traced the role of labour politics in terms of these competing forces, arguing that the dynamics of labour militancy and moderation were a significant but mostly unrecognized aspect of the political polarization process. As a result of these conflicting developments, the labour landscape as it evolved in the 2000s and 2010s was much more complex than suggested by arguments about an inevitable road to decline and political moderation. Instead, this chapter's focus on the conflicts created by the new political scenario shows that while the pull towards political moderation was strong, the forces driving labour militancy continued to exist. With Lula's election to the presidency, union-party relations changed significantly, exerting a moderating influence on organized labour. Significant sectors of the union movement became incorporated in the government after 2003 as many unionists took on ministerial posts and participated in consultative forums, turning organized labour into a strategic political actor within the government. Mobilizing their newly won political influence, the union leadership initially focused on influencing government policy, leading to a preference for negotiation over confrontation. Like many other social movements, the unions also took part in the government's participatory forums to debate major policy areas. Although the political and economic circumstances ostensibly became much more positive for effective labour political strategies, the actual political situation was more complex as some centrist union activists were reluctant to challenge government policies while others criticized this stance, as evident in the case of controversial reform proposals.

The limitations of the moderate approach soon became apparent as subsequent reforms did not meet unionists' high expectations or even hurt key union constituencies, as in the case of public-sector reforms. Political moderation in this period can be explained as a result of the close relationship with the PT in government, which also translated into a reluctance to undermine the left in power. Expectations that the government would act according to the union movement's interests led to an amelioration of their strategies and demands but also sparked internal conflict and protests when this did not materialize. These conflicts resulted in political fragmentation of the union movement and the strengthening of left-wing critics, which increased during the first and second Lula administrations, leading to organizational and political splits between union moderates and militants over negotiating social and labour reforms. The union movement's complicated internal and external trade-offs between political influence, opposition, and protest were therefore a major factor shaping Brazil's political dynamics in the 2000s and 2010s.

As the economy began to deteriorate in the late 2000s, Brazil experienced a new wave of strikes, with labour militancy growing outside of sectors where unions were traditionally strong. Labour mobilization had stagnated up until 2009, both given the adverse economic conditions of the early 2000s and the improving living standards from 2004 onwards as the economy recovered. One area where labour militancy increased was the public sector, a core constituency of the new unionism movement, which was willing to use its strategic power to protest against government policies when they affected their core interests, such as in the case of social security reforms and public spending cuts during the first Lula administration. Labour militancy also increased outside of the main union strongholds, reflecting a worsening economic context and workers' dissatisfaction in non-traditional sectors, such as large infrastructure projects. This renewed labour militancy signalled a growing distance between more moderate union leaders and those grassroots unionists who were willing to go on strike to emphasize their demands. The developments in labour politics since 2003 show that the union movement's growing political power in the formal political arena came at a high price, undermining the unions' ability to mobilize people for political change as organized labour's strategic and symbolical legacy based on the struggle for democracy appeared to fade into the background. Nevertheless, the political dilemmas of this period left considerable space for labour militancy to re-emerge and challenge the apparent moderate consensus.

NOTES

1. The argument that the CUT's most recent political crisis was partly caused by its close relationship with the PT in government is shared by many Brazilian labour scholars. See, for example, Adalberto Moreira Cardoso, "Dimensões da crise do sindicalismo brasileiro," *Cadernos CRH* 28(75) (2015), 502–3; Ruy Braga, "Brazilian Labour Relations in Lula's Era: Telemarketing Operators and their Unions," in *Labour in the Global South: Challenges and Alternatives for Workers*, ed. Sarah Mosoetsa and Michelle Williams (Geneva: International Labour Organization, 2012), 116; Armando Boito Jr. and Paula Marcelino, "O sindicalismo deixou a crise para trás? Um novo ciclo de greves na década de 2000," *Caderno CRH* 23(59) (2010), 336. On the impact of civil society participation on moderation more generally in Brazil, see Evelina Dagnino and Ana C. Chaves Teixeira, "The Participation of Civil Society in Lula's Government," *Journal of Politics in Latin America* 6(3) (2014), 39–66; Hernan B. Gómez, *Lula, the Workers' Party and the Governability Dilemma in Brazil* (New York: Routledge, 2013).
2. Francisco de Oliveira, "O momento Lênin," *Novos Estudos CEBRAP* 75 (2006), 34–5; Ruy Braga, *A política do precariado: Do populismo à hegemonia lulista* (São Paulo: Editorial Boitempo, 2012), loc. 2591; Alvaro Bianchi and Ruy Braga, "Brazil: The Lula Government and Financial Globalization," *Social Forces* 83(4) (2005), 1760–61.
3. Edmund Amann and Werner Baer, "The Macroeconomic Record of the Lula Administration, the Roots of Brazil's Inequality, and the Attempts to Overcome Them," in *Brazil under Lula: Economy, Politics, and Society under the Worker-President*, ed. Joseph L. Love and Werner Baer (New York: Palgrave Macmillan, 2009), 34–5.
4. International Labour Organization, *2014 Labour Overview: Latin America and the Caribbean* (Lima: ILO/Regional Office for Latin America and the Caribbean, 2014), 65.
5. Wendy Hunter, "The Partido dos Trabalhadores: Still a Party of the Left?" in *Democratic Brazil Revisited*, edited by Peter R. Kingstone and Timothy J. Power (Pittsburgh, PA: University of Pittsburgh Press, 2008), 17.
6. Nora Lustig, Luis F. Lopez-Calva and Eduardo Ortiz-Juarez, "Declining Inequality in Latin America in the 2000s: The Cases of Argentina, Brazil, and Mexico," *World Development* 44 (2013), 135.

7. Wendy Hunter and Timothy J. Power, "Rewarding Lula: Executive Power, Social Policy, and the Brazilian Elections of 2006," *Latin American Politics and Society* 49(1) (2007), 15-16.
8. Lustig et al., "Declining Inequality," 135–6.
9. Peter R. Kingstone and Timothy J. Power, "Introduction," in *Democratic Brazil Revisited*, ed. Peter R. Kingstone and Timothy J. Power (Pittsburgh, PA: University of Pittsburgh Press, 2008), 4.
10. Peter Flynn, "Brazil and Lula, 2005: Crisis, Corruption and Change in Political Perspective," *Third World Quarterly* 26(8) (2005), 1223.
11. John D. French and Alexandre Fortes, "Another World is Possible: The Rise of the Brazilian Workers' Party and the Prospects for Lula's Government," *Labor* 2(3) (2005), 11-12.
12. Wendy Hunter, *The Transformation of the Workers' Party in Brazil, 1989-2009* (Cambridge: Cambridge University Press, 2010), 8.
13. David Samuels, "From Socialism to Social Democracy: Party Organization and the Transformation of the Workers' Party in Brazil," *Comparative Political Studies* 37 (9) (2004), 1014. See also William R. Nylen, "The Making of a Loyal Opposition: The Workers' Party (PT) and the Consolidation of Democracy in Brazil," in *Democratic Brazil: Actors, Institutions, and Processes*, ed. Peter R. Kingstone and Timothy J. Power (Pittsburgh, PA: University of Pittsburgh Press, 2000) and Hunter, *Transformation of the Workers' Party*, chapter 4.
14. Hunter, "Partido dos Trabalhadores," 23–4.
15. Hunter, "Partido dos Trabalhadores," 24.
16. Gómez, *Lula, the Workers' Party*, loc. 587.
17. Lecio Morais and Alfredo Saad-Filho, "Snatching Defeat from the Jaws of Victory: Lula, the 'Losers' Alliance, and the Prospects for Change in Brazil," *Capital & Class* 81 (2003): 22; Hunter, "The Partido dos Trabalhadores," 31.
18. Aline Diniz Amaral, Peter R. Kingstone, and J. Krieckhaus, "The Limits of Economic Reform in Brazil," in *Democratic Brazil Revisited*, ed. Peter R. Kingstone and Timothy J. Power (Pittsburgh, PA: University of Pittsburgh Press, 2008), 159.
19. Hunter, *Transformation of the Workers' Party*, 169.
20. André Singer, "Raízes sociais e ideológicas do lulismo," *Novos Estudos CEBRAP* 85 (2009), 84; André Singer, *Os sentidos do lulismo: Reforma gradual e pacto conservador*. São Paulo: Companhia das Letras, 2012.
21. Hunter and Power, "Rewarding Lula," 23.
22. Cesar Zucco, "The President's 'New' Constituency: Lula and the Pragmatic Vote in Brazil's 2006 Presidential Elections," *Journal of Latin American Studies* 40 (2008), 29-31.

23. Luiz Filgueiras, Bruno Pinheiro, Celeste Philigret and Paulo Balanco, "Modelo liberal-periférico e bloco de poder: Política e dinâmica macroeconômica nos governos Lula," in *Os anos Lula: Contribuições para um balanço crítico 2003–2010*, ed. João Paulo de Almeida Magalhães et al. (Rio de Janeiro: Garamond, 2010), 36.
24. See for example, Ricardo Antunes, "A engenharia da cooptação e os sindicatos," *Revista Pegada* 12(1) (2011), 57–8; Hunter, "Partido dos Trabalhadores," 28–30.
25. Salvador Sandoval, "Working-Class Contention," in *Reforming Brazil*, ed. Mauricio Font and Anthony P. Spanakos (Lanham, MD: Lexington Books, 2008); Juan Pablo Ferrero, *Democracy against Neoliberalism in Argentina and Brazil: A Move to the Left* (Basingstoke: Palgrave Macmillan, 2014); and for the wider Latin American context in this period, see Eduardo Silva, *Challenging Neoliberalism in Latin America* (Cambridge: Cambridge University Press, 2009).
26. DIEESE, *Anuário dos Trabalhadores 2005* (São Paulo: DIEESE, 2005), 116.
27. Kathryn Hochstetler, "Organized Civil Society in Lula's Brazil," in *Democratic Brazil Revisited*, edited by Peter R. Kingstone and Timothy J. Power. (Pittsburgh, PA: University of Pittsburgh Press, 2008), 41.
28. Luiz Marinho, "Os trabalhadores e a pauta do crescimento," *Folha de São Paulo*, September 26, 2003.
29. Agência Brasil, "Manifestantes da CUT pedem mudanças na política econômica," Brasília: Agência Brasil, 2004.
30. In 2003, the CUT noted that because economic policy had not changed substantially since Lula's election, state resources had to be devoted to an active industrial policy to promote economic growth. See Executiva Nacional da CUT, "Comentários sobre as 'Diretrizes de política industrial, tecnológica e de comércio exterior (do Governo Lula)" (São Paulo: CUT, December 2003), 6–7.
31. The focus on political participation was not exclusive to the union movement. As Avritzer points out, this focus had its roots in Brazilian civil society's shift towards "the establishment of a broad form of public participation in most areas of public policy" since the mid-1990s. Leonardo Avritzer, "Civil Society in Brazil: From State Autonomy to Political Interdependency," in *Beyond Civil Society: Activism, Participation, and Protest in Latin America*, ed. Sonia Alvarez and others (Durham, NC: Duke University Press, 2017), 57.
32. Ana C. Teixeira, "Até onde vai a participação cidadã?" *Le Monde Diplomatique Brasil* February 2008; for an overview of national-level participatory councils, see Secretaria Nacional da Articulação Social, *Conselhos Nacionais* (Brasília: Secretaria-Geral da Presidência da República, 2010);

for a critical discussion of the participatory initiatives, Cláudia F. Faria, "Estado e organizações da sociedade civil no Brasil contemporâneo: Construindo uma sinergia positiva?" *Revista de Sociologia e Política* 18(36) (2010), 187-204.
33. Instituto Brasileira de Análises Sociais e Econômicas (Brazilian Institute for Social and Economic Analyses).
34. IBASE, "A experiência de Projeto Mapas do monitoramento político de iniciativas de participação do governo Lula," in *Projeto Mapas: Relatório do projeto*, ed. IBASE (Rio de Janeiro: IBASE, 2005), 3.
35. IBASE, "Experiência de Projeto Mapas," 32.
36. To expand civil society and business influence and link monetary policy to economic growth, the CUT together with the business associations Confederação Nacional de Indústrias (CNI) and FIESP unsuccessfully proposed civil society representation in the Conselho Monetário Nacional (CMN) in 2005. See CUT, *Conselho Monetário Nacional: Proposta da CUT para a ampliação e democratização do CMN* (São Paulo: CUT, 2005).
37. Leonardo Avritzer, "Living Under a Democracy: Participation and its Impacts on the Living Conditions of the Poor," *Latin American Research Review* 45 (2010), 173.
38. Brian Wampler, *Participatory Budgeting in Brazil: Contestation, Cooperation, and Accountability* (University Park, PA: University of Pennsylvania Press, 2007), 24, 256.
39. Hochstetler, "Organized Civil Society," 42.
40. Mahrukh Doctor, "Lula's Development Council: Neo-Corporatism and Policy Reform in Brazil," *Latin American Perspectives* 34(6) (2007), 138-9.
41. Lúcio Kowarick, "O Conselho de Desenvolvimento Econômico e Social: Um processo em construção," 2003, http://www.cdes.gov.br/documento/300654/o-conselho-de-desenvolvimento-economico-e-social-um-processo-em-construcao-html, 15.
42. Sérgio Baierle, "Lula's Swamp," *Journal of Iberian and Latin American Research* 11(2) (2005), 113. See also Filgueiras, et al., "Modelo liberal-periférico," 37-9.
43. Sonia Fleury, "O Conselho de Desenvolvimento Econômico e Social do governo Lula," 2006, available from http://app.ebape.fgv.br/comum/arq/ACFBA0.pdf, accessed September 26, 2016.
44. Hochstetler, "Organized Civil Society," 42.
45. Hochstetler, "Organized Civil Society," 44-5; Ferrero, *Democracy against Neoliberalism*, 118-24.
46. There are indications that the government attempted to exploit the differences between public- and private sector unions by distributing information in Congress about the disparities between public- and private sector

pensions, see Vilson A. Romero, "Os 'vilões' da reforma," *Boletim DIAP*, March 17, 2003, http://www.diap.org.br/index.php?option=com_content&view=article&id=5850:os-viloes-da-reforma&catid=46:artigos&Itemid=207, accessed Sept. 28, 2016.
47. Flynn, "Brazil and Lula," 1229–30.
48. Vilson A. Romero, "Previdência: Lula=(FHC)3," *Boletim DIAP*, May 8, 2003, http://www.diap.org.br/index.php?option=com_content&view=article&id=5828:previdencia-lula-fhc-3&catid=46:artigos&Itemid=207, accessed Sept. 28, 2016.
49. Andréia Galvão, "A reconfiguração do movimento sindical no governo Lula," *Revista Outubre* 18 (2009), 182.
50. For details of the CUT's proposals for social security reform, see CUT, "Propostas da CUT para previdência social pública: Diretrizes e ações da CUT para atuação junto aos conselhos de previdência social" (São Paulo: CUT, 2003).
51. Sindicato dos Metálurgicos do ABC, "Pressão no governo e no congresso," June 10, 2003, http://www.smabc.org.br/smabc/materia.asp?id_CON=1703&id_SEC=12&busca=correntes, accessed Sept. 28, 2016.
52. DIEESE, *Política de valorização do Salário Mínimo: Salário Mínimo de 2015 fixado em R$788,00*, Nota Técnica no. 143 (January 2015), 3.
53. Javier Martínez-Lara, *Building Democracy in Brazil: The Politics of Constitutional Change, 1985–95* (London: Macmillan; New York: St. Martin's Press, 1996), 77.
54. Hunter and Power, "Rewarding Lula," 130.
55. CUT, *A agenda dos trabalhadores: Projetos e temas da CUT para o diálogo com os poderes executivo, legislativo e judiciário* (Brasília: CUT, 2005); Rodrigues et al. argue that very little of this agenda resonated with the government, except the minimum wage proposals, see Iram J. Rodrigues, José Ricardo Ramalho and Jefferson J. da Conceição, "Relações de trabalho e sindicato no primeiro governo Lula (2003-2006)," *Ciência e Cultura* 60(4) (2008), 55.
56. DIEESE, *Política de valorização do Salário Mínimo: Salário Mínimo de 2015 fixado em R$788,00*, Nota Técnica 143 (January 2015), 2.
57. Similarly, the land reform marches became a routine feature of rural social movements under the PT-led administrations, leading to negotiation with and support from the government for rural issues. As in the case of the union movement, dissatisfaction with a lack of progress with land reform in particular led to conflicts between grassroots activists and national organizations. See Rebecca Abers, Lizandra Serafim and Luciana Tatagiba, "Changing Repertoires of State-Society Interaction under Lula," in *Brazil under the Workers' Party: Continuity and Change from Lula to Dilma*, ed. Fábio de Castro, Kees Koonings and Marianne Wiesebron (Basingstoke and New York: Palgrave Macmillan, 2014).

58. Galvão, "A reconfiguração," 184–5.
59. Sindicato dos Bancários de São Paulo, "Mais de 20 mil nas ruas em Brasília," 2005, http://www1.spbancarios.com.br/noticia.asp?=589, accessed 18 May 2015. Because minimum wage levels were linked to welfare payments, the increases did affect government spending on social security and public sector pensions.
60. Sindicato dos Bancários de São Paulo, "Mais de 20 mil".
61. Sindicato dos Bancários de São Paulo, "Cerca de 20 mil participam da 3a marcha," December 12, 2006, http://www1.spbancarios.com/br/noticia.asp?c=3998, accessed Nov. 18, 2015.
62. DIEESE, *A situação do trabalho no Brasil na primeira década dos anos 2000* (São Paulo: DIEESE, 2012), 103.
63. DIEESE, "Balanço das greves em 2013." Estudos e Pesquisas 79, December 2015, 42.
64. Eduardo G. Noronha, "Ciclo de greves, transição política e estabilização, 1978-2007," *Lua Nova* 76 (2009), 129–31; DIEESE, "Balanço das greves em 2013," 43; DIEESE. "O movimento grevista em 2004," *Estudos e Pesquisas* 12 (October 2005), 35.
65. Noronha, "Ciclo de greves," 137–8.
66. Associação Nacional dos Funciónarios do Banco do Brasil (ANABB), "Movimento une categoria, mas divide lideranças," *Jornal Ação* 172 (2004). A similar situation occurred in the context of Lula's re-election campaign in 2006, when the CNB attempted to suppress a bankworkers' strike, using the argument that the CNB attempted to avoid instability, Galvão, "Reconfiguração do movimento sindical," 183.
67. DIEESE, "As greves em 2005," *Estudos e Pesquisas* 20 (May 2006), 8–9; DIEESE, "Balanço das greves no primeiro semestre de 2006," *Estudos e Pesquisas* 27 (November 2006).
68. See Hunter, *Transformation of the Workers' Party*, 167–72 for a discussion on how the scandal affected Lula's re-election campaign.
69. Hochstetler, "Organized Civil Society," 50.
70. Armando Boito Jr., "Class Relations in Brazil's New Neoliberal Phase," *Latin American Perspectives* 36(5) (2007), 125.
71. Carlos E. Freitas, "Alterações na regulamentação das relações de trabalho no governo Fernando Henrique," in *Precarização e leis do trabalho nos anos FHC* (São Paulo: CUT/ Secretaria da Política Sindical, 2001): 11–2;
72. Heloísa de Souza Martins and Iram J. Rodrigues, "O sindicalismo brasileiro na segunda metade dos anos 90," *Tempo Social* 11(2) (1999), 176; Michael M. Hall, "The Labor Policies of the Lula Government," in *Brazil under Lula: Economy, Politics, and Society under the Worker-President*, ed. Joseph L. Love and Werner Baer (New York: Palgrave Macmillan, 2009), 155.

73. Mônica Valente, "Sindicato orgânico e projecto sindical," in *Sindicato Orgânico*, Seminários Preparatórios para o 6°. Congresso da CUT (São Paulo: Escola Sindical São Paulo/Secretaria Estadual de Formação, 1997): 12; Kjeld A. Jakobsen, "Modelo sindical e transformações internacionais," in *Sindicato Orgânico*, Seminários Preparatórios para o 6° Congresso da CUT (São Paulo: Escola Sindical São Paulo/Secretaria Estadual de Formação, 1997): 6.
74. The CUT's Arthur Henrique, later elected president, echoed the Lula government's preference for staging the reforms in 2003, see Agência Brasil, "Para dirigente da CUT, reforma sindical deve preceder reforma trabalhista," August 12, 2003, http://memoria.ebc.com.br/agenciabrasil/noticia/2003-08-12/para-dirigente-da-cut-reforma-sindical-deve-preceder-reforma-trabalhista, accessed Sept. 28, 2016; Hall, "Labor Policies," 157. Galvão argues that the flexibilization of labour relations introduced in the 1990s continued despite Lula's comments about the phasing of labour reforms to allow unions to negotiate from a position of strength, Galvão, "Reconfiguração do movimento sindical," 192.
75. Gelsom de Almeida, "O governo Lula, o Fórum Nacional do Trabalho e a reforma sindical," *Revista Katálysis* 10(1) (2007), 57.
76. Flávio Tonelli and Antônio A. Queiroz, "Trabalho e sindicalismo no governo Lula," in *Os Anos Lula: Contribuições para um balanço crítico 2003–2010*, ed. João Paulo Almeida de Magalhães et al. (Rio de Janeiro: Garamond, 2010), 343–4; Almeida, "O governo Lula," 58–9.
77. Almeida, "O governo Lula," 57–8. Critics also suspected that the government was not just a neutral party in the negotiations, fearing that the Ministry of Labour would impose its agenda on the FNT, see ANABB, "Centrais sindicais criticam declarações de Lula sobre CLT," Feb. 13, 2004, http://www.anabb.org.br/mostraPagina.asp?codServico=4&codPagina=4423, accessed July 23, 2015.
78. Sindicato dos Metalúrgicos do ABC (SMABC), "O verdadeiro sindicato," May 28, 2003, http://www.smabc.org.br/smabc/materia.asp?id_CON=493&id_SEC=12&busca=reforma+sindical, accessed July 23, 2015.
79. SMABC, "Reforma sindical: Para completar a democrática," June 4, 2003, http://www.smabc.org.br/smabc/materia.asp?id_CON=1677&id_SEC=12&busca=reforma+sindical, accessed July 23, 2015; Folha de São Paulo, "Reforma sindical democratizará sindicatos, diz Berzoini," *Folha de São Paulo*, May 5, 2005.
80. Câmara dos Deputados, "Trabalho quer votar projeto alternativo à reforma sindical," April 13, 2005, http://www2.camara.leg.br/camaranoticias/noticias/64483.html, accessed Sept. 28, 2016; ANABB, "Protesto contra reforma".

81. Agência Brasil, "Termina sem consenso a primeira rodada de negociações da reforma sindical," Jan. 23, 2004.
82. Hall, "Labor Policies," 159–60.
83. Wagner Gomes, "Avançar na luta é ampliar ainda mais as conquistas," *Jornal Plataforma* 473 (June 2, 2005); see various texts representing criticism of the CUT's position in CUT, *11a Plenária Nacional: Trabalho, salário, emprego e Desenvolvimento, Caderno de textos para debates* (São Paulo: CUT, 2005), 57–108; Agência Brasil, "CUT define 'recuo tático' para aprovação da reforma sindical," May 13, 2005.
84. Rosana da Silva, "Debate reforma sindical: Mobilização social é indispensável," *Teoria e Debate* 63 (July 2015).
85. Marcel Gomes, "Pela união, CUT aceita 'amenizar' fim da unicidade," *Carta Maior* May 12, 2005; Verena Glass, "Marinho espeta esquerda da CUT e apóia reeleição de Lula," *Carta Maior* May 11, 2005.
86. Diego Cruz, "Plenária nacional da CUT ratifica apoio à reforma sindical," Partido Socialista dos Trabalhadores Unificados, May 12, 2005, http://www.pstu.org.br/node/10766, accessed July 23, 2015.
87. CUT, *9o CONCUT—Trabalho e democracia: Emprego, renda e direitos para todos os trabalhadores e trabalhadoras, caderno de textos* (São Paulo: CUT, 2006), 61.
88. Gilson Reis, "A CUT diante um future incerto," Portal Vermelho, June 16, 2006, http://www.vermelho.org.br/coluna.php?id_coluna_texto=190&id_coluna=22, accessed July 17. 2015; Gómez, *Lula, the Workers' Party*, loc. 3602. Oliveira, "Lula in the Labyrinth," 13.
89. Galvão, "Reconfiguração do movimento sindical," 191.
90. Other new national organizations emerged to represent the official unionism and support for corporatist labour relations, see Patrícia Vieira Trópia, Paula R. Pereira Marcelino and Andréia Galvão, "As bases sociais da União Geral dos Trabalhadores," *Revista da ABET* 12(1) (2013), 142–3; Reiner Radermacher and Waldeli Melleiro, "Mudanças no cenário sindical brasileiro sob o governo de Lula," *Nueva Sociedad* 211 (2007), 4.
91. Interview with Geraldo, teachers' union APEOESP and international secretary of Conlutas, São Paulo, June 5, 2009; observations and informal conversations at CTB, São Paulo, June 18, 2009. On the socio-economic background and political profile of Conlutas members, see Patrícia Vieira Trópia, Andréia Galvão and Paula R. Pereira Marcelino, "A reconfiguração do sindicalismo brasileiro nos anos 2000: As bases sociais e o perfil politico-ideológico da Conlutas," *Opinião Pública* 19(1) (2013), 81–117.
92. From 2008 onwards, the Ministry of Labour began to register union affiliations to central union organizations to allocate financial resources. Their figures show that the CUT continued to be by far the largest national organization, followed by Força Sindical, but both began to lose ground

to competing organizations from 2011 onwards, see Departamento Intersindical de Assessoria Parlamentar (DIAP), "Centrais sindicais: Índice de representatividade," 2016, http://www.diap.org.br/index.php/component/content/article?id=17053, accessed September 25, 2016.
93. Ricardo Antunes and Marco A. Santana, "The Dilemmas of the New Unionism in Brazil: Breaks and Continuities," *Latin American Perspectives* 41(5) (2014), 19. See also Galvão, "Reconfiguração do movimento sindical," 188; Alexandre Ferraz, "Novos rumos do sindicalismo no Brasil." *Revista Brasileira de Ciências Sociais* 29 (86) (2014), 109–123; Altamiro Borges, "10 razões contra reforma sindical," DIAP, March 2, 2005, http://www.diap.org.br/index.php?option=com_content&view=article&id=5689:10-razoes-contra-reforma-sindical&catid=46:artigos&Itemid=207, accessed July 30, 2015.
94. DIEESE, "Balanço das greves em 2008," *Estudos e Pesquisas* 45 (July 2009); DIEESE, "Balanço das greves em 2007," *Estudos e Pesquisas* 41 (2008), 2, 6–7; DIEESE, "Balanço das greves no primeiro semestre de 2006"; DIEESE, "As greves em 2005," 9.
95. Matthew S. Winters and Rebecca Weitz-Shapiro, "Partisan Protesters and Nonpartisan Protests in Brazil," *Journal of Politics in Latin America* 6(1) (2014), 137–50.
96. Alfredo Saad-Filho and Armando Boito, "Brazil: The Failure of the PT and the Rise of the 'New Right'," *Socialist Register* (2016), 222–3.
97. Alfredo Saad-Filho, "Mass Protests under Left Neo-Liberalism: Brazil, June-July 2013," *Critical Sociology* 39(5) (2013), 660.
98. Marcelo B. Mattos, "Greves no Brasil: O despertar de um novo ciclo de lutas?" June 10, 2014, http://www.ihu.unisinos.br/noticias/532181-greves-no-brasil-o-despertar-de-um-novo-ciclo-de-lutas, accessed September 26, 2016; Marcelo B. Mattos, "New and Old Forms of Social Movements: A Discussion from Brazil," *Critique* 43(3–4) (2015), 490.
99. Luciana Tatagiba, "1984, 1992 e 2013: Sobre ciclos de protestos e democracia no Brasil," *Política & Sociedade* 13(28) (2014), 40–8.
100. Datafolha, "Manifestação Avenida Paulista: 18/03/2016" (São Paulo: Datafolha, 2016), 6.
101. Hanrrikson de Andrade and Julia Affonso, "Militantes da CUT são agredidos e expulsos de protesto no Rio de Janeiro," *UOL Notícias*, June 20, 2013; Gianpaolo Baiocchi and Ana Teixeira, "Brazil: Back to the Streets?" in *Beyond Civil Society: Activism, Participation, and Protest in Latin America*, ed. Sonia Alvarez and others (Durham, NC: Duke University Press, 2017), 287.
102. José D. Krein and Hugo Dias, "Os caminhos de sindicalismo nos anos 2000," *Revista de Ciências do Trabalho*, 8 (2017), 13.

103. José Schutz, "O movimento sindical de volta ao cenário politico," *Desafios do Desenvolvimento* 9(73) (2012).
104. Esquerda Marxista, "A responsabilidade da direção do PT e da CUT pela atual situação," March 17, 2015, http://www.marxismo.org.br/content/responsabilidade-da-direcao-do-pt-e-da-cut-pela-atual-situacao, accessed March 22, 2016; In an example of the enduring legacy of the CUT's militant past, the document also argued that the strike wave at the end of the 1970s and early 1980s was an example of what protests could achieve.
105. Mattos notes that the connection between the growing labour militancy among precarious workers and the participation of the "precariat" in the 2013 demonstrations alongside middle-class demonstrators. He thereby rejects the distinction drawn between the protestors and precarious workers on strike, arguing that they are manifestations of the same political conjuncture. Mattos, "New and Old Forms of Social Movements," 494–5.
106. DIEESE, "Balanço das greves em 2009 e 2010," *Estudos e Pesquisas* 60 (April 2012), 22–3.
107. Marieke Riethof, "The International Human Rights Discourse as a Strategic Focus in Socio-environmental Conflicts: The Case of Hydroelectric Dams in Brazil," *International Journal of Human Rights* 21(4) (2017).
108. DIEESE, *Copa do Mundo 2014: Algumas considerações sobre a realização do evento no Brasil*, Nota Técnica 110, May 2012, 9; DIEESE, "Balanço das greves em 2012," *Estudos e Pesquisas* 66, May 2012, 6–7.
109. DIEESE, "Balanço das greves em 2012," 7. Out of a total of 45 PAC-related protests in 2013, 19 protests affected industrial port complexes and 18 protests focused on dams in Amazonia, particularly at the Belo Monte, Jirau, Santo Antônio, Teles Pires, and Tapajós dams.
110. For a further discussion on examples of strikes since 2011, Jorg Nowak, "Class Coalitions or Struggles within the Working Class? Social Unrest in India and Brazil during the Global Crisis," *Workers of the World* 1(8) (2016), 71-98; on the Jirau Dam strikes, see Roberto Verás, "Brasil em obras, peões em luta, sindicatos sorpreendidos," *Revista Crítica de Ciências Sociais* 103 (2014): 111–136.
111. Comissão Pastoral da Terra (CPT), *Conflitos no campo Brasil 2013* (Goiânia: CPT, 2014), 22–3.
112. Rede Brasil Atual, "Partidos e movimentos sociais articulam-se para formação de frente de esquerda," Jan. 4, 2015, http://www.redebrasilatual.com.br/politica/2015/01/entidades-sociais-e-partidos-politicos-articulam-se-para-formacao-de-frente-de-esquerda-1518.html, accessed March 22, 2016.

Bibliography

Abers, Rebecca, Lizandra Serafim, and Luciana Tatagiba. 2014. Changing Repertoires of State-Society Interaction Under Lula. In *Brazil Under the Workers' Party: Continuity and Change from Lula to Dilma*, ed. Fábio de Castro, Kees Koonings, and Marianne Wiesebron, 36–61. Basingstoke/New York: Palgrave Macmillan.

Agência Brasil. 2003. Para dirigente da CUT, reforma sindical deve preceder reforma trabalhista, August 1. http://memoria.ebc.com.br/agenciabrasil/noticia/2003-08-12/para-dirigente-da-cut-reforma-sindical-deve-preceder-reforma-trabalhista. Accessed 28 Sept 2016.

———. 2004a. *Manifestantes da CUT pedem mudanças na política econômica*. Brasília: Agência Brasil, July 16.

———. 2004b. *Termina sem consenso a primeira rodada de negociações da reforma sindical*. Brasília: Agência Brasil, January 23.

———. 2005. *CUT define 'recuo tático' para aprovação da reforma sindical*. Brasília: Agência Brasil, May 13.

Almeida, Gelsom de. 2007. O governo Lula, o Fórum Nacional do Trabalho e a reforma sindical. *Revista Katálysis* 10 (1): 54–64.

Amann, Edmund, and Werner Baer. 2009. The Macroeconomic Record of the Lula Administration, the Roots of Brazil's Inequality, and the Attempts to Overcome Them. In *Brazil Under Lula: Economy, Politics, and Society Under the Worker-President*, ed. Joseph L. Love and Werner Baer, 27–43. New York: Palgrave Macmillan.

Associação Nacional dos Funcionários do Banco do Brasil (ANABB). 2004a. Centrais sindicais criticam declarações de Lula sobre CLT, February 13. http://www.anabb.org.br/mostraPagina.asp?codServico=4&codPagina=4423. Accessed 23 July 2015.

———. 2004b. Movimento une categoria, mas divide lideranças. *Jornal Ação* 172: 4–8.

———. 2004c. Protesto contra reforma sindical reúne 8 mil em Brasília, March 25. http://www.anabb.org.br/mostraPagina.asp?codServico=4&codPagina=2974. Accessed 23 July 2015.

Andrade, Hanrrikson de, and Julia Affonso. 2013. Militantes da CUT são agredidos e expulsos de protesto no Rio de Janeiro. *UOL Notícias*, June 20.

Antunes, Ricardo. 2011. A engenharia da cooptação e os sindicatos. *Revista Pegada* 12 (1): 54–59.

Antunes, Ricardo, and Marco A. Santana. 2014. The Dilemmas of the New Unionism in Brazil: Breaks and Continuities. *Latin America Perspectives* 41 (5): 10–21.

Avritzer, Leonardo. 2010. Living Under a Democracy: Participation and Its Impacts on the Living Conditions of the Poor. *Latin American Research Review* 45: 166–185.
———. 2017. Civil Society in Brazil: From State Autonomy to Political Interdependency. In *Beyond Civil Society: Activism, Participation, and Protest in Latin America*, ed. Sonia Alvarez, Jeffrey W. Rubin, Millie Thayer, Gianpaolo Baiocchi, and Agustín Laó-Montes, 45–62. Durham: Duke University Press.
Baierle, Sérgio. 2005. Lula's Swamp. *Journal of Iberian and Latin American Research* 11 (2): 109–116.
Baiocchi, Gianpaolo, and Ana Teixeira. 2017. Brazil: Back to the Streets? In *Beyond Civil Society: Activism, Participation, and Protest in Latin America*, ed. Sonia Alvarez, Jeffrey W. Rubin, Millie Thayer, Gianpaolo Baiocchi, and Agustín Laó-Montes, 283–295. Durham: Duke University Press.
Bianchi, Alvaro, and Ruy Braga. 2005. Brazil: The Lula Government and Financial Globalization. *Social Forces* 83 (4): 1745–1767.
Boito, Armando, Jr. 2007. Class Relations in Brazil's New Neoliberal Phase. *Latin American Perspectives* 36 (5): 115–131.
Boito, Armando, Jr., and Paula Marcelino. 2010. O sindicalismo deixou a crise para trás? Um novo ciclo de greves na década de 2000. *Caderno CRH* 23 (59): 323–338.
Borges, Altamiro. 2005. 10 razões contra reforma sindical. Departamento Intersindical de Assessoria Parlamentar (DIAP), March 2. http://www.diap.org.br/index.php?option=com_content&view=article&id=5689:10-razoes-contra-reforma-sindical&catid=46:artigos&Itemid=207
Braga, Ruy. 2012a. *A política do precariado: Do populismo à hegemonia lulista*. São Paulo: Editorial Boitempo.
———. 2012b. Brazilian Labour Relations in Lula's Era: Telemarketing Operators and Their Unions. In *Labour in the Global South: Challenges and Alternatives for Workers*, ed. Sarah Mosoetsa and Michelle Williams, 109–124. Geneva: International Labour Organization.
Câmara dos Deputados. 2005. Trabalho quer votar projeto alternativo à reforma sindical, April 13. http://www2.camara.leg.br/camaranoticias/noticias/64483.html. Accessed 28 Sept 2016.
Cardoso, Adalberto Moreira. 2015. Dimensões da crise do sindicalismo brasileiro. *Cadernos CRH* 28 (75): 493–510.
Comissão Pastoral da Terra (CPT). *Conflitos no campo Brasil 2013*, 2014. Goiânia: CPT.
Cruz, Diego. 2005. Plenária nacional da CUT ratifica apoio à reforma Sindical. Partido Socialista dos Trabalhadores Unificados, May 12. http://www.pstu.org.br/node/10766. Accessesd 23 July 2015.
CUT. 2003. *Propostas da CUT para previdência social pública: Diretrizes e ações da CUT para atuação junto aos conselhos de previdência social*. São Paulo: CUT.

———. 2005a. *Conselho Monetário Nacional: Proposta da CUT para a ampliação e democratização do CMN*. São Paulo: CUT.

———. 2005b. *A agenda dos trabalhadores: Projetos e temas da CUT para o diálogo com os poderes executivo, legislativo e judiciário*. Brasília: CUT.

———. 2005c. *11a Plenária Nacional: Trabalho, salário, emprego e desenvolvimento, Caderno de textos para debates*. São Paulo: CUT.

———. 2006. *9o CONCUT – Trabalho e democracia: Emprego, renda e direitos para todos os trabalhadores e trabalhadoras, caderno de textos*. São Paulo: CUT.

CUT/Executiva Nacional. 2003. *Comentários sobre as 'Diretrizes de política industrial, tecnológica e de comércio exterior (do Governo Lula)*. São Paulo: CUT, December.

Dagnino, Evelina, and Ana C. Chaves Teixeira. 2014. The Participation of Civil Society in Lula's Government. *Journal of Politics in Latin America* 6 (3): 39–66.

Datafolha. 2016. Avaliação da presidente Dilma Rousseff, 07 e 08/04/2016, April. http://media.folha.uol.com.br/datafolha/2016/04/11/avaliacao-presidente-dilma.pdf. Accessed 27 Sept 2016.

Dataluta. 2014. *Banco de dados da luta pela terra: Relatório Brasil 2013*. Presidente Prudente: NERA/FCT/UNESP.

Departamento Intersindical de Assessoria Parlamentar (DIAP). 2016. Centrais sindicais: Índice de representatividade. http://www.diap.org.br/index.php/component/content/article?id=17053. Accessed 25 Sept 2016.

Departamento Intersindical de Estatística e Estudos Socioeconômicos (DIEESE). 2005a. O movimento grevista em 2004. *Estudos e Pesquisas* 12, October.

———. 2005b. *Anuário dos Trabalhadores 2005*. DIEESE: São Paulo.

———. 2006a. As greves em 2005. *Estudos e Pesquisas* 20, May.

———. 2006b. Balanço das greves no primeiro semestre de 2006. *Estudos e Pesquisas* 27, November.

———. 2008. Balanço das greves em 2007. *Estudos e Pesquisas* 41.

———. 2009. Balanço das greves em 2008. *Estudos e Pesquisas* 45, July.

———. 2011. *Anuário dos trabalhadores, 2010–2011*. DIEESE: São Paulo.

———. 2012a. Balanço das greves em 2012. *Estudos e Pesquisas* 66, May.

———. 2012b. Balanço das greves em 2009 e 2010. *Estudos e Pesquisas* 60, April.

———. 2012c. *Copa do Mundo 2014: Algumas considerações sobre a realização do evento no Brasil*. Nota Técnica 110, May.

———. 2012d. *A situação do trabalho no Brasil na primeira década dos anos 2000*. São Paulo: DIEESE.

———. 2015a. Balanço das greves em 2013. *Estudos e Pesquisas* 79, December.

———. 2015b. *Política de valorização do Salário Mínimo: Salário Mínimo de 2015 fixado em R$788,0sss0*. Nota Técnica 143, January.

———. 2017. Balanço das greves de 2016. *Estudos e Pesquisas* 84, August.

Diniz Amaral, A., Peter R. Kingstone, and J. Krieckhaus. 2008. The Limits of Economic Reform in Brazil. In *Democratic Brazil Revisited*, ed. Peter R. Kingstone and Timothy J. Power, 137–160. Pittsburgh: University of Pittsburgh Press.

Doctor, Mahrukh. 2007. Lula's Development Council: Neo-Corporatism and Policy Reform in Brazil. *Latin American Perspectives* 34 (6): 131–148.

Esquerda Marxista. 2015. A responsabilidade da direção do PT e da CUT pela atual situação, March 17. http://www.marxismo.org.br/content/responsabilidade-da-direcao-do-pt-e-da-cut-pela-atual-situacao. Accessed 22 Mar 2016.

Faria, Claúdia F. 2010. Estado e organizações da sociedade civil no Brasil contemporâneo: Construindo uma sinergia positiva? *Revista de Sociologia e Política* 18 (36): 187–204.

Ferraz, Alexandre. 2014. Novos rumos do sindicalismo no Brasil. *Revista Brasileira de Ciências Sociais* 29 (86): 109–123.

Ferrero, Juan Pablo. 2014. *Democracy Against Neoliberalism in Argentina and Brazil: A Move to the Left*. Basingstoke: Palgrave Macmillan.

Filgueiras, Luiz, P. Bruno, Celeste Philigret, and Paulo Balanco. 2010. Modelo liberal-periférico e bloco de poder: Política e dinâmica macroeconômica nos governos Lula. In *Os anos Lula: Contribuições para um balanço crítico 2003–2010*, ed. João Paulo de Almeida Magalhães et al., 35–69. Rio de Janeiro: Garamond.

Fleury, Sonia. 2006. O Conselho de Desenvolvimento Econômico e Social do governo Lula. Available from http://app.ebape.fgv.br/comum/arq/ACFBA0.pdf. Accessed 26 Sept 2016.

Flynn, Peter. 2005. Brazil and Lula, 2005: Crisis, Corruption and Change in Political Perspective. *Third World Quarterly* 26 (8): 1221–1267.

Folha de São Paulo. 2005. Reforma sindical democratizará sindicatos, diz Berzoini. *Folha de São Paulo*, May 5.

Freitas, Carlos E. 2001. Alterações na regulamentação das relações de trabalho no governo Fernando Henrique. In *Precarização e leis do trabalho nos anos FHC*, ed. CUT/Secretaria da Política Sindical. São Paulo: CUT/Secretaria da Política Sindical.

French, John D., and Alexandre Fortes. 2005. Another World Is Possible: The Rise of the Brazilian Workers' Party and the Prospects for Lula's Government. *Labor* 2 (3): 13–31.

Galvão, Andréia. 2009. A reconfiguração do movimento sindical no governo Lula. *Revista Outubre* 18: 177–200.

Glass, Verena. 2005. Marinho espeta esquerda da CUT e apóia reeleição de Lula. *Carta Maior*, May 11.

Gomes, Marcel. 2005a. Pela união, CUT aceita 'amenizar' fim da unicidade. *Carta Maior*, May 12.

Gomes, Wagner. 2005b. Avançar na luta é ampliar ainda mais as conquistas. *Jornal Plataforma* 473, June 2.
Gómez, Hernan B. 2013. *Lula, the Workers' Party and the Governability Dilemma in Brazil.* New York: Routledge.
Hall, Michael M. 2009. The Labor Policies of the Lula Government. In *Brazil Under Lula: Economy, Politics, and Society Under the Worker-President*, ed. Joseph L. Love and Werner Baer, 151–165. New York: Palgrave Macmillan.
Hochstetler, Kathryn. 2008. Organized Civil Society in Lula's Brazil. In *Democratic Brazil Revisited*, ed. Peter R. Kingstone and Timothy J. Power, 33–53. Pittsburgh: University of Pittsburgh Press.
Hunter, Wendy. 2008. The Partido dos Trabalhadores: Still a Party of the Left? In *Democratic Brazil Revisited*, ed. Peter R. Kingstone and Timothy J. Power, 15–32. Pittsburgh: University of Pittsburgh Press.
———. 2010. *The Transformation of the Workers' Party in Brazil, 1989–2009.* Cambridge: Cambridge University Press.
Hunter, Wendy, and Timothy J. Power. 2007. Rewarding Lula: Executive Power, Social Policy, and the Brazilian Elections of 2006. *Latin American Politics and Society* 49 (1): 1–30.
Instituto Brasileira de Análises Sociais e Econômicas (IBASE). 2005. A experiência de Projeto Mapas do monitoramento político de iniciativas de participação do governo Lula. In *Projeto Mapas: Relatório do projeto*, ed. IBASE. Rio de Janeiro: IBASE.
International Labour Organization. 2014. *2014 Labour Overview: Latin America and the Caribbean.* Lima: ILO/Regional Office for Latin America and the Caribbean.
Jakobsen, Kjeld A. 1997. Modelo sindical e transformações internacionais. In *Sindicato orgânico, seminários preparatórios para o 6 Congresso da CUT.* São Paulo: Escola Sindical São Paulo/Secretaria Estadual de Formação.
Kingstone, Peter R., and Timothy J. Power. 2008. Introduction. In *Democratic Brazil Revisited*, ed. Peter R. Kingstone and Timothy J. Power, 1–12. Pittsburgh: University of Pittsburgh Press.
Kowarick, Lúcio. 2003. O Conselho de Desenvolvimento Econômico e Social: Um processo em construção. Available from http://www.cdes.gov.br/documento/300654/o-conselho-de-desenvolvimento-economico-e-social-um-processo-em-construcao-html. Accessed 26 Sept 2016.
Kowarick, Lúcio, and André Singer. 1993. A experiência do Partido dos Trabalhadores na prefeitura de São Paulo. *Novos Estudos CEBRAP* 35: 195–216.
Krein, José Dari, and Hugo Dias. 2017. Os caminhos de sindicalismo nos anos 2000. *Revista de Ciências do Trabalho* 8: 1–17.
Lustig, Nora, Luis F. Lopez-Calva, and Eduardo Ortiz-Juarez. 2013. Declining Inequality in Latin America in the 2000s: The Cases of Argentina, Brazil, and Mexico. *World Development* 44: 129–141.

Marinho, Luiz. 2003. Os trabalhadores e a pauta do crescimento. *Folha de São Paulo*, September 26.
Martínez-Lara, Javier. 1996. *Building Democracy in Brazil: The Politics of Constitutional Change, 1985-95.* London/New York: Macmillan/St. Martin's Press.
Martins, Heloísa de Souza, and Iram J. Rodrigues. 1999. O sindicalismo brasileiro na segunda metade dos anos 90. *Tempo Social* 11 (2): 155–182.
Mattos, Marcelo B. 2014. Greves no Brasil: O despertar de um novo ciclo de lutas? May 16. http://www.ihu.unisinos.br/noticias/532181-greves-no-brasil-o-despertar-de-um-novo-ciclo-de-lutas. Accessed 26 Sept 2016.
———. 2015. New and Old Forms of Social Movements: A Discussion from Brazil. *Critique* 43 (3-4): 485–499.
Morais, Lecio, and Alfredo Saad-Filho. 2003. Snatching Defeat from the Jaws of Victory: Lula, the 'Losers' Alliance, and the Prospects for Change in Brazil. *Capital & Class* 81: 17–23.
Noronha, Eduardo G. 2009. Ciclo de greves, transição política e estabilização, 1978-2007. *Lua Nova* 76: 119–168.
Nowak, Jörg. 2016. Class Coalitions or Struggles within the Working Class? Social Unrest in India and Brazil During the Global Crisis. *Workers of the World* 1 (8): 71–98.
Nylen, William R. 2000. The Making of a Loyal Opposition: The Workers' Party (PT) and the Consolidation of Democracy in Brazil. In *Democratic Brazil: Actors, Institutions, and Processes*, ed. Peter R. Kingstone and Timothy J. Power, 126–143. Pittsburgh: University of Pittsburgh Press.
Oliveira, Francisco de. 2006a. O momento Lênin. *Novos Estudos CEBRAP* 75: 23–47.
———. 2006b. Lula in the Labyrinth. *New Left Review* 42: 5–22.
Radermacher, Reiner, and Waldeli Melleiro. 2007. Mudanças no cenário sindical brasileiro sob o governo de Lula. *Nueva Sociedad* 211: 1–24.
Rede Brasil Atual. 2015. Partidos e movimentos sociais articulam-se para formação de frente de esquerda, January 4. http://www.redebrasilatual.com.br/politica/2015/01/entidades-sociais-e-partidos-politicos-articulam-se-para-formacao-de-frente-de-esquerda-1518.html. Accessed 22 Mar 2016.
Reis, Gilson. 2006. A CUT diante um futuro incerto. *Portal Vermelho*, June 16. http://www.vermelho.org.br/coluna.php?id_coluna_texto=190&id_coluna=22. Accessed 17 July 2015.
Riethof, Marieke. 2017. The International Human Rights Discourse as a Strategic Focus in Socio-environmental Conflicts: The Case of Hydro-electric Dams in Brazil. *International Journal of Human Rights* 21 (4): 482–499.
Rodrigues, Iram J., José Ricardo Ramalho, and Jefferson J. da Conceição. 2008. Relações de trabalho e sindicato no primeiro governo Lula (2003-2006). *Ciência e Cultura* 60 (4): 54–57.

Romero, Vilson A. 2003a. Previdência: Lula=(FHC)3. *Boletim DIAP*, May 8. http://www.diap.org.br/index.php?option=com_content&view=article&id=5828:previdencia-lula-fhc-3&catid=46:artigos&Itemid=207. Accessed 28 Sept 2016.
———. 2003b. Os 'vilões' da reforma. *Boletim DIAP*, March 17. http://www.diap.org.br/index.php?option=com_content&view=article&id=5850:osviloes-da-reforma&catid=46:artigos&Itemid=207. Accessed 28 Sept 2016.
Saad-Filho, Alfredo. 2013. Mass Protests Under Left Neo-Liberalism: Brazil, June-July 2013. *Critical Sociology* 39 (5): 657–669.
Saad-Filho, Alfredo, and Armando Boito. 2016. Brazil: The Failure of the PT and the Rise of the 'New Right'. *Socialist Register*: 213–230.
Samuels, David. 2004. From Socialism to Social Democracy: Party Organization and the Transformation of the Workers' Party in Brazil. *Comparative Political Studies* 37 (9): 999–1024.
Sandoval, Salvador. 2008. Working-Class Contention. In *Reforming Brazil*, ed. Mauricio Font and Anthony P. Spanakos, 195–215. Lanham: Lexington Books.
Schutz, José. 2012. O movimento sindical de volta ao cenário politico. *Desafios do Desenvolvimento* 9 (73): 48–57.
Secretaria Nacional da Articulação Social. 2010. *Conselhos Nacionais*. Brasília: Secretaria-Geral da Presidência da República.
Silva, Eduardo. 2009. *Challenging Neoliberalism in Latin America*. Cambridge: Cambridge University Press.
Silva, Rosana da. 2015. Debate reforma sindical: Mobilização social é indispensável. *Teoria e Debate* 63, July.
Sindicato dos Bancários de São Paulo. 2005. Mais de 20 mil nas ruas em Brasília. http://www1.spbancarios.com.br/noticia.asp?=589. Accessed 18 May 2015.
———. 2006. Cerca de 20 mil participam da 3a marcha, December 12. http://www1.spbancarios.com/br/noticia.asp?c=3998. Accessed 18 Nov 2015.
Sindicato dos Metalúrgicos do ABC. 2003a. Pressão no governo e no congresso, June 10. http://www.smabc.org.br/smabc/materia.asp?id_CON=1703&id_SEC=12&busca=correntes. Accessed 28 Sept 2016.
———. 2003b. Reforma sindical: Para completar a democrática, June 4. http://www.smabc.org.br/smabc/materia.asp?id_CON=1677&id_SEC=12&busca=reforma+sindical. Accessed 23 July 2015.
———. 2003c. O verdadeiro sindicato, May 28. http://www.smabc.org.br/smabc/materia.asp?id_CON=493&id_SEC=12&busca=reforma+sindical
Singer, André. 2009. Raízes sociais e ideológicas do lulismo. *Novos Estudos CEBRAP* 85: 83–102.
———. 2012. *Os sentidos do lulismo: Reforma gradual e pacto conservador*. São Paulo: Companhia das Letras.
Tatagiba, Luciana. 2014. 1984, 1992 e 2013: Sobre ciclos de protestos e democracia no Brasil. *Política & Sociedade* 13 (28): 35–62.

Teixeira, Ana C. 2008. Até onde vai a participação cidadã? *Le Monde Diplomatique Brasil*, February 4.
Tonelli, Flávio, and Antônio A. Queiroz. 2010. Trabalho e sindicalismo no governo Lula. In *Os anos Lula: Contribuições para um balanço crítico 2003–2010*, ed. João Paulo Almeida de Magalhães et al., 329–350. Rio de Janeiro: Garamond.
Trópia, Patrícia Vieira, Andréia Galvão, and Paula R. Pereira Marcelino. 2013a. A reconfiguração do sindicalismo brasileiro nos anos 2000: As bases sociais e o perfil politico-ideológico da Conlutas. *Opinião Pública* 19 (1): 81–117.
Trópia, Patrícia Vieira, Paula R. Pereira Marcelino, and Andréia Galvão. 2013b. As bases sociais da União Geral dos Trabalhadores. *Revista da ABET* 12 (1): 141–163.
Valente, Mônica. 1997. Sindicato orgânico e projecto sindical. In *Sindicato Orgânico, Seminários Preparatórios para o 6° Congresso da CUT*. São Paulo: Escola Sindical São Paulo/Secretaria Estadual de Formação.
Verás, Roberto. 2014. Brasil em obras, peões em luta, sindicatos sorpreendidos. *Revista Crítica de Ciências Sociais* 103: 111–136.
Wampler, Brian. 2007. *Participatory Budgeting in Brazil: Contestation, Cooperation, and Accountability*. University Park: University of Pennsylvania Press.
Winters, Matthew S., and Rebecca Weitz-Shapiro. 2014. Partisan Protesters and Nonpartisan Protests in Brazil. *Journal of Politics in Latin America* 6 (1): 137–150.
Zucco, Cesar. 2008. The President's 'New' Constituency: Lula and the Pragmatic Vote in Brazil's 2006 Presidential Elections. *Journal of Latin American Studies* 40: 29–49.

CHAPTER 7

Conclusion: Labour and the Ambiguities of Power

The fortunes of the Brazilian union movement have reflected the country's recent political history in many significant respects, particularly the conflicts that emerged from labour's active participation in a rapidly changing political environment. Although trade unions became a formidable opponent to military rule in the 1970s and 1980s, like many other labour organizations around the world, they also faced the debilitating effects of the economic crisis which continued into the 1990s. In the 2000s, this political dynamic changed when Lula was elected to the presidency, providing union representatives with unprecedented access to political influence, but also creating intractable conflicts when government policies clashed with labour interests. Since the late 2000s, Brazilian politics has witnessed a renewed wave of labour mobilization and political polarization, which spread to the wider Brazilian population during the mass demonstrations that have taken place from 2013 onwards. The central argument presented here is that the political dilemmas evident in organized labour's political agenda can explain these waves of political polarization and moderation. The union movement's political engagement has therefore shaped key political events, as evident in organized labour's key political role from the democratic transition to the left coming to power. Instead of facing inevitable decline in the face of globalization, workers' political influence should therefore not be discounted.

© The Author(s) 2019
M. Riethof, *Labour Mobilization, Politics and Globalization in Brazil*,
Studies of the Americas,
https://doi.org/10.1007/978-3-319-60309-4_7

Throughout Brazil's recent political history, militant trade union strategies have emerged at the intersection of political and economic change at a global and a national level, which means that the position of Brazilian labour can be understood in terms of its responses to these changes. Moreover, a focus on trade unions' active involvement in the political arena emphasizes organized labour's agency rather than treating labour as a passive subject of global, political, and economic change. While the polarizing combination of rapid economic and political change in Brazil provoked confrontational strategies, they also heightened internal conflicts regarding the desired direction of political change, which often resulted in the political fragmentation and gradual ideological and strategic moderation of a movement that already represented a wide variety of political ideas and socio-economic interests. Consequently, episodes of heightened labour mobilization also shaped subsequent political choices and organizational developments, underlining the book's argument about the significance of political ideas and debates in understanding labour strategies. Labour militancy can, therefore, be understood as evolving in response to both political and economic developments, and as mediated by the movement's internal debates. Adopting this longer-term perspective focused on the ebbs and flows of radicalism and pragmatism within the union movement provides insights not only into the conditions which have changed labour political strategies, but it also helps to explain why countries such as Brazil have returned to political polarization after long stretches of relative moderation.

Many progressives saw the events of 2016 as the end of a cycle in Brazilian politics, starting with the opening up of the democratic process in the 1980s and concluding with the impeachment of a democratically elected president. The latest political crisis has also marked the decline of progressive governments, reflecting the evolution of the union movement's political agenda since the late 1970s. Leading up to the crisis, Brazilian politics underwent seismic changes, in which labour agitation and gradualism played a crucial but thus far underappreciated role. These momentous events not only raise serious questions about Brazil's political culture, both for those who celebrated and mourned Dilma's impeachment, but also regarding the political position of the new unionism movement, a movement which became such a central actor in the country's recent history. Since the late 1970s, Brazil has experienced periods of heightened labour militancy (in the 1980s, the early to mid-1990s, and from the late 2000s onwards) and moderation (from the late 1990s until the late 2000s) as labour political strategies split into two directions: one pulled activists towards radicalism and the other towards pragmatism. These changes draw our attention to how the union movement itself has experienced a thorough process of renewal and transformation, escaping at key moments from social, economic, and political constraints to decisively influence the course of political change.

To understand the longer-term implications of workers' involvement in Brazilian politics, their position cannot be analysed without reference to the evolution of corporatism and national developmentalism as well as the legacies of democratization. The state-labour relationship that emerged in the early- to mid-twentieth century provided trade unions with legal recognition and access to political influence. However, corporatism also depoliticized unions by curtailing the right to strike, thereby severely restricting the extent to which trade unionists could use their structural and associational power to exert political influence. During the same period, the shift towards national developmentalism helped create a growing urban working class, underlining the argument that labour militancy emerged at the intersection of national and global economic developments. To a significant extent, the trade union movement which materialized at the end of the 1970s was a product of rapid state-led industrialization, as the strike wave took place in multinational corporations, sectors which the military regime considered economically strategic. As a result, trade unionists experienced high levels of structural and associational power, which they managed to translate into significant political influence. Despite the restrictive political context, the driving forces behind the strike movement in this period show how union strategies became politicized, as striking workers translated their wage demands into protests against authoritarianism. Together with these workers' experiences with authoritarian labour practices in the growing industrial sector, the military regime's highly repressive attitude to labour opposition meant that the new unionism movement ended up rejecting corporatism, circumventing the restrictions on union action with novel strategies, such as sit-in strikes and community action. These new strategies contributed to strengthening the union movement's position in the wider pro-democratic movement, while its connections to social movements explain the emphasis on grassroots activism and internal democracy.

Building on the strike movement's achievements, Brazilian trade unions turned into a crucial actor in the democratization process during the late 1970s and 1980s, formulating a democratic agenda that started with the principle that workplace and industrial relations needed to be democratized. This connection between a pro-democracy agenda and workers' demands for higher wages and better working conditions underlines the fundamentally political nature of union action at the time. However, the evolving democratization process also generated significant debates among union activists regarding the political ramifications of the new unionist principles, the establishment of a national union organization, and the question of how to translate the strike movement's achievements into an effective political agenda in a democratic context. The debates about the desirability and objectives of labour's political participation signalled internal conflicts which centred on the extent to which unions should maintain their political autonomy or make use of the opportunities to negotiate the rules of democracy and participate in elections. In the late 1970s and early 1980s, autonomy involved developing a political agenda that departed from past labour politics, including the rejection of both corporatism and populism. In the immediate aftermath of the transition to civilian rule, trade union and social movement opposition became more explicitly political as they pushed for a more comprehensive democratization agenda, as in the campaign for direct presidential elections in 1983–1984 and the writing of a new constitution in 1987–1988. Combined with widespread dissatisfaction the impact of the economic crisis, the opportunity for union activists to shape political events during this period meant that the number of strikes rose despite increasingly adverse economic conditions.

During the 1990s, however, a more defensive trade unionism emerged, as reflected in the declining number of strikes and workers' increasing focus on the maintenance of wage and employment levels, rather than workplace democratization and progressive wage demands. The developments in labour militancy in this period demonstrate that although the political context and the legacy of effective militancy spurred high numbers of strikes in the 1980s, the economic difficulties of the 1990s began to limit the unions' mobilizational power. While the economic chaos of the 1980s had constrained trade union activity to some extent, during the following decade workers faced increasing pressures on their wages and job security, affecting their willingness to engage in militant strikes. Controversially, the national union organizations, including the CUT, had the opportunity to enter into negotiations with the government regarding economic policies, while attempting to pressurize the government into responding to social demands by organizing large-scale political strikes. However, the Plano Real's relative success in stabilizing the Brazilian economy undermined the unions' opposition to the economic reform programme, leading to more than a decade of stagnation and an increasingly moderate labour agenda. Meanwhile, many unions—including those in the multinational industries that had been at the heart of the strike movement in the late 1970s—began to focus on negotiating company restructuring, including performance-related pay, flexible contracts and working hours. In addition, as the failure to reverse privatization shows, it became increasingly difficult to reconcile the ideological positions that dominated the union debate at a national level with the need to formulate union strategies to deal with the practical problems faced by workers in privatized companies. This dynamic highlights the argument that the implications of rapid political and economic change manifested themselves internally in—sometimes debilitating—conflicts about radical and pragmatic strategies.

When the PT came to power in 2003, the unionists who helped found the party struggled with new challenges as organized labour had to reposition itself politically, which generated significant internal conflicts about political strategies. Despite high expectations that a progressive government would introduce reforms to alter Brazil's unequal socio-economic structures, party supporters soon became disillusioned by the lack of progress. This changing political scenario created new strategic dilemmas for the union movement, which had gained political access through new participatory decision-making forums and with former trade unionists in key government posts. The close union-party relationship made militant opposition to controversial reforms exceedingly complicated because protests could destabilize the government, while labour activists risked losing their hard-won political influence. However, rather than resulting in straightforward co-optation by the government, unions continued to mobilize against proposals for social security and labour reform, even if their protests were rarely successful. At a grassroots level, although labour conflicts stagnated at first in the context of Brazil's growing economy, when economic growth began to decline in 2009 the number of strikes increased exponentially, peaking with the mass demonstrations that were held in 2013. The developments in the 2000s and 2010s signalled that while the national union organizations, including the CUT, took a pragmatic turn under the PT-led governments, the underlying causes of labour conflict remained present, which also helps explain the trend towards renewed political polarization from the late 2000s onwards.

The evolution of labour strategies in recent Brazilian history has indicated three political dilemmas that are central to the union movement's trajectory: the inheritance of past strategies, the relationship between the national union leadership and grassroots activists, and the trade-off between political autonomy and political influence. Firstly, the crucial role of trade unions in opposing the military regime left a legacy of militant action, which was highly valued within the new unionism movement. The radical strategies developed by new unionists in the 1980s continued to shape subsequent debates, even though it had proved difficult to influence austerity policies during this period, particularly when unions faced repression or when workers feared job losses. Other longer-term constraints, such as corporatism's continuing impact, also influenced strategic choices and debates, while support for corporatist labour relations among significant sectors of the union movement sparked major internal disagreements. Secondly, strike action not only fluctuated in relation to economic and political crises but also often coincided with a strengthening of grassroots unionism. For example, in the late 1970s and 1980s, grassroots activism was central to the strike wave and the emergence of new unionism, while in the 2000s, rank-and-file union members began to distance themselves from what they saw as a pragmatic turn, contributing to the escalation of labour conflicts from the late 2000s onwards. The relationship between union leaders and rank-and-file activists therefore helps explain why the number of strikes increased in adverse economic conditions when one would expect labour mobilization to decline.

The third key dilemma refers to the extent to which the labour activists could maintain political autonomy while pursuing a wider agenda for social and political change. Whereas the political context changed fundamentally between the 1970s and the 2010s, organized labour's relationship with the formal political arena continued to generate significant internal divisions. Even if union action was inherently political, wage demands and workplace representation did not automatically translate into an effective political agenda, thereby how to engage with the political arena became the focus of internal discussions. These debates focused both on the desirability of entering political negotiations with the government and on union-party relations, with the latter resulting in some union leaders absorbing electoral and governmental logics. Other activists questioned whether unions should pursue their political demands through a party, which involved turning the union agenda into one of the many constituencies that the party appealed to and risked watering down essential labour demands. As the debates about government negotiations in the early 1990s illustrate, many unionists preferred to pressurize the government into making concessions through protests, even if the national union leadership considered bargaining a significant political opportunity. Moreover, the highly fractious debates about labour reforms in the 2000s highlight how the electoral and governmental logics shared by many new unionists clashed with demands that others considered fundamental, including maintaining an autonomous stance in relation to political parties.

In a Latin American context, as the cycle of the new left governments is likely to come to a close, the Brazilian case contributes significant insights into the rise and fall of progressive governments. While the PT governments were generally considered politically moderate compared to the more radical left in other countries, such as Venezuela, Bolivia, and Ecuador, the nature of union-party relations as well as the implications for union political strategies with the left in power can explain similar predicaments in other countries. As these governments often came to power supported by social movements, activists experienced similar dilemmas, in particular whether to try to achieve social demands by continuing to protest for change or to use the newly available political channels to campaign from within the government. From 2003 onwards in Brazil, the new unionism movement's close association with the government combined with increasing levels of labour militancy and political divisions among the Brazilian left, contributing to a growing polarization that subsequently escalated into a major political crisis. Union activists found themselves in a strategic quandary regarding their relations with a progressive government, leading to splits between those who believed in collaborating with the government and those who were dissatisfied with the limitations of institutionalized politics. As the 2016 impeachment crisis highlighted, when the PT-led government experienced corruption scandals in the context of a deepening recession, this political dilemma quickly spiralled out of control.

Though the subject of much debate and scrutiny in the aftermath of the rise of new unionism and the democratic transition in the 1980s, labour's political role has received much less scholarly attention recently. The lessons from the Brazilian case, with its multiple parallels to other experiences in the global south, show that despite discourses about labour's political marginalization, trade unions have continued to act as a powerful component of civil society, while their support for the PT remained contingent upon the extent to which union activists believed their demands were heard. Understanding the impact of the ambiguities of power requires an analysis of the reasons why labour's strategies became politicized given the potential to challenge the status quo and under what conditions trade unions developed militant and moderate strategies. Labour movement theories offer a framework to understand the interaction between structural conditions—such as the diverse labour market, socio-economic inequalities, and corporatism—and the ability of unions to mobilize their structural, associational, and symbolic power to achieve workers' core demands. The Brazilian labour movement's trajectory illustrates that labour's political power is a key element of this dynamic as labour strategies have responded not only to economic conditions but, crucially, labour militancy has often fluctuated alongside changing political contexts. Although social movement theories have often disregarded trade unions as representative of the "old" left, there are many parallels and overlaps between labour and social movements in the political arena, thereby leaving ample space for a productive dialogue between their respective theoretical traditions. Labour's trajectory also shows that protest cycles can be understood as generating their own dynamics, which bequeathed strategic and political legacies that subsequently shaped the labour agenda. Despite the widespread pessimism about labour's fortunes in a globalized economy, the Brazilian case demonstrates that labour's political struggle has in fact been highly dynamic, thereby influencing the course of political change at crucial moments.

Index[1]

A
ABC region (municipalities of Santo André, São Bernardo do Campo, São Caetano in Greater São Paulo), 1, 88–89, 91, 95–96, 100, 112, 134, 136, 149
Abertura (opening), *see* Democratization
Aliança Renovadora Nacional (National Renewal Alliance, ARENA), 72
Alliances, 26–31, 35–36, 63, 69, 100, 106–112, 137–139, 182, 197
  in civil society, 9, 12, 29–31, 62–63, 154–155, 181–182, 186
  government, 27–28, 36, 107, 137, 154
  with political parties, 27, 69, 100, 106–108, 116n37
Armed forces, *see* Military regime
Articulação (political group in Central Única dos Trabalhadores and Partido dos Trabalhadores), 134, 160n31, 198, 210n32
Associação de Engenheiros da Petrobras (Association of Petrobras Engineers, AEPET), 164n83, 167n106
Associação de Professores de Ensino Oficial do Estado de São Paulo (Teachers' Association of the State of São Paulo, APEOESP), 159n28, 215n91
Autênticos ("authentic" group within new unionist movement), 93–94, 102, 118n47

B
Banco Nacional de Desenvolvimento Económico e Social (National Economic and Social Development Bank, BNDES), 153, 158n18, 165n86

---

[1] Note: Page numbers followed by 'n' refer to notes.

© The Author(s) 2019
M. Riethof, *Labour Mobilization, Politics and Globalization in Brazil*, Studies of the Americas, https://doi.org/10.1007/978-3-319-60309-4

Barbosa, Mario dos Santos, 90, 95, 115n24
Bargas, Osvaldo, 95, 98, 115n22, 118n44, 119n62
Berzoini, Ricardo, 197
Boletim Nacional (Partido dos Trabalhadores magazine), 2, 102, 104
Bolsa Família, 183
  See also Social policies
Bourdieu, Pierre, 27
Brasília, 70, 111, 155, 190
Bureaucracy, *see* State; Trade unions

C
Cardoso, Fernando Henrique (president, 1994–2002), 6, 79n53, 96, 143, 147–148, 156
Carneiro, Gilmar, 140
Carvalho, Durval de, 141, 162n55
Catholic Church, 92–96
Central dos Trabalhadores e Trabalhadoras do Brasil (Brazilian Workers' Central, CTB), 199, 215n91
Central Única dos Trabalhadores (Unified Workers' Central, CUT), viii, 3–4, 85, 87, 100, 102–111, 129–131, 133–146, 148, 150–152, 154–156, 158n16, 158n22, 159n25, 160n29, 162n54, 167n108, 179, 184–189, 191–193, 195–200, 202, 203, 205, 217n104, 230–231
  See also New unionism; Trade unions; Union–party relations
Centro Pastoral Vergueiro, 116n32
Cesário, Nilson Viana, 149
Citizenship rights, 16n16, 27–28, 67–68, 78n32, 187

Civil society, 3–4, 27–28, 73–74, 99, 185–188
  and 2013 protests, 200–203
  and democratization, 23, 28, 34–35, 74, 86–87, 92, 99, 111
  and privatization, 83, 147, 164n83
  and PT, 3–4, 9, 31, 96–97, 104, 138–139, 179, 185–188
  and trade unions, 27–28, 31, 92, 137, 142, 233
Class, 3, 24, 28, 33–34, 37–38, 40, 50n48, 65–67, 102–106, 116n37, 138
  conflict and struggle, 37, 40, 44, 104, 139, 145
  interests, 34, 38, 40, 65
  middle, 67, 106, 136, 217n105
  relations, 33, 139
  working class, 24, 59, 61–62, 70–71, 75, 85, 89, 95, 102, 109, 183, 229
  See also Labour; Trade unions
Clientelism, 63, 131, 147, 165n87
Clube de Investidores (Investors' Club), 152
Coffee, ix, 63
Collective bargaining, 25–27, 41, 44, 66–68, 73, 111, 195–197
  See also Labour power; Trade unions; Wages; Working conditions
Collor de Melo, Fernando (president, 1990–1992), 6, 131, 147
Comandos de greve (strike commamdos), 95
  See also Strikes
Comissão Nacional Pró-CUT, 102
Commodity prices, 62
Communities, 5, 16n16, 28, 42, 74, 85, 87, 88, 92, 95, 96, 229
  See also Grassroots activism

INDEX 237

Companhia Siderúrgica Nacional (CSN), 148, 152–153
Companhia Vale do Rio Doce (CVRD), viii, 147–148, 153, 161n40, 165n88, 165n89
Confederação Nacional das Indústrias (National Confederation of Industries, CNI), 211n36
Confederação Nacional dos Bancários (National Bankworkers' Confederation, CNB), 192, 213n66
Confederação Nacional dos Metalúrgicos (National Confederation of Metalworkers, CNM), 144
See also Metalworkers' unions
Confederação Nacional dos Trabalhadores na Agricultura (National Agricultural Workers' Confederation, CONTAG), 160n29
Congresso Nacional da Central Única dos Trabalhadores (CUT National Congress, CONCUT), 134, 136, 138, 140, 160n29, 162n54
Congresso Nacional das Classes Trabalhadoras (National Congress of the Working Classes, CONCLAT), 97–99, 102, 144
Conselho de Desenvolvimento Econômico e Social (Socio-Economic Development Council, CDES), 187–188
Conselho Monetário Nacional (National Monetary Council, CMN), 211n36
Conselho Nacional de Relações de Trabalho (National Labour Relations Council, CNRT), 197
Consolidação das Leis do Trabalho (Labour Code, CLT), 43–44, 64–68

See also Corporatism
Constituent Assembly, 97, 107, 111
Constitution (1988), 13, 67, 190
Coordenação dos Movimentos Sociais (Social Movement Coordination, CMS), 188
Coordenação Nacional de Lutas (National Struggle Coordination, CONLUTAS), 199
Corporatism, 12, 22, 24–25, 28, 34, 60, 64–70, 93–94, 112, 187–188, 229–230
and labour laws, 24, 60, 65
and militancy and moderation, 37, 43–44, 47n10, 59–60, 67–69, 88, 98
and new unionism, 74–75, 91, 93–94, 98, 117n39, 146, 229, 232
and reform, 97–98, 111–112, 178, 195–198
and state control, 27, 64, 68
state–labour relations, 12, 59, 62, 64, 88, 195
and trade unions, 12, 37–38, 64, 195, 232
Corrente Sindical Classista (Class-based Union Movement, CSC), 117n39, 198–199, 203
Corruption, 14, 131, 134, 141, 146, 151, 161n48, 165n87, 183, 193–194, 197, 199–203, 233
See also Lava Jato (Car Wash) investigations; *Mensalão* scandal

D

Delegacia de Ordem Social (Social Order Delegation, DOS), 115n19
Democracy, 24, 31, 40, 73, 83, 95–99, 140–141
internal, 38, 44, 136, 229

Democracy (*cont.*)
  pro-democracy movement,
    12, 27–28, 85–88, 92, 95,
    100, 137, 230
  workplace, 12, 92, 197
  See also Democratization
Democratization, 6, 12–13, 20, 24,
    28–29, 34–36, 73–75, 86–89, 99,
    140, 197, 229–230
  and political participation, 8
  and protests, 87, 89
  and strikes, 44, 85–95, 230
  and trade unions, 8, 13, 20, 23,
    28–29, 44–45, 60, 86, 108,
    112–113, 230
  See also Military regime;
    New unionism
Demographic changes, 69
Departamento Intersindical
  de Estatísticas e Estudos
  Socioeconômicos (Interunion
  Department of Statistics and
  Socio-Economic Studies,
  DIEESE), viii, 6, 16n18,
  89, 204–205
Developing countries, 7, 11, 21–22,
  35, 63
Developmentalism, 60, 62, 71, 229
  See also Industrialization
Diretas Já (campaign for direct
  presidential elections,
  1983–1985), 107–108
Dutra, José Eduardo, 147

E
Education, 32, 36, 71, 91, 100, 136,
  138, 148, 181, 201, 205
  See also Strikes; Trade unions
Eldorado dos Carajás massacre, 155
Elections, 35, 86, 95–96, 106–112,
  156, 183, 194, 201, 230
  and democratization, 86, 95, 99,
    228, 230

  electoral considerations,
    10, 113, 133
  local, 106
  presidential, 35, 87, 103, 106–112,
    131, 141, 156, 162n54, 177,
    183, 201, 230
  union, 68, 70, 93–94, 117n40,
    136, 140, 152
  See also Diretas Já (campaign for
    direct presidential elections,
    1983–1985)
Electoral College
  (*Colégio Eleitoral*), 108
Employers, 1–2, 11, 26, 88, 112,
  114n10, 134, 139, 155, 158n18,
  163n73, 163n78, 197
  and collective bargaining, 19–20,
    26, 39–41, 43, 98–99, 129,
    145, 159n26
  and corporatism, 24, 60, 64–69
  and trade unions, 88–89,
    91–94, 100–101
Employment, 71, 97, 134, 155,
  167n102, 180, 191, 230
  and trade union strategies, 5, 23,
    100, 155, 159n26, 163n58
  and union membership, 32, 142,
    148, 162n58
Entendimento Nacional,
  133, 135, 136
Erundina, Luiza, 133
Estado Nôvo (1937–1945), 62
Exports, 22, 62–63, 73, 76n6, 142,
  146, 159n26, 194

F
Factory commissions (*comissões de
  fábrica*), 41, 69, 89, 91, 93–94,
  100–101, 120n71, 159n26
Federação das Indústrias do Estado de
  São Paulo (Federation of
  Industries of the State of São
  Paulo, FIESP), 134, 211n36

Federação dos Metalúrgicos de São Paulo (São Paulo Metalworkers' Federation, FMSP), 91
Federação Única dos Petroleiros (Unified Federation of Oil Workers, FUP), 149, 167n107
Felício, João, 191, 198
Figueiredo, Ernesto (president, 1979–1985), 102
Fleury, Sonia, 188
Força Sindical (Union Force, FS), 138–140, 151–152, 154, 161n45, 161n48, 168n124, 196, 199, 215n92
Ford motor company, 91, 100, 115n22, 120n69
Formal sector, *see* Workers
Fórum Nacional do Trabalho (National Labour Forum, FNT), 196–198
See also Labour reforms
Fórum Sindical dos Trabalhadores (Union Labour Forum, FST), 197
See also Labour reforms
Free Trade Area of the Americas (FTAA), 186

G
Geisel, Ernesto (president, 1974–1979), 74
Globalization, 7–8, 20–22, 34, 42, 143, 164n80, 227, 234
  and developing countries, 7, 11, 21–22, 35, 63
  and labour, 7, 8, 20–22, 25, 42, 46n1, 234
  national variations, 22
  structural explanations, 11, 19, 21–22, 25
Goulart, João (president, 1961–1964), 70–71
Government policy, 10, 23, 30, 63, 71, 87–89, 103, 146, 200, 210n30
  exchange rates, 63, 109
  exports, 63, 73, 142, 146, 180
  fiscal, 63
  imports, 63, 142
  minimum wage, 4, 14, 64, 71, 178, 183, 189–193
  monetary, 63, 211n36
  and participation, 20, 178–190, 206, 211n36
  planning, 63, 70, 100, 102
  privatization, 13, 129–131, 134–135, 138, 142, 146–154, 156, 231
  and protests, 87–89, 102–103, 143, 183–184, 186–193, 203
  stabilization, 6, 71, 73, 110, 141, 186
  wages, 14, 23, 87, 101
  See also Industrialization; Neoliberal reforms; Political participation; Social policies
Grassroots activism, 35, 60, 73–74, 87, 112
grassroots labour activism, 7, 28, 37–38, 41, 46, 87–96, 100–101, 104–106, 131, 154, 185, 192–194, 198, 204–207, 229, 231–232
  in the PT, 100, 104–106
  in social movements, 28, 35, 60, 73–74, 87, 112, 212n57
  See also Social movements; Trade unions
Great Depression, 24, 62–63

H
Henrique, Arthur, 198, 214n74
Historical sociology, 24, 45
  See also Democratization; Labour movement theory

Human rights, 74, 92
Hydroelectric dams, 217n107, 73

I

Impeachment, 6, 7, 14, 35, 141, 179, 201–203, 206, 228, 233
  See also Collor de Melo, Fernando (president, 1990–1992); Rousseff, Dilma (president, 2010–2016)
Import-substitution industrialization (ISI), 60
Industrialization, 59–61, 63–64, 73–75, 229
  See also Developmentalism; Import-substitution industrialization (ISI)
Inequality, 4, 25, 180, 181, 183, 234
Inflation, 6, 13, 70–71, 89, 91, 99, 101, 108, 141, 143, 144, 180–181, 190
Informal sector, *see* Workers
Infrastructure, 64, 199, 204, 205
Institutional Act (Ato Institucional, 1964), 72
  See also Military regime
Instituto Brasileira de Análises Sociais e Econômicas (Brazilian Institute for Social and Economic Analyses, IBASE), 122n105, 187, 211n34
International Monetary Fund (IMF), 101–102, 108, 146, 180
Investment, 63, 70, 146, 179
  See also Multinational corporations

J

Juventude Operária Católica (Catholic Workers' Youth, JOC), 94

K

Keynesianism, 63
Kubitschek, Juscelino (president, 1956–1961), 70–71

L

Labour, 3, 5, 7–11, 21–22, 35–44, 62, 68, 70, 72–75, 87–89, 99–100, 102, 111, 129–130, 178, 194, 202–203, 228, 232–233
  activism, 2, 5, 13, 23, 96
  activists, 23, 27, 29, 43, 60, 75
  collective action, 23, 39
  commodification of, 41–42
  decline, 5, 7–8, 19, 21, 25, 38, 41, 42, 46, 205
  demands, 2, 10, 12, 21, 23, 26, 31, 46, 65, 69, 71–73, 75, 85–90, 95, 99, 100, 102, 103, 105, 109–113, 131–132, 134, 144, 149, 150, 182–186, 188–190, 193, 201, 204–205, 207, 229–230, 232–234
  and globalization, 7–8, 19–45, 46n1, 47n9, 48n24, 49n39, 50n52, 51n68, 227
  grassroots, 7, 35, 73–74, 87, 89, 91–94, 96, 100, 154, 185, 194, 198, 205, 207, 231–232
  and judicial system, 68
  legislation, (*see also* Corporatism), 23, 60, 67–68, 72, 75, 194–195
  market, 19, 21, 23, 26, 27, 42, 47n10, 67, 69, 195–196, 234
  organized, 3, 7, 8, 10–11, 13, 20–22, 26–27, 29, 32, 38, 59–61, 71, 75, 87, 97, 103, 137, 155, 158n18, 178, 203, 206–207, 227–228, 231–232

INDEX 241

political dimensions of, 4–7, 22–25, 38, 149
structural explanations, 11, 19, 21–22, 25
and workers' rights, 8, 27, 88–89, 98, 111, 129, 143, 195
See also Trade unions
Labour mobilization theory, 38
Labour movement theory, 23–33, 37–44, 234
Labour power, 20, 25–29, 31–32, 34–35, 39, 45
  and agency of labour, 7, 10, 25, 228
  and associational power, 26–27, 32, 42, 88, 98, 107, 185, 229
  and mobilizational power, 25, 135, 139, 140, 202, 230
  and political power, 2, 20–21, 26–29, 32, 62–63, 95, 98, 106, 184, 193–194, 200, 207, 234
  subjective and ideational dimensions, 10, 21, 26, 31–33, 35–40, 44–45, 65
  and social power, 26–27, 32, 74–75, 87, 92, 154–156
  structural factors, 11, 21–22, 32, 44–46
  and symbolic power, 27, 111, 190, 205–207, 234
Labour reforms, 4, 10, 97, 102, 111, 114n10, 178–179, 185, 193–199, 207, 214n74, 231, 233
See also Corporatism; Trade unions
Land reform, 13, 138, 212n57
Lava Jato (Car Wash) investigations, 201
See also Corruption
Left-wing politics, 6, 8–9, 20–21, 36, 38, 44, 69, 105–106, 111, 116n37, 147, 182–185, 192, 198–199, 203, 205–207, 228, 231, 233
See also Political ideologies

Legitimacy, 38–39, 48n24
  in labour conflicts, 39
  and political legitimacy of trade unions, 3, 13, 22, 27, 85–86
  of pro-democracy opposition, 27, 80n63
  of regime or government, 70, 73–74, 80n63, 108, 196
Lopes, Fernando, 144, 163n72
Lula da Silva, Luiz Inácio (president, 2003–2010), 1–6, 87, 131, 144, 162n54, 180–193
  and labour reforms, 89, 94, 97, 195–199
  as leader of the PT, 87, 131, 156, 180
  as president, 3–6, 9, 11, 14, 31, 45, 119, 156, 178, 180–193, 202, 207–208, 227
  as union leader, 1–2, 89, 91, 94, 97, 115n26, 118n45

M
Magri, Antônio Rogério, 139
Marcolino, Luiz Claúdio, 191
Marinho, Luiz, 98, 119n63, 189, 196, 210n28
Medeiros, Luis Antonio, 152
Meneguelli, Jair, 101, 110, 122n112, 133, 135, 151, 196
Mensalão scandal, 197
See also Corruption
Mercedes-Benz motor company, 91, 100, 120n70
Metalworkers' unions, 1, 77n21, 88–89, 91, 94–96, 98, 101–102, 115n26, 118n46, 134, 136, 142, 144, 152, 157n12, 158n16, 159n26, 161n43
See also Sindicato dos Metalúrgicos do ABC (ABC Metalworkers' Union, SMABC); Trade unions

Migration, 67, 69, 94, 118n45
Militancy, 4–12, 28–31, 35–44,
  60–62, 87–88, 91–92, 98–103,
  129–130, 178–179, 191–192,
  199–200, 204–205, 228–230,
  233–234
  and attitudes to democracy, 74, 88,
    150–151, 229
  and confrontation, 74, 93, 112,
    139, 145, 154, 202, 206
  debates about, 7, 11, 13, 20–21, 32,
    39, 42–43, 86–87, 95–96, 100,
    102–103, 112–113, 133, 140,
    179, 184, 230, 233
  government response to, 24, 34–65,
    87, 92, 98, 102
  legacy of, 28, 43, 112, 230, 232
  and politics, 4–9, 35–44, 71,
    76, 88, 112, 130, 155,
    179, 184, 193
  and pro-active strategies,
    5, 130, 184
  and radicalism, 2, 41, 60, 65, 69,
    97, 137, 228–229
  and resistance, 21, 42, 59–61,
    145, 154
  in the early twentieth century,
    24, 38, 60–64
  and trade union strategies, 8, 11,
    20, 35–36, 38, 41, 66, 69, 86,
    88, 142, 228
  See also Political ideologies
Military regime, 72–75, 87–92
  1964 coup, 85
  authoritarianism of, 12, 21, 22, 45,
    73, 90, 102, 112, 139, 229
  and democratic transition, 5, 13, 28,
    34, 45, 86, 97–98, 108, 112,
    227, 233
  and human rights, 74, 92
  and repression, 8, 12, 24, 28,
    41–42, 44, 72–75, 86–87, 90,
    92, 101, 149
  and trade unions, 2, 12, 29, 35,
    42, 44, 60, 64, 66, 67,
    72–75, 87–92
Minimum wage campaign,
  178, 190, 193
Mobilization, 12–13, 26–27, 33,
  131–132
  and democracy, 74–75, 106, 108
  grassroots, 44, 60, 74, 94, 193,
    207, 232
  labour, 4, 6, 26, 42, 44, 110, 112,
    134–135, 143–145, 155,
    178–179, 182, 184–186, 190,
    193, 198, 200, 204–205, 207,
    227–228
  social and political, 9, 27, 33, 43, 60,
    131–132, 138–141, 200, 203
Moderation, 2–5, 8–10, 24, 29–30,
  35–44, 97, 99, 106, 109, 112,
  131, 182–183, 186, 194, 206,
  227–228
  accommodation (to the
    government), 3, 14, 40, 61, 129
  debates about, 2, 9, 41, 137, 156
  and defensive strategies, 5, 20
  pragmatism, 2, 9, 31, 37–38,
    40–42, 93–94, 130, 136–139,
    145, 154–156, 177, 183, 232
  reformism, 9, 62, 109, 185, 207
  and trade union strategies, 8, 11,
    35–36, 41, 66, 69
  See also Political ideologies; Trade
    unions
Movimento Brasil Livre (Free Brazil
  Movement, MBL), 202
Movimento Democrático Brasileiro
  (Brazilian Democratic Movement,
  MDB), 72, 96, 116n37
Movimento dos Trabalhadores Rurais
  Sem Terra (Landless Workers'
  Movement, MST), 3, 31, 138,
  155, 160n39, 165n89, 169n138,
  186, 188, 203

INDEX 243

Movimento dos Trabalhadores Sem Teto (Homeless Workers' Movement, MTST), 203
Movimento Passe Livre (Free Fare Movement, MPL), 200, 202
Movimento Vem Pra Rua (Come to the Streets Movement, MVR), 202
Multinational corporations, ix, 20, 42, 73, 142, 155, 229
  See also Investment; Metalworkers' unions

N
National Development Plan (Plano Nacional de Desenvolvimento, 1974–1979), 73
Nationalism, 59–60, 62–63, 71, 73, 147
National security doctrine, 72
National Truth Commission (Comissão Nacional da Verdade, CNV), 70
Neoliberal reforms, 3, 5–6, 20–22, 34, 42, 46, 135, 146–148, 150
  impact on labour, 12–13, 20, 25, 40, 130–134
  impact on trade union strategies, 142–146, 148–154
  in the 1990s, 129, 131, 142–146
  See also Privatization
Neto, Rafael Freire, 138
Neves, Tancredo, 108
New unionism, 12–13, 30–31, 37, 39–40, 85–86, 94, 101, 112, 130–131, 135, 154, 179, 190, 207, 228–229, 232–233
  and corporatism, 93–95, 111–112, 146, 195–197
  and democratization, 13, 85, 87, 229, 233
  and Força Sindical, 139–140, 161n45
  internal divisions within, 86, 105, 135–139, 143–144, 151, 156, 232
  origins, 73–75, 86, 92
  and social movements, 28, 92, 94–96, 103, 107–109, 111–112, 138–139, 169n138
  and the strike movement, 42, 85–95, 99, 102, 104, 112–113, 229–231
  union–party relations, 9, 29, 31, 96, 104–105, 177, 232–233
  See also Central Única dos Trabalhadores (Unified Workers' Central, CUT); Metalworkers' unions; Partido dos Trabalhadores (Workers' Party, PT); Trade unions

O
Oposições sindicais (union oppositions), 93, 96, 98, 117n39–40, 141
  See also Central Única dos Trabalhadores (Unified Workers' Central, CUT); New unionism

P
Paim, Paulo, 109
Participação nos Lucros e Resultados (Participation in Profits and Results, PLR), 163n77, 195
  See also Collective bargaining; Wages
Participatory democracy, 16n16, 182, 185
Partido Comunista Brasileiro (Brazilian Communist Party, PCB), 69, 96, 117n37, 117n38

Partido Comunista do Brasil
(Communist Party of Brazil,
PCdoB), 199
Partido do Movimento Democrático
do Brasil (Brazilian Democratic
Movement Party, PMDB),
116n37
Partido dos Trabalhadores (Workers'
Party, PT), 2–5, 9, 12–14, 30–31,
45, 95–97, 100, 103–108,
131–133, 138, 150, 178–187,
191, 194–200, 231–233
  Diretório Nacional (National
  Executive), 105, 110
  federal government, 3–6, 9,
  132–133, 178–195, 202,
  206, 208n1
  foundation, 2, 86, 95–97
  local government, 132–133,
  170n141, 182, 185
  núcleos (grassroots circles),
  100, 104–106
  party activists, 110, 138
  party supporters, 182, 231
  political divisions, 15n9, 95–99,
  105, 233
  voters, 105–106, 182–183, 202
  See also Lula da Silva, Luiz Inácio
  (president, 2003–2010); New
  unionism; Rousseff, Dilma
  (president, 2010–2016);
  Union–party relations
Partido Social Democrático (Social
Democratic Party, PSD), 65
Partido Socialismo e Liberdade
(Socialism and Freedom Party,
PSOL), 189, 199
Partido Socialista dos Trabalhadores
Unificado (Unified Socialist
Workers' Party, PSTU), 199,
215n86
Partido Trabalhista Brasileiro
(Brazilian Labour Party, PTB), 65

Pastorais operárias (workers' pastoral
commissions), 92
Pauta do Crescimento (Platform for
Growth), 186
Pelego (official, corporatist unionism or
trade unionist), 37, 65, 66, 102
  See also Corporatism; Trade unions
Pension reforms, 185, 193
Pereira de Sousa, Washington Luís
(president, 1926–1930), 61
Perón, Juan, 65
Petrobras, 149–150, 167n103,
167n108, 199, 203
Plano de Aceleração do Crescimento
(Growth Acceleration Plan, PAC),
204, 217n109
Polanyi, Karl, 42
Policy forums, 178, 186–188, 193, 206
  Conselho Monetário Nacional
  (National Monetary Council,
  CMN), 211n36
  Conselho Nacional de Relações
  de Trabalho (National Labour
  Relations Council,
  CNRT), 197
  Fórum Nacional do Trabalho
  (National Labour Forum,
  196–198
  See also Political participation
Political ideologies, 35, 37–41, 45, 65,
97, 104–105, 130, 139–141,
156, 228, 231
  anarchism, 36, 38, 69, 202
  communism, 36, 38, 62,
  69–72, 117n37
  conservatism, 4, 202
  and militancy, 39, 44–45, 129, 228
  and moderation, 37–41, 130, 139,
  156, 228
  socialism, 38, 108, 117n39
Political incorporation
(of workers), 24–25, 60–61, 185
  See also Corporatism

Political liberalization, 73–74, 87–88
  See also Democratization
Political participation, 4–5, 28–30,
    59–61, 64, 74, 85–87, 95, 99,
    181, 188, 190
  and corporatism, 25
  and democratization, 13, 59,
    74, 107–108
  and political power of unions, 28, 45
  and trade unions, 4–5, 8–9, 61,
    85–87, 99, 107–108, 133–135,
    155, 184, 186, 190, 230
Political polarization, 14, 60, 70–71,
    178–179, 202, 204, 206,
    227–228, 231
Pont, Raul, 105
Populism, 24, 25, 34, 60, 65, 94,
    131, 230
Poverty, 4, 34, 36, 69, 177
Privatization, 129–131, 134–135,
    146–154, 189, 199, 231
  and employment, 148, 153, 166n94
  as government policy, 142, 147–150
  opposition to, 13, 23, 135,
    138, 146–148, 164n83,
    165n86, 199
  and trade unions, 23, 148–154, 199
Protest waves,
  see Social movement theory
Protests, 10–14, 28, 33–35, 37–39,
    42–43, 99, 107, 128, 130–132,
    138, 141–142, 155
  2013–2016 mass protests, 7, 179,
    200–206, 217n105, 231
  and democratization, 61, 87–89,
    107–108, 138–139
  repression of, 71, 75, 88–89,
    91, 101
  and social movement theory, 32–35,
    38, 42–43, 45
  and strikes, 5, 64, 102, 134–135,
    137, 145, 148–149
  and trade unions, 6–7, 26–28,
    37–39, 45–46, 87–89, 135

Protest waves,
  see Social movement theory
Public sector, 31, 97, 129–130,
    146–154
  reform, 129, 185, 188–189, 207
  strikes, 6, 109, 132–133, 167n102,
    191–192, 194, 204–205
  trade unions, 111, 114n13, 131–132,
    136, 142, 149–151, 154, 155,
    189, 196, 199, 204–205, 207
  workers, 97, 149, 151, 167n108,
    189, 199, 204
Public sphere, 68, 74, 92

R
Repression, 33–35, 41–44, 60, 62,
    72–75, 86–92, 94–95, 97,
    99–102, 106–107, 149, 200
  and labour militancy, 8, 12, 75,
    87–92, 94–95, 100–102, 106,
    112, 118n49, 149–150, 232
  under military dictatorship, 12, 28,
    41–44, 60, 72–75, 87–92
  and social movement theory,
    33–35, 42
  state repression before 1964, 24, 62
Revolutionary politics, 37, 61, 71–72,
    105, 116n37, 117n39, 182
  See also Left-wing politics; Political
    ideologies
Rossi, Waldemar, 94–96,
    118n44, 118n52
Rousseff, Dilma (president,
    2010–2016), 5, 6, 14, 15n12,
    35, 179, 201–202

S
Sarney, José (president, 1985–1990),
    108, 132, 147
Silva, Vicente Paulo da (Vicentinho),
    viii, 42, 134, 142, 150, 161n48,
    162n65, 162n66, 213n61

246 INDEX

Sindicato dos Bancários de São Paulo (Bankworkers' Union of São Paulo, SBSP), 136, 140, 159n27, 191, 213n59, 213n61
Sindicato dos Metalúrgicos do ABC (ABC Metalworkers' Union, SMABC), 1–2, 88–89, 94, 98, 120n71, 142, 145, 158n16, 159n26, 163n77, 214n78, 214n79
See also Metalworkers' unions
Sindicato dos Trabalhadores na Indústria Petróleo no Estado de Rio de Janeiro (Petroleum Workers' Union of Rio de Janeiro, SINDIPETRO-RJ), 164n85
Sindicato dos Trabalhadores nas Indústrias de Prospecção, Pesquisa e Extração de Minerios (Union for Workers' in the Mineral Prospecting, Research and Extraction Industries, SINDIMINA), 147–148, 166n92
Sindipetro Duque de Caxias, 149
Social movement theory, 32–35, 42, 45, 230
and class, 33
and democratization, 8, 35, 87
and identity-based, 11–34
political opportunities, 33–34
and protest waves, 28
and repertoires of collective action, 33, 38
rural social movements, 212n57
subjective dimensions, 32
Social movement unionism, 28, 48n27
See also New unionism
Social movements, 9, 30–31, 33–35, 137–138, 169n136, 185–188, 191, 193–194, 201–203, 212n57
and democratization, 74, 87, 229
and the PT, 30–31, 36, 103–104, 182, 185–188, 233

and trade unions, 5, 13, 22, 27–28, 36, 38, 74, 85, 92, 103, 107, 137–138, 154–155, 206, 229
See also Grassroots activism; Movimento dos Trabalhadores Rurais Sem Terra (Landless Workers' Movement, MST); Movimento dos Trabalhadores Sem Teto (Homeless Workers' Movement, MTST); Social movement theory
Social policies, 4, 177, 180–181, 183, 201
Social security reforms, 188–189, 193–195, 199, 207, 231
State, 20–24, 27–29, 40, 43, 59–64, 88, 98, 131, 142, 146, 184–187, 229
budget cuts, 147, 191
control of labour, 24, 67–69
federal, 63, 64, 164n82, 186, 195
institutions, 22, 24, 27, 43, 64, 72, 88, 108
intervention, 6, 12–13, 22, 28, 63–64, 73, 85, 87, 146, 151, 164n82, 187, 195
state–labour relations, 12, 24, 48n13, 59–60, 64, 195, 229
state-led development, 75
state-owned companies, 63, 73, 101, 109, 130, 146–147, 149, 151, 153–154, 162n61, 165n86–88, 166n94, 179, 191
union autonomy from, 85, 92–93, 104, 111, 134, 151, 154, 195, 198
See also Corporatism; Trade unions
Strikes, 5–7, 12–13, 22–23, 26, 28, 35, 37, 40–41, 44–45, 62, 66–68, 80n64, 86–95, 99–104, 117n43, 130–137, 144–146, 155, 178, 182, 191–192, 203–206, 229–231

construction sector, 104, 204
education sector, 29, 100
general strikes, 13, 93, 101–103, 107–110, 112, 121n87, 132, 135, 139, 150, 158n16, 203
government response to, 24, 42, 59, 62, 65, 87–88, 90
industrial sector, 5, 40–41, 75, 91, 204, 229
leaders, 1–2, 26, 44, 90–91, 93, 95, 100, 102, 110
metalworkers, 1, 91, 95, 98, 101–102, 113n2, 117n38
oil workers, 101–102, 146–154, 156
picketing, 95
political strikes, 157n4
private sector, 6, 99, 100, 109, 132, 191–192, 204
public sector, 109, 132, 146, 167n102, 189, 191–192, 194, 199
public transport, 133
repression, 41, 87–95, 101–102, 106, 112, 149
Saab-Scania strike, 89–91
solidarity, 101
statistics, 5, 15n15, 16n17
See also New unionism, and the strike movement

T
Telebras, 148
Tendências (political groupings in the union movement and the Partido dos Trabalhadores), 93–95, 97, 102, 104–105, 117n39, 136, 156
See also New unionism; Partido dos Trabalhadores (Workers' Party, PT); Political ideologies
Teoria e Debate (Partido dos Trabalhadores magazine), 36

Trabalhismo (labourism), 59–60, 65
See also Corporatism; Populism; Vargas, Gétulio (president, 1930–1945, 1951–1954)
Trade unions, 7–14, 21–33, 40–41, 43–44, 64–69, 73–74, 87, 103–104, 131–132, 134–135, 143–145, 155, 184, 188–189, 193, 201, 227–229, 232–234
activists, 9, 20, 23, 27–29, 38–40, 43, 60, 66, 105, 148, 230, 232, 233
and authoritarianism, 45, 87, 229
bankworkers, 140, 191
classista (class-based), 106
cooptation, 2, 4, 11, 14
and democratization, 8, 13, 20, 23, 44, 74, 87–88, 129, 229, 230
and fragmentation, 3, 10, 178, 184, 195, 228
grassroots, relations with, 92, 100, 131, 194, 198, 232
and internal conflicts, 10–11, 25, 39, 131, 145–146, 155, 179, 182, 193, 228, 230
internal democracy of, 38, 44, 229
leadership, 1, 38, 44, 67, 69, 72, 89, 93, 100, 110, 130, 134, 148, 151, 154, 178–179, 182, 185, 189, 198–199, 204, 206, 232, 233
membership, 3, 25, 32, 40, 44, 68, 195
metalworkers, 1, 77n21, 88–89, 94, 113n6, 115n26, 118n46, 134, 142, 152, 158n16, 159n26, 161n43
under military rule, 20, 72–75, 87–92
mining, 63, 147
official (*pelego*), 37, 65, 68, 75, 91–94, 117n37, 117n40, 197, 215n90
oil workers, 101, 149–150

Trade unions (*cont.*)
  political activism, 13, 22–25, 27–29
  political strategies, 24, 29, 33, 44, 46, 90, 130, 233
  public sector, 129, 131–132, 142, 150–151, 189, 191
  services sector, 138, 142
  sindicalismo de resultados ("results unionism"), 37, 139
  and social movements, 3, 8–9, 11, 13, 27–28, 33, 35, 43, 45, 74, 85, 99, 155, 179, 182, 185, 188, 194, 201–203, 229–230, 234
  strategies, 8, 11, 20, 22–23, 35–36, 38, 41, 66, 69, 86, 142, 228
  telecommunications, 148
  white-collar, 136, 138
  See also Collective bargaining; Corporatism; Labour power; New unionism
Tribunal Superior de Trabalho (Supreme Labour Court, TST), 149, 167n99

U
Unemployment, 5, 13, 26, 41, 45, 99–100, 113, 131, 135, 142–145, 148, 166n94, 180, 185, 194, 232
Unicidade sindical (monopoly on union representation), 66, 111, 195
Unidade Sindical (Union Unity, UnS), 93, 97–98, 107, 197
  See also Corporatism
Union reforms, *see* Corporatism; Labour reforms

Union tax (*impôsto sindical*), 66, 93, 111, 196–197
  See also Corporatism
Union–party relations, 9, 22, 29–31, 103, 110, 178, 189, 193, 231–233
  See also Central Única dos Trabalhadores (Unified Workers' Central, CUT); New unionism; Partido dos Trabalhadores (Workers' Party, PT)
Usiminas, 151, 153

V
Vargas, Gétulio (president, 1930–1945, 1951–1954), 59, 61–63, 65–66, 68, 70–71, 114n13
Volkswagen motor company, 90–91, 115n22, 115n24, 144, 163n75

W
Wages, 4, 64, 67, 70–71, 73, 75, 88–89, 158n14, 180–184
  and globalization, 19, 25, 42
  and strikes, 1–2, 88–89, 92, 100–101, 149, 205
  and trade union strategies, 23, 42–43, 70, 88–89, 92, 97–101, 130, 144–145, 157n4, 189–190, 230
  See also Collective bargaining; Minimum wage campaign
Wall Street Crash, 62

INDEX 249

Workers, 8, 12–13, 21, 25–28, 33, 38–39, 41–46, 70–75, 87, 96–102, 131–132, 143, 197, 207, 227, 229, 232
  and corporatism, 64–68
  formal sector, 61, 67
  industrial, 12, 41, 69, 74, 79n42, 136, 142
  informal sector, 67, 106, 138
  rural, 67, 106, 138, 160n29, 196
  working class (*classe operária*), 106
    See also Labour; Trade unions
Working class, *see* Class
Working conditions, 22–23, 25, 27, 43, 88–89, 97, 130, 139, 145, 166n97, 200, 204–205, 230
Workplace activism,
  see Grassroots activism;
  New unionism;
  Trade unions

CPSIA information can be obtained
at www.ICGtesting.com
Printed in the USA
LVHW07*1605190518
577811LV00003B/6/P